GREAT BRITAIN AND THE OPENING OF JAPAN
1834–1858

Great Britain

and

The Opening of Japan

1834 – 1858

W. G. BEASLEY

JAPAN
LIBRARY

GREAT BRITAIN AND THE OPENING OF JAPAN
1834–1858

First published 1951 by Luzac & Co.

First paperback edition published 1995 by
JAPAN LIBRARY
Knoll House, 35 The Crescent
Sandgate, Folkestone, Kent CT20 3EE

Japan Library is an imprint of Curzon Press Ltd
St John's Studios, Church Road
Richmond, Surrey TW9 2QA

British Library Cataloguing in Publication Data
A CIP catalogue record for this book is available
from the British Library

ISBN 1–873410–43–3

Printed and bound in England by Redwood Books, Trowbridge, Wiltshire

CONTENTS

ERRATA

For Townshend Harris *read* Townsend Harris throughout, that is, on the following pages/lines: xi/14, 156/
19, 166/16, 166/24, 171/8, 177/27, 179/9, 217/23,
218/31, 220/3, 220/24, 224/col, 2/41, and also in the
following notes, 116/n.17, 183/n.43, 184/n.46.

p. xiv, n.2, *for* yielded a revenue *read* produced an
estimated crop

p. 7, n.14, *for* Pondon *read* London

p. 38/29, *for* Shimazu Saihin *read* Shimazu Nariakira

p. 40/13, *for* the senior of the *read* one of the senior

p. 59/17, *for* irrestible *read* irresistible

p. 108/20, *for* revenues *read* crop values

p. 108, n.55, *for* fief revenues *read* fief values

p. 121, n.30, *for* Galhoku *read* Gaikoku

p. 150/3, *for* enentitle *read* entitle

p. 177/16, *for* ōmetuke *read* ōmetsuke

PREFACE TO THE PAPERBACK EDITION

This monograph was written in the aftermath of a war in which Britain was one of the victors and Japan one of the vanquished. In those circumstances its subject-matter was conceived to be an early chapter in a story which ended with that war, leading through alliance to conflict in the relations between Britain and Japan, while making it steadily more apparent over time that the lead taken by America in the world's dealings with Japan was not just the product of mid nineteenth-century opportunity.

The perspective today is very different. The Pacific War of 1941–45 marked the irreversible decline of British power in East Asia, shortly (1997) to be completed by the surrender of Hong Kong. For Japan it initiated a new phase in both domestic and international policies. Between 1850 and 1900 Japanese governments had pursued the goal of 'national wealth and strength' in Western guise, treating trade and industry for the most part as a contribution to the country's military potential. After 1945, however, the emphasis shifted. Wealth itself became a prime objective, both as a means of repairing a society shattered by defeat and as a route to international reputation. Historians responded to that change. They concerned themselves more with the origins and nature of the 'economic miracle', hardly at all with nineteenth-century diplomacy.

In such a context an account of the British contribution to the opening of 'closed' Japan does not seem to have a great deal to contribute. After all, a narrative ending in 1858 touches only at the margins of those forces which were to shape Japanese development for the rest of the century and beyond. The ten years after 1858 were more important. Similarly, for the study of British imperialism, which the book also addressed, Japan proved to be too inconsiderable an issue in the making of policy for an examination of the decisions taken concerning it to throw much light on key general questions, such as the comparative significance of economic ambitions and strategic interests. For these purposes China is much the better object of attention.

Nevertheless, it does not follow that no useful purpose is served by turning back to the events which are here described. The treaties of the 1850s, in the making of which Britain played a considerable part, both directly as an actor and indirectly as a looming threat off-stage, had a lasting effect on Japanese attitudes towards the outside world, helping to make Britain a model of 'wealth and strength' in Japanese eyes for much of the modern period. From a different viewpoint, Britain's own contrasting experience in China and Japan, dating from these years, laid the foundations for a continuing ambivalence in British policy with respect to those two countries. One can still usefully distinguish between Old China Hands and Old Japan Hands among British diplomats. It is useful, too, to be reminded of changing patterns: of how greatly personal and local initiatives determined Western actions in that distant part of the world before the days of the telegraph and telephone; of how recently Japanese political structures were predominantly feudal; of what was then a close, but is now a fast-disappearing relationship between naval power and trade.

In the text of this book, as originally published, there were a number of errors. Some of these were typographical, but two in particular were mistakes on the author's part: the consistent misspelling of the given name of the American consul, Townsend (not Townshend) Harris; and the assumption (on three occasions) that the official valuation of Japanese feudal territories was a statement of revenue (whereas it was in fact the tax collector's estimate of total crop). These errors have been corrected in the list of errata included in the present edition.

TWICKENHAM, 1995   W.G.B.

JAPANESE NAMES, TITLES AND DATES

Japanese names. Japanese personal names are given in the usual Japanese order, i.e. family name followed by given name (e.g. Ii Naosuke, where Ii is the family name).

Japanese titles. With few exceptions, the formal titles of Japanese feudal lords have no geographical significance and are therefore given in the Japanese form, e.g. Kamon-no-kami (Ii Naosuke's title) or Bitchū-no-kami (Hotta Masayoshi's title). Where titles are descriptive, i.e. designate the actual fief or province held by a feudal lord, it has been thought better to translate them. For example, Ii Naosuke can also be described as ' lord of Hikone ' and Hotta as ' lord of Sakura '.

Japanese dates. The dates found on Japanese documents of this period are usually in the form of references to year-periods (*nengō*), with month and day according to the Japanese lunar calendar. Where such documents are cited in footnotes, the date is wherever possible changed to the exact Gregorian equivalent. In some documents, however, only month and year are given, and these do not correspond exactly with those of Western calendars. Where these are cited, therefore, the year is given first according to the Gregorian calendar, followed by the Japanese (lunar) month and (in brackets) the Gregorian equivalents for the first and last days of that month, e.g. 1856, 8th. month (30 August–28 September).

THE SEVENTEENTH CENTURY

FOR over two hundred years, under Tokugawa rule, the ports of Japan were closed to Western ships and commerce, save only for a limited trade conducted by the Dutch at Nagasaki. In 1853, however, Commodore Perry of the United States Navy led his squadron of "Black Ships" into Edo Bay to deliver a letter from the President and request a treaty of commerce and friendship with Japan. In the following year, having given the Japanese time to consider his proposals and meditate upon his display of force, he returned to conclude the first of the nineteenth-century conventions with that country. The work Perry began was completed by Townshend Harris in July 1858, when the Treaty of Kanagawa opened Japan to American trade ; and the lead so given was followed by other Western countries anxious to establish treaty relations. After 1854, and again after July 1858, British, French, Russian and Dutch representatives hastened to conclude similar agreements. For Britain, Rear Admiral Sir James Stirling negotiated at Nagasaki in 1854 and Lord Elgin at Edo in 1858. Neither succeeded in making any important change in the treaty-pattern established by the Americans.

The fact of American leadership in the opening of Japan has long been recognised. The negotiations of Perry and Harris, and the events which led up to them, have accordingly been investigated in some detail. Much less attention has been paid to British actions, however, and no general agreement has been reached on the nature and objectives of British policy, especially for the two decades before 1854. This study has been undertaken in an attempt to trace an accurate narrative of British policy towards Japan in the years 1834 to 1858. Most of the events to which it refers

—the voyages of the *Morrison*, *Samarang* and *Mariner*, the negotiations of Stirling and Elgin—have been described before. But taken alone, the evidence of events is often conflicting. Visits of British warships to Japan in 1845 and 1849 seem to argue the existence of an interest and a purpose not in fact borne out by the results of those visits. The negotiations of Stirling and Elgin, in that they followed closely those of Perry and Harris both in time and in achievement, suggest that Britain attempted only to emulate American success : yet it has recently been shown that Stirling's actions were brought about largely by the Crimean War, while those of Elgin depended on events in China. Study of the Foreign Office and Admiralty papers adds the evidence of intentions to the evidence of results. It establishes new relationships between some of the events, an apparent lack of connection between others, which enable us to resolve many of the existing ambiguities and contradictions.

It must be emphasised that this is not primarily a study of British opinion about Japan, but of official plans and official negotiations. It is therefore concerned chiefly with the Foreign Office and its representatives in China, to a lesser degree with the Admiralty and the commanders of the East Indies station. Other factors are treated only in so far as they impinge on this problem of official policy.

The period chosen has a certain unity in that its central theme is the attempt to initiate relations with Japan, in particular to initiate trade. It ends, therefore, in 1858, with the conclusion of a commercial treaty. Like all " periods " in history, however, it is arbitrary and has certain disadvantages. To end at the point where full treaty relations begin makes this very largely a study of plans and intentions, of a policy formulated in the abstract rather than one modified by the impact of everyday problems. To this extent it presents a distorted picture. The conclusions to which it leads do not necessarily hold good for the period after 1858. The opening of trade inevitably brought fresh influences to bear on Foreign Office policy, a consideration of major importance, for example, in any discussion of " imperialist " tendencies in the British approach to Japan. Within the chronological limits here imposed, one can properly attempt no more than an analysis of the motives which led Britain to establish relations with Japan, and of the " initial prejudices " from which later British policy was to develop.

Similarly the year 1834, which saw the abolition of the East India Company's monopoly of the China trade, is a convenient starting-point because it makes it possible to concentrate on the Foreign Office as the controlling agent in the formulation of policy. But it is not intended thereby to suggest that 1834 saw either the beginning or even a revival of British interest in Japan. In fact, British traders founded a factory in Japan as early as 1613. Earlier contacts provided a background against which nineteenth-century policy was worked out, and were occasionally cited in the discussions of the years 1834 to 1858. It has therefore been thought convenient to include here a brief account of the failure of the Hirado factory and the East India Company's subsequent attempts to renew the trade.

It was not until the seventeenth century that Dutch and English traders extended their commerce to the southern ports of Japan. They found a ready welcome there. Late in the sixteenth century, after generations of intermittent civil war, the country had been united under the rule of Toyotomi Hideyoshi, a brilliant soldier whose lowly birth alone prevented him from becoming Shōgun, the office held for centuries by successive dynasties of *de facto* military rulers who governed in the Emperor's name. Hideyoshi died in 1598, and was succeeded by Tokugawa Ieyasu, who soon took the title of Shōgun and settled down to the task of consolidating his own and his family's position. In that task, he realised, the wealth and guns brought by foreign trade could play an important part. He was, therefore, willing to grant generous privileges to European traders.

In 1613, four years after the arrival of the Dutch, John Saris reached Japan to open trade on behalf of the English East India Company. He found a friend at court in the person of Will Adams, an Englishman who had first reached Japan in Dutch employ and had subsequently entered the service of Ieyasu. With his help, Saris obtained permission to trade. Against Adams' advice, however, he elected to settle his factory not at Edo,[1] where he would have been sure of Ieyasu's patronage and protection, but at Hirado on the west coast of Kyūshū, where the Dutch were already established and the *daimyō*[2] had shown himself very friendly. By this decision the factory was handicapped from the outset in its struggle against Dutch competition.

The English factory lasted only ten years. In 1623 it was withdrawn because its trading had consistently failed to show a profit, a fact that requires some explanation. Even before Saris arrived Adams warned the Company that as a result of Dutch imports, cloth had become ' as cheap in Japan as in England '[3] and that the market was principally for spices and Chinese goods. Adams' advice was suspect because of his long connection with the Dutch, but in this his English colleagues soon proved him right. Richard Cocks, whom Saris had left in charge of the factory, found it difficult to supply the kind of goods Japanese were willing to buy. His efforts to open trade with Cochin China and Siam met with little success, while the bribes he lavished on Chinese merchants trading in Japan, in an attempt to secure a foothold in the China trade itself, yielded nothing but promises to the end—to the considerable indignation of his superiors at Bantam. In January 1617 he wrote to the Court of Directors :—

> ' My greatest sorrow is I lye in a place which hitherto hath byn chargable and not benefitiall to your Worships . . . And were it not for the hope of trade into China, or for procuring som benefit from Syam, Pattania and (it may be) Cochinchina, it were noe staying in Japan. Yet it is certen here is silver enough, and may be carried out

---

[1] Ieyasu's capital, renamed Tōkyō in 1868.
[2] A feudal lord. *Daimyō* was the highest general category in the Japanese feudal system, and was reserved for lords whose fiefs yielded a revenue of 10,000 *koku* (about 50,000 bushels) or more of rice a year.
[3] P. Pratt, *History of Japan compiled from the records of the English East India Company* . . . 1822, I, 16-20, Adams to President at Bantam, 12 Jan. 1612/3.

at pleasure ; but then must we bring them comodeties to
ther lyking, as the Chinas, Portingales and Spaniards doe,
which is raw silke and silke stuffs, with Syam sapon and
skins.'[4]

Dutch rivalry made Cocks' task doubly difficult. Dutch
factors constantly cut their prices to drive English goods
from the market. Moreover, the Dutch controlled the seas
and did not hesitate to use their power. For some years,
Cocks complained, the only English ships to reach Japan
were brought in as Dutch prizes, while in Hirado itself the
English factory was only protected from attack by the
intervention of Japanese officials. And after 1616 the
English traders ceased to enjoy the Shōgun's favour.
Ieyasu himself had seen in the activities of Catholic priests
and converts a potential threat to the political stability he
was so anxious to maintain. His son Hidetada went still
further. Foreign trade was undoubtedly a source of
strength to a strong ruler, but under a weaker man guns and
wealth might find their way into the hands of a disgruntled
vassal and so enable him to defy the Tokugawa. If political
safety demanded the suppression of Christianity, it also
required the rigid control of trade, and viewed in this light,
the privilege of trading freely to all the ports of Japan,
which Ieyasu had granted to the English company in 1613,
seemed fraught with danger. In 1616 Cocks was told that
the old privileges were revoked. For a time trade was
confined to Hirado, and even the re-opening of Nagasaki
in 1619 brought little improvement.

It had become painfully obvious to the East India
Company's council in Java that the Japan factory was losing
money and had little hope of future profits. Indeed, Cocks'
own behaviour and accounts were thought to need investigation. He was therefore ordered to close the factory and
return to the Indies, and in 1623 he did so, leaving the
Dutch, ironically enough, to collect all outstanding debts
due to the Company.

In announcing his departure to the *daimyō* of Hirado,

---

[4] *Diary of Richard Cocks* (2 vols., Hakluyt Soc., London, 1883), II, 279-88,
Cocks to Court of Directors, 1 Jan. 1616/7.

Cocks had expressed the hope that he might return 'if the next yeare shall produce any better encouradgement '.[5] There were others equally optimistic in the years that followed. In 1627 the President of the council at Batavia, arguing that the severe winter climate of Japan would ensure a market for English cloth, urged an attempt to re-open trade,[6] but found that the Company's records belied his estimate. In 1632 the tale was taken up by Thomas Smethwick, a disappointed adventurer in the Joint Stock, who accused the Governor and Committees of gross mis-management and attempted fraud on the grounds that they had abandoned a promising opening because their private interests in the Levant trade would have been seriously affected by success in China and Japan. He took part in some acrimonious exchanges before the Court of Directors before his charges were finally dismissed by the Attorney General.[7] The Company's rivals in England sometimes followed Smethwick's example in citing failure in Japan as an argument against the monopoly. Both the Courteen Association and the Assada Merchants, for example, announced their intention of trading with Japan, though neither attempted to put its plans into practice.

Shortly before the Restoration, the East India Company decided to make another attempt to trade in Japan. Plans were made in 1658 but were abandoned because of the outbreak of war with Holland, and discussions between London and Bantam in 1664 and 1668 proved equally abortive. Then, early in 1671, Samuel Baron, a native of Tonquin of mixed European descent, approached the Company with proposals for a voyage to Japan. Some of his proposals were dismissed as 'dishonourable', but in April it was decided to adopt the remainder, and later in the year the *Experiment*, *Zant* and *Return* sailed from London bearing letters from the King and Company.

In the summer of 1672 the *Experiment* and *Return* called

---

[5] Cocks, *Diary*, II, 345-6.

[6] *Calendar of State Papers* (*East Indies*) 1625-9, pp. 371-80, President Hawley to Court, 18 July 1627.

[7] *Calendar of State Papers* (*E. Indies*) 1630-4, pp. 335, 374-7 and 383.

at Taiwan (Formosa) to found a trading factory. By so doing they lost the last of the southerly monsoon, which made it impossible for the expedition to reach Japan until the following year, a delay that was put to good use by the Dutch at Nagasaki.

After the withdrawal of the English factory in 1623, the Tokugawa had become increasingly hostile to European traders, especially those of Portugal and Spain. An overwhelming suspicion of the political implications of Christianity led Hidetada and his successor Iemitsu into savage and widespread persecution of Catholic priests and converts, and part of this suspicion transferred itself to the merchants who sometimes smuggled missionaries into the country. Moreover, the search for political security so dominated Tokugawa policy as to outweigh even the advantages to be gained from foreign trade. Better no trade at all than foreign help to a disgruntled vassal. In 1624, therefore, when Spanish intrigue with some of the northern *daimyō* was reported, the ports of Japan were closed to Spanish ships. In 1638, because they were suspected of complicity in a revolt which had broken out at Shimabara in Kyūshū, the Portuguese were ordered to leave the country and never to return. Death was to be the penalty for disobedience. Soon after, to show that this was no idle threat, the Shōgun executed the members of a Portuguese embassy sent from Macao to seek re-admittance to the trade.

By 1641 the Tokugawa " seclusion policy " was in full operation. Japanese were forbidden to travel or trade abroad, and although Dutch and Chinese were still allowed to visit Nagasaki, they were subject to the strictest supervision. The Dutch, in fact, were transferred to the tiny artificial island of Deshima in Nagasaki harbour, where they lived in isolation, almost prisoners.

The seclusion policy rapidly became a tradition, and by the time Simon Delboe entered Nagasaki in the *Return* in June 1673, the Japanese needed little persuasion to refuse all requests for trade. The Dutch, who had received early warning of the English plans, were careful to point out that by Charles II's Portuguese marriage England had entered into alliance with Japan's traditional enemy. This provided an admirable reason for refusing to honour the privileges Ieyasu had granted in 1613, a copy of which Delboe brought with him. After weeks of waiting at Nagasaki, Delboe was informed that he could not be admitted to trade, and Japanese officials held out little hope that success would attend any future English efforts. Once given, they said, the Shōgun's decision was irrevocable.[8]

The direct attempt to open trade had failed, but the Company did not at once relax its efforts. The Court of Directors attributed the failure largely to Dutch intrigue, and hoped that success might still come from some indirect approach to Japan. In 1674 the Bantam agents were ordered to seek the intercession of the rulers of Bantam or Taiwan to explain away the difficulties that had arisen. Meanwhile, they were to make every effort to push the sale of English goods among native merchants having access to the Japan market, ' that soe if possible by our trading to Tywan it may be in effect as if we did trade to China, Japan and the Manilhaes '.[9] Similar attempts were made through Amoy and Siam. In 1681 the Company tried to transmit letters to Japan through the good offices of a number of eastern rulers, but found that the Chinese merchants, who alone could act as messengers, dared not convey a letter for a private individual, much less one addressed to the officials. The same fears prevented them from co-operating in a plan to found a Chinese colony at Madras and use it to carry on trade with Japan. In 1684 the Siam factory, in its turn, was instructed to arrange a voyage if it could see any prospect of success, but the ship which was to have been sent from England for this purpose lost the season and was diverted to Bengal. For some years no new plans were made.

The events of 1688 gave England a Dutch king and a Protestant queen. To the sanguine it appeared that this

---

[8] A short account of this mission appears in *Calendar of the Court Minutes of the East India Company* 1671-3 (intro., pp. viii-ix), the relevant papers being in that volume and Pratt, *op. cit.*, vol. II. See also C. R. Boxer, ' Anglo-Dutch Rivalry in Japan ', *Trans. Asiatic Soc. Japan*, 2nd Ser., VII (1930).

[9] *Cal. Court Min.* 1674-6, p. xix, citing Court to Bantam, 23 Oct. 1674.

would remove both Dutch and Japanese opposition, and that the trade should therefore be attempted once again. The Company, however, had at last been discouraged by the constant failure of its efforts. It was content simply to remind the Madras Presidency of the changed circumstances, while explicitly withholding permission to fit out an expedition at the Company's expense. Instead, the trade was thrown open to the 'country' merchants, the licensed traders in India.[10]

There is no evidence that any of the 'country' merchants were sufficiently interested to plan a voyage to Japan. After 1700 the Company itself devoted most of its attention to India, where French competition ensured that it had little thought for the lands further east. The Japan trade was noticed briefly and with little enthusiasm in 1701 when a temporary foothold was secured in the Chusan Islands, but thereafter, for more than seventy years, Japan was hardly mentioned in English books and records.[11]

[10] For the attempts at indirect trade after 1673 see *Cal. Court Min.* 1677-9. pp. xvii-xviii, and Pratt, *op. cit.*, II, 195-205.

[11] For the eighteenth century see J. F. Kuiper, *Japan en de buitenwereld in de achtiende eeuw* ('s-Gravenhage, 1921), especially pp. 198-200.

CHAPTER I

COMPANY AND CROWN

DURING the greater part of the eighteenth century British merchants made no attempt to renew their former connection with Japan. The closing decades of the century, however, saw a revival of interest in the north Pacific and the China seas stemming from a variety of political and economic causes. British successes in the Seven Years War freed the East India Company for a time from its enforced preoccupation with the affairs of India. The loss of the American colonies accentuated the growing emphasis on commercial rather than colonial development, while the failure to find new markets in Terra Australis, and the phenomenal increase in trade with China,[1] concentrated attention on the possibility of commercial expansion in areas where a start had already been made. That, in its turn, almost inevitably brought to mind the " closed " markets of Siam, Cochin China and Japan. Four times between 1791 and 1819, British ships reached Japan in search of trade.

The story of the Hirado factory and the voyage of the *Return* continued to play a part in moulding British attitudes towards the Japan trade. Detailed accounts of both were made readily accessible to English readers. In 1793, for example, the East India Company published a report on the Japan trade which outlined much of its early history.[2] A diary of the *Return's* voyage appeared in John Pinkerton's

[1] The Company's exports of tea from Canton more than quadrupled between 1775 and 1785. See Morse, *Chronicles of the East India Company trading to China*, II, 11, 50, 111, 119.

[2] East India Co., *Third Report of the Select Committee Appointed to take into Consideration the Export Trade from Great Britain to the East Indies*, London, 1793.

Collection of Voyages and Travels (London, 1808), and in 1822 Peter Pratt published his *History of Japan*, which included long excerpts from the Company's seventeenth-century archives. The privileges granted to the Company by Tokugawa Ieyasu were even referred to in the correspondence columns of *The Times* during 1846 and 1847. Not everybody, of course, drew the same conclusions from the facts available. The Company argued that the market was difficult of access and that history showed it to be unprofitable. Others rejected all such evidence and chose to assume the value of the trade. They urged, rather, that since the withdrawal of the Hirado factory had been a peaceful and voluntary act, the privileges of 1613 still entitled Britain to trade and would, indeed, operate to overcome Japanese objections. Both points of view were still in evidence in 1834, when the Foreign Office assumed responsibility for the direction of British policy in the China seas. The conviction with which they were urged, however, and by the same token the degree to which they were likely to influence the Foreign Office, was largely conditioned by the plans and voyages of the period 1790 to 1830.

One characteristic of this period was the active interest shown by private merchants. Their first venture arose out of the newly-established fur trade across the Pacific between Nootka and Canton. In May 1790 James Colnett, in command of the ship *Argonaut*, reached Canton with a cargo of pelts, only to find that the Chinese officials would not allow him to sell them there. Daniel Beal, his company's agent at Macao, suggested that a market might be found for them in Korea and Japan, and in July 1791 gave him instructions to make a voyage to those countries. His plans envisaged something more than a single voyage. If the Japanese did not immediately turn him away, Beal wrote, Colnett must be particularly careful to inform them that his ship and crew were English and that he came ' for the purpose of obtaining permission to trade Annually to the Port of Nangasaque or any other belonging to Japan.'[3]

[3] Beal to Colnett, 25 July 1791, in *The Journal of Captain James Colnett aboard the Argonaut* (Champlain Society, Toronto, 1940), pp. 234-9.

During August 1791 Colnett cruised up the west coast of Kyūshū and at several points tried to establish communication with the Japanese. On each occasion, *Argonaut* or the boats she sent away towards shore were met by Japanese craft which signalled them to depart. Her Chinese interpreter proved useless. At last, Colnett wrote in his journal that he had made six such overtures ' without any prospect of communication or Trade with the natives, but by force of Arms, which in my present situation . . . I did not think proper to attempt.'[4] The failure led him to certain general conclusions. He could see small prospects of success for any private venture to open trade with Japan. The attempt, if made, he thought, should be in a vessel sufficiently well-manned and well-armed to command respect, but it was even so ' too doubtful and hazardous an Undertaking for two or three Merchants to Enter into, nor should it be thought on without an exclusive privilege to the trade granted by Charter.'[5]

Although Colnett's only published reference to this voyage[6] was much less calculated to discourage further efforts than the opinions expressed in his journal, the experiences of two other expeditions tended to confirm the difficulties in the way of trading with Japan. In 1803 Captain Stewart, an American who had visited Japan in the service of the Dutch, persuaded some merchants in India to fit out two ships for Nagasaki. When the attempt was made, however, Stewart's British colleague, Captain Torey, was dismissed without ceremony and Stewart himself was eventually turned away without permission to trade.[7] Fifteen years later, Captain Peter Gordon of the brig *The Brothers* stood into Edo Bay in search of trade. He had chosen his destination with care, hoping that at the capital he might find more willingness to relax the seclusion laws than among hidebound provincial officials at Nagasaki, but in the event he

---

[4] Colnett, *Journal*, pp. 250-1.
[5] Colnett, *Journal*, pp. 278-81.
[6] J. Colnett, *A Voyage to the South Atlantic and round Cape Horn into the Pacific Ocean* (London 1798), in the introduction to which (pp. iii-iv) he implied that the venture was only abandoned because of the damage *Argonaut* suffered in a typhoon.
Murdoch, *History of Japan*, III, 510-1.

achieved no more than Colnett or Torey. His views on the subject were quoted by the *Quarterly Review* in the following year. Like the Java factors in 1627, he believed that if access were once obtained, the severity of the Japanese winter would ensure a demand for British woollens and that Japanese ore would supply an ample return. But the *Quarterly* completely disagreed. It regretted Britain's failure to establish relations with Japan, but this was ' not so much because we lost the opportunity of extending our commerce (for we believe the wants of this people are few and their superfluous produce neither great nor valuable), as that we let slip the occasion of convincing this proud and jealous government that the few Dutchmen, on whom they were long accustomed to trample, are not the best specimen of Christian Europe.'[8] There was little in this to encourage further ventures. Even the Whig *Edinburgh Review* viewed the trade with indifference.[9]

If private merchants had tried and failed, the East India Company was little disposed to try at all. In 1792, at the government's request, it had produced a report on the Japan trade[10] which made it abundantly clear that in the Company's view the trade could never become ' an Object of Attention for the Manufactures and Produce of Great Britain'. In a singularly unconvincing argument, the report pointed out that even at the time of the Hirado factory Japan had never provided a market for British goods, while the returns from the trade, if any, must largely be in copper, a commodity that would compete in India with the output of British mines. Thus, any profits made by the Company would be at the expense of the mining interests at home. Moreover, the Hirado factory had never made any profits. To the Company, such considerations were unanswerable.

It is not surprising, then, to find that no fresh plans were made at East India House. The fact that British ships

---

[8] *Quarterly Review*, XXII (July 1819), p. 119 and note. For a further account of Gordon see *Chinese Repository*, VII (March 1839), pp. 588 94.
[9] *Edinburgh Review*, XXIX (Nov. 1817), pp. 39-52.
[10] East India Co., *Third Report of the Select Committee Appointed to take into Consideration the Export Trade from Great Britain to the East Indies*, London 1793.

found their way to Japan under the Company's colours in 1813 and 1814 was due entirely to the energy and enthusiasm of Thomas Stamford Raffles, one of the Company's officials in the East whom Lord Minto appointed Lieutenant-Governor of Java when that island was conquered from the Dutch in 1811.

It is not clear what caused Raffles' interest in Japan. It is certain, however, that it existed some months before he reached Java. In June 1811 he wrote to Lord Minto from Malacca urging that an attempt be made to open an English trade with Nagasaki. He admitted that the Japan trade was ' by no means equal to that of many neglected countries in Asia ', but still thought it worth a trial because of ' the prospect of it being opened on a more extensive scale, an event . . . very likely to be accelerated by the aggressions of Russia '. He said, too, that the intrigues and misrepresentations of the Dutch would condemn to failure any open attempt to trade. The attempt must therefore be made ' by gaining to our interest the present Dutch Resident in Japan and the Japanese Corps of Dutch interpreters, at whatever price it may cost '.[11]

As Lieutenant-Governor in Java, Raffles was in a position to put this plan into practice, and in 1813 he sent two ships to Nagasaki. Waardenaar, a Dutchman formerly at the Deshima factory, went as ostensible Chief, but he was accompanied by Dr. Ainslie, who was to assume command as soon as it seemed safe to reveal that a British trade was openly to be substituted for the Dutch connection. In fact, the latter object was never attained. Hendrik Doeff, the *opperhoofd* at Deshima, refused to take orders from Raffles and persuaded Ainslie that any attempt to reveal the truth of the situation would jeopardise both the safety of the ships and the lives of their crews. With the connivance of the Japanese interpreters, trade was carried on under Dutch colours, but Doeff remained at Deshima. An attempt to remove him in 1814, when Raffles sent Waardenaar back with one ship, met with no greater success.

[11] *Sir T. S. Raffles' Report on Japan to the Secret Committee of the East India Company*, pp. 1-4, Raffles to Minto, June 1811.

Meanwhile Raffles was meeting considerable opposition in India. Minto had returned home in 1813, and the new Governor-General objected to both the scope and the nature of the Japan project. He wrote to Java deprecating the great expense, undertaken 'without having more satisfactory grounds for assuming that the experiment was likely to succeed and that the advantages to be derived . . . were likely to be such as to justify great pecuniary sacrifices in the prosecution of the attempt'. Moreover, any plan that depended for its success on deceiving the Japanese must be fraught with danger. In fact, the letter summed up, 'the Governor-General in Council is of opinion that the attempt to establish an intercourse should have been open and avowed, that it should have been in the first instance at a small expense, and that if serious obstacles were found to exist the idea should for the time have been relinquished'.[12]

Some months later, when the reports and balance-sheet of the 1813 voyage reached India, the reaction was still more hostile. The Accountant-General in Calcutta claimed that money had been lost on the venture and objected that he could see more difficulties than advantages in the trade ; the Governor-General ordered Raffles to take no further steps 'without special authority and instructions from the Supreme Government or from the Public Authorities in England'.[13]

Raffles remained optimistic, however. He maintained that the voyages, especially that of 1814, had shown a respectable profit, and that future prospects far outweighed present disadvantages. Unable to convince the authorities in India, he appealed to the Company in England. In London, of course, his plans aroused little enthusiasm. The Court of Directors expressed a hope that the Japan connection would be maintained if at all practicable, but in May 1815, some weeks before the arrival of Raffles' letter, the Governor-General had been informed that the final decision would be left to his discretion, in the expectation that he would be guided by the results of the 1814

[12] *Raffles Report on Japan*, pp. 71-4, Gov.-Gen. to Raffles, 29 Jan. 1814.
[13] *Raffles Report on Japan*, pp. 191-201, Gov.-Gen. to Raffles, 11 June 1814 and encls.

voyage.[14] Before any action could be taken on these instructions, the war with France had come to an end and preparations were being made to hand Java back to the Dutch. Thereafter, to Raffles' mind, further interference in Japan became impossible.

Raffles' attempt sprang from a very personal enthusiasm. More typical of the Company's servants were the views expressed in India and England. Responsible officials were willing to admit that the opening of Japan was a desirable objective, but they did not think it an important one, certainly not one in which the returns were likely to repay the outlay of any great effort or expense. A similar attitude characterised the actions of the British government.

In the years 1791 and 1792 the government had shown signs of taking steps to end Japanese seclusion. Late in 1791, with the Company's monopoly under fierce attack from merchants in England, it had called for reports on the trade with China, Persia and Japan to enable it ' to judge what prospect there may be of extending or opening such Trade with any of those Countries '.[15] The discouraging report produced by the Company was not enough to stifle this ambition. It had already been decided that Lord Macartney should go to China and try to effect some improvement in the conditions under which British trade was carried on at Canton. In his final instructions, he was given discretionary powers to visit Japan as well. Circumstances, he was told, seemed to favour such a visit, which might at least operate to make the Chinese more amenable to reason, by indicating that Japan was an alternative source of supply for many of the goods hitherto obtained at Canton. He was therefore given letters to Japan, which he might ' either deliver, send or suppress ' as he thought advisable.[16]

These were not very positive directions, to be sure, but Macartney made every effort to carry them out. When he landed in China in the summer of 1793 he at once ordered

---

[14] *Raffles Report on Japan*, pp. 206–7, Raffles to E.I.Co., 10 Dec. 1814, received Pondon 24 June 1815 ; pp. 210-1, Court to Bengal, 5 May 1815.
[15] East India Co., *Court Minute Book*, vol. 100, minutes of 7 Dec. 1791.
[16] Morse, *Chronicles of the E. India Co.*, II, 241.

H.M.S. *Lion* to Japan. Her commander was to make the usual nautical surveys, find out whether the reports of Japanese aversion to foreigners had been exaggerated, how far they were likely to purchase British manufactures, and what goods or raw materials, apart from copper, might profitably be exported in return. He was also to deliver a letter from the ambassador. But if no reply was forthcoming within two weeks, he was to sail so as to meet Macartney at Macao early in May 1794.[17]

The *Lion* did in fact sail for Japan, but was forced back by stress of weather. Before she could try again, Macartney had found it necessary to cancel her instructions. His negotiations in China had broken down, and news of the outbreak of war with France made it imperative that the *Lion* should convoy home the Company's ships from Canton.

The war also explains, in part, why no attempt was made to follow up this abortive expedition. True, Broughton visited the northern coast of Japan in 1796 and 1797,[18] while H.M.S. *Phaeton* entered Nagasaki harbour in 1808, seized hostages to ensure the prompt supply of stores, and sailed before the ill-prepared Japanese garrison could launch any attack.[19] But neither of these visits implied the existence of any government policy with regard to trade. Broughton was engaged in exploration, while the *Phaeton's* object was the capture of two Dutch ships believed to be bound for Nagasaki—a normal function of war-time naval operations.

With the end of the war in Europe, the British government was free once more to turn its attention to commercial interests in the East. By this time, however, there was less reason for it to concern itself with Japan. The failure of Raffles' plans had shown the undertaking to be difficult. Public discussions and debates over the renewal of the East

---

[17] Staunton, *An Authentic Account of an Embassy from the King of Great Britain to the Emperor of China*, I, 507.
[18] Murdoch, *History of Japan*, III, 510.
[19] W. G. Aston, ' H.M.S. Phæton at Nagasaki', *Trans. Asiatic Soc. Japan*, 1st Ser., VII (1879), pp. 323-36 : C. Mutō, *Nichi-ei kōtsū-shi* (*A Study of the History of Anglo-Japanese Relations*), pp. 92-4, 246-435 ·

India Company's charter in 1813 had revealed no wide-spread demand for action about Japan—even Daniel Beal, who had drafted the *Argonaut's* instructions in 1791, neglected the opportunity of introducing the subject when called on to give evidence before a Parliamentary committee. Moreover, the new charter threw open the trade with India, an ample field for private endeavour. The China trade, which continued as an East India Company monopoly, might benefit from government intervention, but when Lord Amherst was sent to China in 1816, there was no mention of Japan in his instructions.

During the next decade, at least, there was no sign of a change in the government's attitude, though British whaling vessels began to visit the Japanese coast in considerable numbers. Many of the whalers were unscrupulous men, not averse to attacking isolated settlements when it seemed both safe and profitable to do so. Some, on the other hand, driven to seek Japanese harbours for shelter or fresh water, found themselves ordered away or even attacked without warning. In such circumstances, occasional clashes were inevitable.[20] There is no evidence, however, that such incidents caused any immediate outcry at home, or even that the whalers tried to secure government protection. Interference in Japan, it seemed, would require some more powerful motive.

By 1830, then, the wheel had almost come full circle. The primary responsibility for action still rested with the Company, and to the Company, recent failures served only to underline the lessons it had learnt in the seventeenth century. Moreover, the government and the private traders, who had once seemed willing to attempt the opening of Japan, no longer seemed inclined to force action upon it. But in this the analysis is incomplete. Neither Cabinet nor merchants looked to the Company as the agent of future action because the Company's charter would expire in 1834. Widespread opposition to the theory of monopoly trading

---

[20] One such incident is described in detail in E. W. Clement, 'British Seamen and Mito Samurai in 1824', *Trans. Asiatic Soc. Japan*, 1st Ser., XXXIII (1905), pp. 86-131 ; and Mutō, *Nichi-ei kōtsū-shi*, pp. 467-83.

made it inevitable that the China trade monopoly would be abolished, and in that event British policy in the China seas would become a matter of government action. How far that policy would concern itself with Japan seemed likely to depend on the ideas expressed in the charter negotiations and debates of the years 1830 to 1834.

In 1830 both houses of Parliament appointed select committees to enquire into the affairs of the Company and its eastern trade. The merchants and others who gave evidence before them were almost all hostile to the East India Company. Most emphasised the Company's failure to find markets for the increasing volume of British manufactures ; especially had it failed to extend its trade to many countries of the East which might—indeed would —furnish profitable outlets. Japan was cited as a notable example. John Aken, former master of a ' country ' ship, held that an embassy should be sent to Japan, for if successful it would undoubtedly pave the way for an immense trade.[21] Another witness, John Deans, who had lived in the East for twenty years and knew much about the Dutch trade with Japan, doubted whether the Japanese government would be influenced by such a mission. But he had no doubt that there was a market for British goods in Japan. Once the monopoly were abolished, that market would be developed whatever the attitude of the Japanese authorities, either through Chinese middlemen or as a direct but illegal trade ; ' our enterprizing countrymen ', he said, ' generally manage to conduct a trade with every part of the world which they can get to '.[22]

Both witnesses believed that these views were widely held in the East. Certainly they were known to, and apparently respected by, the East India Company's select committee at Canton. In a letter to the Court of Directors in January 1831 they discussed a project for using the Bonin Islands as a base for opening trade with Japan, Korea and

[21] Parliamentary Papers 1830, vol. V (Sess. No. 644), *First Report from the Select Committee on the Affairs of the East India Company (China Trade)*, p. 140, minutes of evidence, Mr. John Aken, 4 Mar. 1830.
[22] *ibid*, p. 242, evidence of Mr. John Deans, 16 Mar. 1830.

Loochoo. This they recommended not as a potential source of profit to the Company, but because ' it seems a great desideratum at the present moment to find some means of satisfying the British Mercantile and Manufacturing community with a legitimate prospect of extending their trade in these Eastern Countries '.[23] Of more immediate political importance, the few merchants interested in Japan received powerful support from the *Edinburgh Review*. The Whig periodical published an article maintaining that Japan's hostility to trade had been much exaggerated ; once her coasts were being regularly visited by merchants anxious only to bring the benefits of friendly commerce, ancient fears and suspicions would entirely disappear.[24]

Future trade expansion, however, remained a minor issue in the discussions between Company and Cabinet to decide the terms on which the charter should be renewed. The Company, in a last attempt to retain its privileges, claimed that the China monopoly was not open to the objections usually advanced against the theory of monopoly trading. It was not so employed as to restrict sales and raise prices. It made possible control over British merchants and seamen, essential when dealing with distant and jealous peoples like the Chinese, whose hostility once aroused might easily put an end to trade altogether. Finally, the supposed market for British goods was illusory ; the Company was often forced to sell them at a loss, while the Americans provided purchase-money for their return cargoes not by the sale of manufactured goods but by importing specie into China.[25] Charles Grant, President of the Board of Control, refused to accept this reasoning. Monopoly trading, he wrote, was undesirable in principle, and the Company's arguments were not strong enough to justify the government in making an exception of the China trade. The

---

[23] Foreign Office, General Correspondence, *China* (F.O. 17 : hereafter cited as F.O. *China Corres.*), vol. 2, Canton to Court, 26 Jan. 1831, quoted in a memoir on the China trade prepared by the East India Co.

[24] *Edinburgh Review*, LII (Jan. 1831), pp. 310-3.

[25] East India Co., *Papers respecting the negotiations with His Majesty's Ministers on the subject of the East India Company's Charter* (1833), pp. 5-10, minutes, Secret Comm. of Correspondence, 2 Jan. 1833.

abolition of the monopoly must be accepted, or it would be imposed.[26]

Grant's ultimatum decided the broad outlines of the settlement. The rest of the discussions concerned only points of detail, and neither Company nor Board of Control showed interest in the extension of trade to Japan or any other neglected area of the East. It remained to be seen whether the government would do so in bringing the new charter before Parliament or in drafting detailed instructions for the officials it must eventually send to China.

On 13 June 1833 Sir George Staunton, supporting the East India Company, moved a number of resolutions on the China trade in the House of Commons. These set out once again the difficulties of Eastern trade caused by the exclusion policies of oriental governments, in particular those of Japan and Cochin China, and attributed the relative ill-success of the China trade to the existence of similar sentiments in China rather than to any inefficiency on the part of the Company. In fact, Staunton argued, the Company exerted a most beneficial influence. That influence should only be removed if there were to be substituted for it an effective system of protection based on a national treaty with China, and an embassy to obtain such a treaty would be a far more valuable measure than the abolition of the monopoly.[27] His arguments had little effect. Grant, who introduced the terms of the new charter in a tone of optimism, observed that such an embassy as Staunton proposed might only serve to alarm the Chinese and thus defeat its own ends. It would be better to let the normal working of free enterprise bring a gradual improvement. Meanwhile, representatives of the Crown could control the trade as effectively as had the Company ; more so, in fact, for the Chinese would not hold them responsible for the alarming British advances in Nepal and Burma, which had been directed by the Company not by the Crown.[28] This last

[26] *ibid*, pp. 14-53, Grant to Chairs, 12 Feb. 1833.

[27] Hansard, *Parliamentary Debates*, 3rd Ser., XVIII, cols. 698-700 (13 June 1833).

[28] Hansard, XVIII, cols. 700-18 (13 June 1833).

distinction was to prove a little too subtle to be understood in China and Japan.

The debates that followed were of little moment. The most noticeable feature, commented on by nearly every speaker, was the lack of interest shown in the question both in Parliament and outside it. The East India interest in the Commons, weakened by the Reform Act, was able to put up only feeble opposition, and the East India Company's monopoly of the China trade was abolished by a half-empty House of Commons.

The government had now to work out the details of a new organisation for the China trade. No one department was solely responsible for this task. The India Board and the Foreign Office were first to consider the problem, and there were later a number of meetings between members of the government. The Treasury, as was to be expected, took the initiative on questions of salaries and funds for the new establishment. Lord Auckland, President of the Board of Trade, was present at some of the discussions, but his department concerned itself only with such practical details as port facilities and shipping dues at Canton.[29] The chief responsibility lay with Grant and Palmerston.

At the beginning of November 1833 Grant sought the assistance of the Chairman and Vice-Chairman of the East India Company. He sent them drafts of the commissions and general instructions for the new Superintendent of Trade in China, together with a number of proposed Orders in Council relating to the new establishment.[30] They found little with which to quarrel in the drafts. Noting that the Governor-General of India was to receive copies of correspondence passing between the Superintendency and the Foreign Office, they emphasised that India and China must now be regarded as separate problems. Both had previously been the concern of the Company, but that, the sole connection, was now to be severed, and it must not therefore be

[29] India Board, Secret Dept., *China*, vol. 7, Grant to Auckland, private, 14 Nov. 1833 ; Auckland to Grant, 14 Nov. 1833. Board of Trade, *Minutes* (B.T. 5), vol. 41, *passim*, e.g. minutes of 22 and 26 Nov., 6 and 17 Dec. 1833.
[30] East India Co., *Letters from the Board of Control*, vol. 9, Board to Chairs 1 Nov. 1833.

thought ' that the resources of India are the natural means with which any line of Policy may be enforced by His Majesty's Servants at Canton '.[31] With this reservation and one or two criticisms on points of detail the Chairs were content. In fact, they expressed much gratification that the government had followed so closely the policy which the Company had long enjoined on its own servants at Canton.

While the general lines of policy were thus worked out by the government in consultation with the East India Company, the responsibility for its detailed execution lay with the Foreign Secretary. Accordingly, in addition to the instructions given under the Sign Manual, Lord Palmerston issued more particular instructions in a series of dispatches written in January 1834, in the drafting of which he consulted Lord Napier, who had been appointed Chief Superintendent in the previous month. In these instructions, too, the influence of the East India Company is clearly seen.

The first dispatch concerned only the Canton trade, by far the most important of the new Foreign Office responsibilities. Palmerston, however, was the Foreign Secretary of a Whig government which had abolished the East India Company's monopoly, ostensibly, at least, to make possible an extension of British trade. He could not, had he wished it, completely ignore the criticisms which had been directed against the Company in the previous four years, particularly the charge that it had neglected opportunities to open new markets in the East for British goods. In his second dispatch Palmerston turned his attention to this problem. He cautiously directed Napier to take every safe opportunity of encouraging the extension of trade with China. Trouble might be caused by ships attempting to explore the China coast in search of new markets, but while he was not to give public support to such adventures, the Superintendent must clearly understand that he had no authority to prevent or interfere with them. He must investigate the need for surveys of the China coast and the adjacent islands, an

---

[31] East India Co., *Letters to the Board of Control*, vol. 12, Chairs to Board, 14 Nov. 1833.

indispensable concomitant of trade expansion, but was to take no action in the matter without reference home. Finally, in equally guarded terms, direct reference was made to Japan :—

> " Observing the same prudence and caution . . . you will avail yourself of every opportunity which may present itself for ascertaining whether it may not be possible to establish commercial intercourse with Japan, and with any other of the neighbouring countries, and you will report to this Department from time to time the results of your observation and enquiries."[32]

The Foreign Office papers give no direct indication of the origin of this instruction.[33] Yet its origin may be inferred. The Foreign Office had only once before dealt directly with the problem of relations with China, on the occasion of Lord Amherst's special embassy in 1816, and thus had very few records which might act as a guide to future policy. It apparently relied for most of its information on a long memorandum detailing the history of the China trade, which was drawn up by the East India Company.[34] Almost inevitably, therefore, its China policy showed strong traces of the influence of East India House. One might reasonably expect a similar tendency in its attitude to Japan. The Company had long ceased to show interest in the Japan trade except when under attack from merchants and manufacturers at home ; but such attacks had been revived in the period 1830 to 1834, and in a sense constituted pressure upon the government to work for an extension of trade when the monopoly should end. Palmerston himself had been impressed with the importance of encouraging trade in his student days at Edinburgh. In the circumstances, it is not very surprising that there should have been some reference to Japan in Napier's instructions.

[32] F.O. *China Corres.*, vol. 5, For. Off. to Napier, No. 2, 25 Jan. 1834.

[33] Except the question of surveying, which had first been raised by Napier on the basis of a report from Captain Horsbrugh, Hydrographer to the East India Co. Palmerston had been inclined to authorise it, but the Admiralty urged that nothing be done until Napier had reached China and decided whether surveying could be carried out without alarming the Chinese. See F.O. *China Corres.*, vol. 4, Napier to Palmerston, 31 Dec. 1833 ; For. Off. to Adty., 3 Jan. 1834 ; Adty. to For. Off., 6 Jan. 1834.

[34] F.O. *China Corres.*, vols. 1 and 2.

In the same way, one can account for the note of caution sounded in those instructions. The Company's influence would be against direct and decisive action. Nor was there any consistent attempt by any other interests to force a trade with Japan. The *Edinburgh Review*, the most influential supporter of the idea, had mentioned the subject but once. Other equally powerful opinion, which found expression in the *Quarterly Review* later in 1834, was opposed to any rash undertaking. The *Quarterly* held that the trade of Japan was no longer worth the effort required to obtain it, long the East India Company's belief. Even the trade of the Dutch, it said, had become ' rather matter of curiosity and habit, than of commercial profit '. Moreover the opposition of the Japanese presented a serious obstacle, so serious that it seemed much more likely ' that the sole remaining link between Europe and Japan, the Dutch connexion, should be severed by violence or obliterated by disuse, than that either force or persuasion should devise a new one between this country or any of its dependencies and that empire.'[35] Trade with Japan, by this estimate, was neither practicable nor desirable.

We see, then, that Lord Palmerston, still a relatively in-experienced Foreign Secretary, refrained from committing himself too deeply in the wording of his instructions about Japan. Napier was to observe and report. He was to take no action without reference home. The Foreign Secretary thus showed proper respect for the views of his political supporters but did nothing to arouse the ire of his oppon-ents. His attitude to the proposed annexation of the Bonin Islands and to the *Morrison's* visit to Japan lends colour to this interpretation of his policy.

For some years Englishmen had discussed the advisability of establishing an island base off the China coast. The idea attracted some as being the best protection for the Canton trade, providing a secure refuge for the ships and merchants engaged in it, free from the oppressions of Chinese law. There were others, however, who were more ambitious.

[35] *Quarterly Review*, LII (Nov. 1834), pp. 293-4.

They regarded such a base as one from which trade could be extended directly to North China and even to Japan, and it was from this group that there came a number of proposals for the annexation of the Bonin Islands.

These islands, some twelve hundred miles east of Taiwan and seven hundred from the south coast of Japan, were too far from China to be of value in the Canton trade. They might, however, prove useful for trade to the north and northwest. They had been known to the Japanese as early as the sixteenth century, when they were used for a time as a prison colony, but in 1823, when they were visited by an American whaling vessel, they were uninhabited. Captain Beechey of H.M.S. *Blossom* called there four years later and claimed them formally for Great Britain. In 1830 a group of Europeans of various nationalities formed a settlement on the islands, hoping to raise fresh provisions for sale to the whaling crews who used them as a base for the Japan fisheries, and to any merchant ships that might call on their way to the coasts of China and Japan. The venture had the support of Mr. Charlton, British consul in the Sandwich Islands. Ignorant of the real distance of the Bonins from Japan, he thought it possible to persuade Chinese junks to call there on the run from Canton to Nagasaki, which would enable them to pick up British goods for the Japan market at a port free from the heavy duties imposed in China. At about the same time the Canton committee of the East India Company also remarked on the islands as being a convenient centre for the northern trade, far enough from Canton not to endanger British interests there.[36] Neither the Company nor the Foreign Office took any action on these reports.

The matter was not allowed to rest, however, for the settlers themselves began to seek British protection. In April 1834, Francis Stavers of Peckham Rye sought permission to found a colony on Bonin under British authority and protection, to be a port of refuge for whalers and for

[36] F.O. *China Corres.*, vol. 2, quoting Canton Comm. to Court, 26 Jan. 1831. Foreign Office, Embassy and Consular Archives, *China* (F.O. 228; hereafter cited as F.O. *China Emb. Arch.*), vol. 153, Charlton to For. Off., No. 5, 1 Dec. 1831, encl. in For. Off. to Bonham, No. 97, 24 Nov. 1853.

the British shipping 'which may be expected to endeavour to drive a Trade in those Seas both to the Coast of China and to Japan'. Stavers claimed that he had a friend already established there. None the less, the Colonial Office declined to offer its protection, on the grounds that the islands were outside the range of ordinary naval assistance. It contented itself with commending the idea of such a settlement and hoping that no harm would come to it for lack of official protection.[37]

At the end of the same year a British ship, the *Volunteer*, was damaged in a typhoon and put in to Port Lloyd in the Bonin group to effect repairs. On his arrival at Macao, Robert Edwards, her owner, gave an account of his visit and of the settlement to Captain Charles Elliot, one of the three Superintendents of Trade. He in his turn drew up a report for the Chief Superintendent, Sir G. B. Robinson.[38] After describing the islands and the origin of the settlement Elliot proceeded to urge their value as a base for opening up trade 'with the richest part of the Chinese Empire, and with the South coast of Japan'. Moreover, the settlers themselves needed protection, he thought. The whaling vessels which often visited Port Lloyd were manned by lawless crews whose violence and occasional piracy should be suppressed before their 'acts of depredation' on the coasts of Japan incurred the wrath of the Japanese. Robinson, who found Elliot's argument impressive enough to recommend that a naval vessel be sent to investigate the islands, forwarded a copy of this report to the Governor-General of India in February 1835.[39]

The problem of a formal occupation, of course, had to be decided in London. The Foreign Office took no immediate steps in the matter, but the question was raised again later in 1835 by the Colonial Office and Board of Trade. In November the Board of Trade received a peti-

[37] F.O. *China Emb. Arch.*, vol. 153, For. Off. to Bonham, No. 97, 24 Nov. 1853, enclosing Stavers to Colonial Office, 10 Apr. 1834, and Col. Off. to Stavers, 16 Apr. 1834.

[38] Napier had died in 1834 and was succeeded first by J. F. Davis and then, in Jan. 1835, by Robinson.

[39] F.O. *China Corres.*, vol. 9, Robinson to Gov.-Gen., 21 Feb. 1835.

tion from two of the original Bonin settlers, Millichamp and Mozaro, asking directly for the recognition and protection of the colony by the British government.[40] The Board consulted the Admiralty and then wrote to the two petitioners to explain that no action could be taken as 'the Island of Bonin is beyond the Limits to which British Cruizers ordinarily go '.[41] This reply, substantially the same as that made to Stavers by the Colonial Office over a year before, was never sent because the addresses could not be found, but a few days later the Admiralty announced that a ship was to be sent to the islands from the East Indies station, and the whole correspondence was forwarded to the Colonial Office.[42]

Charles Grant, now Lord Glenelg and head of the colonial department, decided that the question was one on which the Foreign Office must be consulted, as the colony, if recognised, would derive its only importance from its proximity to the coast of China. Palmerston made a non-commital reply to his letter. Bonin was far enough from China, he wrote, and its occupation need not prove a source of embarrassment in British relations with that country.[43] Glenelg, however, wanted something more definite than this, and on 1 February emphasised that he had no intention of recommending the annexation of the Bonin Islands unless, in the opinion of the Foreign Office, possession of them would be of positive advantage to the China trade. At this, Palmerston revealed that the question had also been raised by the Chief Superintendent in China. Since a ship was being sent to investigate, he proposed that the matter be allowed to rest until the result of this visit be known.[44]

It is significant that throughout this correspondence the

[40] Bd. Trade, *Minutes*, vol. 43, minutes, 13 Nov. 1835.

[41] Bd. Trade, *Minutes*, vol. 43, minutes, 27 Nov. 1835. Bd. Trade, *Out Letters* (B.T. 3), vol. 26, Board to Adty., 21 Nov. 1835 ; Board to Millichamp and Mozaro, 3 Dec. 1835.

[42] Bd. Trade, *Minutes*, vol. 43, minutes, 11 Dec. 1835. Bd. Trade, *Out Letters*, vol. 26, Bd. Trade to Col. Off., 23 Dec. 1835.

[43] Col. Off., *East Indies*, vol. 45, Col. Off. to For. Off., 7 Jan. 1836 ; For. Off. to Col. Off., 14 Jan. 1836.

[44] Col. Off., *East Indies*, vol. 45, Col. Off. to For. Off., 1 Feb. 1836 ; For. Off. to Col. Off., 20 Feb. 1936.

three home departments concerned not once referred to Japan either in letters or minutes. Consul Charlton, the Canton select committee, Stavers, Millichamp and Mozaro, Captain Elliot, even Sir George Robinson, all regarded the Bonins chiefly desirable as affording or facilitating access to the markets of North China and Japan. The government ignored this aspect of the question. The Colonial Office was concerned only with their value as a colony, the Foreign Office and Board of Trade with the effect annexation might have on the existing trade at Canton. It was a period, of course, when British statesmen viewed with disfavour the idea of acquiring any new colonial territories, other than those valuable as naval and commercial centres. One concludes that the commercial prospects of the Bonin Islands were not obvious enough to arouse enthusiasm—a view, judging by the tone of the earlier instructions to Lord Napier, which applied equally to the other small countries of the western Pacific.

Robinson's recommendation had been enough to secure a promise that Captain Quin of H.M.S. *Raleigh* should visit the Bonin settlement. An attempt was made at the end of 1835, but the *Raleigh* lost a mast in a typhoon and was forced to put back. Other duties intervened to cause delay, and it was not until the summer of 1837 that Captain Quin finally reached the islands. He reported at length on their resources and topography, but found no evidence that they were used as a base for piratical excursions into Japanese waters, or that they were in any danger from the Japanese, and he concluded that no formal occupation would be necessary. The appointment of a vice-consul would be sufficient safeguard, he thought, ' in the present infant state of the settlement '.[45] In the event, even this suggestion was not adopted.

Quin made no reference to the prospects of opening a trade with Japan from the Bonin Islands. This was not necessarily because, like Palmerston and Glenelg, he thought the issue unimportant. More probably it was

[45] F.O. *China Corres.*, vol. 21, Quin's report of 9 Aug. 1837, enclosure in Elliot to For. Off., No. 58, 4 Sept. 1837.

because he knew that a direct attempt to break down Japanese seclusion was already in progress.

This new attempt, rather surprisingly, had originated with the Hudson's Bay Company. Late in 1832 a Japanese junk, on a coasting voyage from Owari to Edo, had been driven east by a typhoon. Its unseaworthy construction—the result of the seventeenth-century seclusion laws—ensured that it could not make its way back to Japan, and in January 1834 it was wrecked on the northwest coast of America. Three sailors, Kyūkichi, Iwakichi and Otokichi, the only survivors of a crew of fourteen, were made prisoners by the Indians, but news of this reached John McLoughlin, the Hudson's Bay Company's factor at Fort Vancouver, who arranged for their release and had them brought to his trading post. These men, he believed, were the first Japanese to have fallen into British hands, and McLoughlin did not wish such an opportunity to be wasted. Rather than send them to the Sandwich Islands to await a ship bound for China, he decided to send them to London, in the expectation that the British government would gladly avail itself of such a chance to open communication with Japan and to impress on the three castaways 'a respectable idea of the grandeur and power of the British nation'.[46]

The three Japanese reached London in June 1835. The Governor of the Hudson's Bay Company at once laid McLoughlin's plan before the government—probably before Lord Palmerston, with whom he certainly corresponded on other matters. Judging by the tone of his subsequent letter to Fort Vancouver, the response was not encouraging. McLoughlin was commended for his humanity, but rebuked for putting the Company to fruitless trouble and expense. It would have been better, the Governor said, to have sent the men home via the Sandwich

---

[46] Hudson's Bay Company Archives, *Vancouver Fort, Correspondence Books Out* (B. 223), b. 10, McLoughlin to Company, 18 Nov. 1834. (Printed in E.E. Rich, ed., *The Letters of John McLoughlin from Fort Vancouver to the Governor and Committee, First Series*, 1825-38, pp. 128-9). See also C. M. Drury, 'Early American Contacts with the Japanese', *Pacific Northwest Quarterly*, XXXVI (Oct. 1945), pp. 319-21.

Islands, 'His Majesty's Government not being disposed to open a communication with the Japanese Government thro' the medium of three shipwrecked Seamen '.[47] There remained the problem of what to do with the men now they were in England. This was quickly solved. They were sent aboard the *General Palmer* for passage to Macao at the Hudson's Bay Company's expense, and her captain was requested to arrange their return thence to their own country.[48]

This was not by any means the end of the story, however. When the *General Palmer* reached the Canton estuary in December 1835, her captain was faced with the problem of arranging passage to Japan for his three passengers. He sought the help and advice of the Chief Superintendent. As a first step, Robinson put the three men under the care of the indefatigable Chinese Secretary, Dr. Gutzlaff, who lodged them at his own house and at once began to learn their language. Captain Elliot, now Second Superintendent and impatient with his superior's " quiescent " policy towards China, saw in this an opportunity of extending British influence in the East, and perhaps of gaining reputation for himself. He proposed that the castaways be returned to Japan aboard a British ship of war. The voyage, if undertaken, must have as its ostensible aim nothing more than the return of the three men, and the envoy entrusted with the mission—Elliot suggested that he might go himself—must be careful to avoid the appearance of any other motives. Even so, with careful handling, a correspondence could be started which might lead in time to the opening of trade. Secrecy, of course, must be strictly maintained. Moreover, the ship should go direct to Edo, the capital. The home of the sailors, he thought, was close enough to Edo to enable such a course to be followed without arousing undue suspicion, while to choose the

---

[47] Hudson's Bay Co., *London Correspondence, Outward, Official* (A. 6), vol. 23, Company to McLoughlin, 28 Aug. 1835.

[48] Hudson's Bay Co., *London Correspondence, Outward, General* (A. 5), vol. 11, Company to Mr. Wade, 11 June 1835. Also S. Sakamaki, ' Japan and the United States 1790-1853 ', *Trans. Asiatic Soc. Japan*, 2nd Ser., XVIII (Dec. 1939), p. 13 and note.

alternative of going to Nagasaki would be to leave the way open for Dutch intrigue.[49]

Robinson claimed to be delighted at finding himself for once in agreement with Captain Elliot. Early in 1836 he forwarded copies of Elliot's memorandum to the Foreign Office and the Governor-General in India, recommending that a warship be sent and Elliot put in charge of the expedition.[50] He reported that an American frigate was about to visit Japan,[51] and boasted that the possession of the three Japanese gave Britain an introduction which both Americans and Dutch would be glad to possess. It ought not to be wasted. Support could be expected from India, where Elliot was marshalling influential friends to back the project, and Robinson hoped that the Foreign Office would at least approve the immediate steps he had taken to keep the Japanese in Macao, and thus preserve the initial advantage Britain had gained.

Elliot and Robinson did not know that a similar plan had already been discussed in London and rejected as beneath the dignity of a British government. Nor had anything happened to change Foreign Office opinion since the previous summer. On the contrary, just before Robinson's dispatch was received, the *Quarterly Review* had again denounced Japan adventures in the strongest possible terms. In July 1836 it reviewed Doeff's *Herinneringen uit Japan*, which included a long account of Raffles' attempt to open trade with Japan in 1813 and 1814. The reviewer accused Raffles of over-optimism in thinking that any change could easily be effected in the trade and policy of the Japanese. He also condemned those who more recently

---

[49] F.O. *China Corres.*, vol. 14, Elliot to Chief Supt., 25 Dec. 1835, encl. in Robinson to Gov.-Gen , 16 Jan. 1836 : Sakamaki, *op. cit.*, p. 13.

[50] F.O. *China Corres.*, vol. 14, Robinson to For. Off., No. 16, 1 Mar. 1836 ; Robinson to Gov.-Gen., 16 Jan. 1836.

[51] F.O. *China Corres.*, vol. 14, Robinson to For. Off., No. 16, 1 Mar. 1836, presumably a reference to Roberts' mission. Roberts had been sent secretly by President Jackson to negotiate with Siam and Japan some years before. He succeeded in Siam, but because of certain conflict in the wording of his instructions, had returned to America for additional orders before visiting Japan. In 1835 he set out openly to complete the mission, but died at Macao in June 1836 before reaching Japan. His presence at Macao cannot have been the cause of Elliott's plan, however, as he did not arrive there until 1836.

had come to believe something of the same kind. Nothing said the *Quarterly*, could be done except by force, and the use of force was morally unjustifiable ; for 'some great and sweeping revolution must disorganize [Japan's] government and obliterate her institutions before we can approach her coasts in any other guise than that of invaders of an unoffending, we wish we could add unoffended, nation '.[52] In contrast, the Whig *Edinburgh Review* kept silent about Japan. Since 1831 it had made no comment on that subject, and when eventually it did so in 1838, it was with no evidence of enthusiasm.[53]

Once again there was no important group in London sufficiently concerned about the Japan trade to bring pressure to bear on the Foreign Secretary. Left thus to make his own decision, Palmerston did not wait for any recommendation from India. Elliot had been instructed to relieve Robinson, and on 14 September 1836 the tersest of replies was sent to his proposals. Without explanation or preliminary, the new Superintendent was ordered ' to send these men quietly home in any Chinese junk bound for Japan '.[54]

Elliot found it impossible to carry out these instructions. Chinese junks going to Japan sailed not from Canton but from Chapoo, some six hundred miles distant, and in any case no Chinese dared accept passengers so calculated to arouse the hostility of Japanese officials. There was an alternative, however. Elliot and Gutzlaff had not been alone in recognizing the opportunity offered by the return of the three seamen. C. W. King, an American merchant, and Dr. S. Wells Williams, head of the American Board Mission Press, both wanted to visit Japan. When Elliot's plan was vetoed by Palmerston and the official American expedition was abandoned on the death of Roberts, they suggested that these castaways, together with four others who had been sent from Manila, might be returned to Japan in the American brig *Himmaleh*, shortly expected back from a cruise to the

[52] *Quarterly Review*, LVI (July 1836), pp. 436-7.
[53] *Edinburgh Review*, LXVIII (Oct. 1838), pp. 46-75.
[54] F.O. *China Corres.*, vol. 14, For. Off, to Elliot, No. 18. 14 Sept. 1836.

Malay archipelago. Elliot was reluctant to concede to the Americans an advantage which he had hoped to gain for his own countrymen. Yet there seemed no other way of carrying out his instructions. However, when he finally gave way to American persuasions, it was only on condition that the three Japanese for whom he was responsible should be given the opportunity of transferring to a Japanese junk when the *Himmaleh* reached the Loochoo Islands.[55]

It was arranged that Gutzlaff should join the party as interpreter, and take charge of the three castaways from London. As he was leaving almost at once in H.M.S. *Raleigh* to visit the Fukien coast, and it would then be most convenient for him to sail direct to Loochoo, there was no time to wait for the *Himmaleh*. A rendezvous was arranged at Napa and King hurriedly fitted out another ship, the *Morrison*, for Japan. A doctor was added to the expedition, and when she finally sailed, the *Morrison* carried medicines, tracts and trade goods in addition to the seven Japanese. King, hoped, in fact, to open an American trade with Japan, and drafted letters asking permission to do so, which he planned to present when the castaways were returned to their " grateful " fellow-countrymen.[56] Such optimism was to prove ill-founded.

Gutzlaff, as a British official, had to ask formally for permission to accompany the expedition, and since there was no time to refer to London, Elliot had to grant it on his own responsibility. He had, however, been convinced by the previous correspondence on the subject that the Foreign Office had no wish to be involved officially in any attempt to communicate with Japan. He therefore made it quite clear that Gutzlaff would be expected on his return to provide a report on any matters of general interest that came to his notice during the voyage, but must in other respects remember that he would technically be on leave of absence

---

[55] F.O. *China Corres.*, vol. 20, Elliot to For. Off., No. 43, 3 July 1837 ; C. W. King and G. T. Lay, *The Claims of Japan and Malaysia upon Christendom*, I, ix-xvi.

[56] S. W. Williams, ' Narrative of a voyage . . . to Lewchew and Japan ', *Chinese Repository*, VI (Dec. 1837), pp. 210-1 ; King and Lay, *op. cit.*, I, xvi-xxii.

from the time he left the *Raleigh*. He emphasised that the chief consideration must at all times be the safety of the castaways. They were to be warned of the risk they ran in breaking Japanese laws, and if they chose to remain with the *Morrison* till she reached Japan, were to be landed with the utmost caution, secretly if possible. ' Generally, in all your proceedings with regard to these individuals ', he wrote, ' you will bear in mind that their secure return to their own Country is the single object to which His Majesty's Government attach any importance ; and I feel assured that nothing would seem less pardonable to Lord Palmerston, than the least disposition to postpone that consideration to any views or purposes whatever '.[57] Clearly, Elliot had no intention of risking another snub from London. Nor did he wish to do anything that might enable the Americans to secure trading privileges in Japan.

At Loochoo the *Morrison* was the object of much interest and some suspicion. The actions of Williams, whose investigations into Loochoo life and customs were persistent and unwelcome, and of the doctor, who forcibly demonstrated the efficacy of vaccination, might almost have been designed to alarm the officials. The arrival of a British warship—the *Raleigh* bringing Gutzlaff to join the others—gave the expedition something of the appearance of an international conspiracy. Suspicion was heightened when it was learned that she was to proceed next to the Bonins, with the probable intention of annexing those islands. It became certainty when the Loochoo authorities discovered that there were Japanese aboard the *Morrison*. News of the expedition, and of its supposedly hostile intentions was at once dispatched to Japan.

With commendable caution the seven Japanese refused to take passage in a Japanese junk, and on 30 July 1837 the *Morrison* dropped anchor off Uraga, at the entrance to Edo Bay. Her arrival was greeted by some firing ashore, thought to be warning guns, but this soon stopped and crowds of Japanese came out to inspect the ship. King

[57] F.O. *China Corres.*, vol. 20, Elliot to Gutzlaff, 21 June 1837, enclosed in Elliot to For. Off., No. 43, 3 July 1837.

wished to communicate with the officials in order to hand over the letters he had prepared, but to all his enquiries he got the same answer—orders must first come from the capital. At night all visitors went ashore. At dawn the next day, without any warning, coast batteries opened fired on the ship. The *Morrison*'s guns had been dismantled and left behind at Macao, in order to emphasise the peaceful nature of her errand, and as she was unable to return the fire, there was no alternative but to withdraw. She left Edo Bay, pursued for a time by Japanese war-junks, to try again at Kagoshima, a port in the extreme south of Kyūshū and capital city of the Satsuma fief. There the same reception awaited her. On 27 August, the expedition arrived back at Macao, having succeeded neither in its public nor in its secret plans.

King maintained that the experiences of the *Morrison* showed that the time had come for government intervention to protect American shipping in Japan. In closing his account of the voyage, he urged that an American naval squadron be sent there to exact guarantees of good behaviour for the future and of better treatment for American seamen wrecked on the Japanese coast. No less a measure could possibly succeed. The insult to the American flag gave sufficient cause, providing 'an occasion too valuable to be lost for bringing national influence to bear on the point where private effort . . . failed to make any impression '.[58] Dr. Williams, as became his calling, was more moderate. He felt that at least part of the blame must be born, by the whaling crews who had at times attacked the Japanese coast. The expedition, he said, had proved that the Japanese still pursued their policy of isolation without question and without deviation. None the less, and at whatever cost, the missionaries must be prepared to try again.[59]

When Elliot sent an account of the expedition to London, he was able to report that he had once more taken charge of the three Japanese, now apparently permanent exiles, and had found work for them in Macao, thus relieving the pub-

[58] King and Lay, *Claims of Japan and Malaysia*, I, 178.
[59] Williams, ' Voyage . . . to Lewchew and Japan ', pp. 376-7.

lic funds of the cost of their upkeep. He forwarded Gutzlaff's report without comment. Gutzlaff was in sympathy with King, and thought the treatment meted out to the *Morrison* a new and intolerable development of the seclusion policy. Whatever the laws of Japan, he said, her rulers must be constrained to observe the law of nations, and not treat all foreigners as enemies. The people themselves seemed friendly and industrious. In fact, the government was the only obstacle to the development of friendly intercourse. Should that obstacle prove insurmountable, it should still be possible to develop Napa as a centre for an illegal trade with Japan—the people of Satsuma, the fief which claimed suzerainty over the Loochoos, would certainly welcome such an opportunity. The greatest difficulty would be ' to convince the people of Loochoo, that trade is our sole object and to silence their suspicion of ulterior views '. To accomplish this would require a great and prolonged effort.[60]

Palmerston made no comment on this report. He did, however, give his full approval to Elliot's arrangements, and made this the occasion to re-state the policy which he had originally embodied in his instructions to Lord Napier. Collecting information about potential new markets was still to be considered one of the duties of the Superintendency. In particular, should it be known that one of H.M. ships planned a cruise among the islands off the China coast, it would be well for a competent member of the establishment to go with her, ' in order to collect information as to the Commerce and Statistics of these Islands ; their present intercourse with any foreign Nation ; and the best means of establishing or increasing the intercourse of British Traders with them '.[61]

Thus in 1834, and again in 1838, Palmerston issued instructions which looked to the expansion of British trade —even specifically with Japan—as a desirable object. Yet

[60] F.O. *China Corres.*, vol. 21, Elliot to For. Off., No. 58, 4 Sept. 1837, and Gutzlaff's report enclosed therein.
[61] F.O. *China Corres.*, vol. 25, For. Off. to Elliot, No. 4, 2 June 1838.

in the same period he failed to take advantage of opportunities to further that end by annexing the Bonins or by sending a British ship to return the Japanese seamen. Despite appearances, there is no real contradiction between these facts.

The Bonin question has only indirect reference to Japan, and Palmerston's inaction can readily be explained. Many Englishmen, Palmerston among them, disliked the prospect of further territorial expansion. Britain seemed to have already in India and Canada more territory than she could efficiently exploit, while the secession of the thirteen colonies still served as a dreadful warning of the ingratitude of colonists. Only commercial and naval stations were needed in the new age of commercial empire. The Bonins were not, and could never become, a strategic centre of the same value as Aden, Ceylon or Singapore ; they were too far from the China coast to be of value in the Canton trade ; and their significance for the future, problematical as it was, was no argument to overcome a deep-rooted prejudice.

No such consideration entered into the *Morrison* affair. It is unlikely that the insignificance of the occasion—the return to their homeland of three common sailors—would alone have been enough to prevent action had Palmerston seriously wanted it. The fact is that there is no evidence that Palmerston was ever really interested in Japan, or even saw it as a distinct and individual problem. His instructions to Napier were couched in general terms such as might have been expected from any Whig Secretary of State. Palmerston himself was less interested in commerce than in questions of boundaries, constitutions and national prestige while the increasing work of the office can have left him little leisure to plan expeditions for relatively unimportant commercial ends. Moreover, the affairs of Europe were more important to him than those of the Far East. Until 1839 he gave but little attention to China, where British interests were both valuable and well-publicised. It is only natural that Japan should have seemed more remote and even less important. His refusal to entertain Elliot's proposals is not surprising. Napier had been ordered to report not to act. Action might, perhaps, have been taken if the Japanese had appeared to relent or if pressure had been brought to bear on the Foreign Secretary in England. But there was no sign of such change in either country. In England, indeed, the opponents of direct action seem to have been more powerful, or at least more vocal, than its supporters.

Palmerston's policy towards Japan—if his attitude can be so described—was one which involved the minimum of political and diplomatic risk. In this it paralleled that of the East India Company before 1834. The abolition of the monopoly had brought no immediate attempt to open the ports of Japan to British trade. New factors, however, were soon to be introduced into the situation. In 1839 Canton became the scene of a dispute over opium which precipitated war between China and Great Britain, and this war, in turn, made radical alterations in Britain's position on the China coast. The fact was to play a prominent part in the history of Anglo-Japanese relations.

CHAPTER II

THE OPIUM WAR IN ANGLO-JAPANESE RELATIONS

THE events of the years 1834 to 1838, and especially the preliminaries to the *Morrison* expedition, indicate that the transfer of responsibility from the East India Company to the Foreign Office had made no marked change in Britain's official attitude to Japanese seclusion. Her China policy, too, had at first remained essentially the same. In China, however, a valuable trade already existed, and such minor changes as were caused by the substitution of Crown for Company had far-reaching effects. In the past, arrangements for trade and the settlement of disputes had been effected on both sides through merchants, a method which conformed admirably to the Chinese scale of social and economic values in which trade and traders had a very lowly place. Yet Napier was ordered to announce his arrival to the Canton viceroy. This was, in effect, a claim to diplomatic status as the representative of an equal and independent state, and one which no Chinese official could admit. It led to an immediate dispute, and unable to break the resulting deadlock, Napier withdrew to Macao. He died soon after, and his successor, J. F. Davis, decided to await further instructions from London, making no attempt to force a decision or even to resume relations with the Chinese until they arrived. In the absence of orders from the Foreign Office, this policy of " quiescence " was pursued by the Superintendency for the next two years.

After December 1836 Captain Charles Elliot, the new Superintendent of Trade, tried without success to re-establish communication with the Canton officials. Meanwhile, disputes and grievances on both sides remained unsettled. British discontent with both the conditions and terms of trade increased, and opium smuggling grew apace. In 1839 a Chinese attempt to suppress the opium traffic brought conflict to a head. Before the end of the year local hostilities had broken out in the Canton estuary, and in 1840 these developed into open war.

British victory was rapid and complete. Sir Henry Pottinger, Elliot's successor as Superintendent and Plenipotentiary, forced the Chinese to accept his terms at Nanking in August 1842 and amplified them in a supplementary agreement signed in 1843. By these two treaties Britain secured most of the benefits long sought by her merchants. The island of Hongkong was ceded to her in full sovereignty ; five ports—Canton, Foochow, Amoy, Ningpo and Shanghai—were opened to trade ; a fixed tariff was established at a level favourable to the foreign trader ; and Britain was granted partial jurisdiction over her subjects in China and the right to participate in any privileges granted for the future to other foreign powers. The trade of China had at last been opened, and it seemed that the stage was set for a new phase of British expansion in the Far East. To none did this seem more likely than to the Japanese.

Since the closing of the country in the seventeenth century, the Tokugawa had if anything grown more suspicious of the motives of foreign visitors. Russian attacks in the north,[1] the *Phaeton's* visit to Nagasaki, and occasional clashes with whaling crews, had all been taken as evidence of foreign designs on Japanese territory. In 1825, after one of these clashes, and as a result of the alarming discovery that in some areas coast-dwellers were regularly providing the whalers with stores, the seclusion laws were revised. The new decree was more drastic even than the old. For the future, all foreign ships approaching the coast were to be driven off by force, without stores or

---

[1] In 1804 a Russian mission had reached Nagasaki in search of trade. As a result of Japanese refusal to permit trade, there followed a number of Russian visits to the Kuriles and Hokkaidō, sometimes leading to armed conflict. See Murdoch, *History of Japan*, III, 511-7, 522-3.

water, without even an opportunity of stating their business.[2]

Many Japanese realised that the new policy must inevitably arouse resentment abroad—and that Japan was in no condition to resist attack. Economic changes, visible in the growth of towns and the evolution of a merchant-financier class, were undermining the feudal basis of Tokugawa society. The Bakufu[3] and many of the *daimyō* were near bankruptcy, and their exactions pressed ever more heavily on the peasants and lower ranks of the feudal hierarchy, attacking at once their livelihood and their loyalty. At the same time political opposition to the Tokugawa was crystallising. The great *tozama* lords,[4] direct vassals of the Emperor, had never been fully reconciled to Tokugawa rule ; nor had the Court nobles at Kyōto, who could never hope to regain their former wealth and privileges while Japan was ruled by a Shōgun. Together they formed the core of the anti-Tokugawa movement.

For the time, however, political action was confined to the debates and disputes of scholars and pamphleteers. Three groups in particular are important for our purpose, in that they played a major part in moulding Japan's reactions to British Far Eastern policy. The *Wagakusha* stood for the revival of native Japanese learning and traditions as opposed to the Chinese culture which had so firm a hold on Tokugawa Japan. They attacked the very foundations of Tokugawa power by re-asserting the divinity and authority of the Emperor. The *Rangakusha*, or ' Dutch ' scholars, on the other hand, studied Western thought and science, taking their name from the fact that the books they used were imported through the Dutch factory at Deshima. Both groups were in bitter conflict with the *Jusha*, the Confucian scholars who were advisers to the Bakufu and

---

[2] Kobayashi, *Bakumatsu-shi* [History of the late-Tokugawa period], pp. 76-9. A translation of the decree appears in Murdoch, *History of Japan*, III, 528.

[3] *Bakufu.* The term for the government of Japan under the rule of a Shōgun, as distinct from that of an Emperor.

[4] *Tozama daimyō*. The descendants of those lords who had opposed Ieyasu after the death of Hideyoshi in 1598 and submitted only after their defeat at Sekigahara in 1600. They remained subject to close supervision and were permanently excluded from all administrative offices.

many fiefs, advocates of Chinese learning and uncompromising opponents of all things new.

The Rangakusha led the way in the new discussions of foreign policy. Their work had begun in the eighteenth century with an emphasis on the study of Western medicine, but investigation of this soon led them to other subjects. By the end of the century they were turning to discussion of foreign relations and military technique. At first they concerned themselves with the problem of countering Russian attacks in the north ; it was not until after 1830, notably after the visit of the *Morrison* in 1837, that fear of Britain became a major theme in their books and pamphlets.

Two men, in particular, were responsible for this change of emphasis. They were Watanabe Kazan, son of a *samurai* of the Tawara fief in central Honshū, and Takano Chō-ei, a former pupil of Siebold who had abandoned medicine to concentrate on his writing and translating. Both these men were convinced that Japan was in imminent danger of attack from overseas. Late in 1838 they found occasion to make their views public. In November of that year they came into possession of a document, reputedly copied from the Bakufu archives, which stated that the British warship *Morrison* was about to visit Japan in order to bring back seven Japanese castaways, and that the Bakufu had resolved to permit no relaxation of the seclusion laws in her favour. The exact nature of this document is not clear,[5] but Takano and Watanabe decided that it contained notable errors both of fact and of policy. These they planned to correct. Watanabe wrote a pamphlet on the subject, which he never published, and Takano produced the famous *Yume Monogatari* (The Story of a Dream), which was widely read and aroused considerable interest.[6] It told

[5] It was presumably a report connected in some way with the visit which had taken place in the previous year and of which the Rangakusha apparently knew nothing. It may well have been written in *sōrobun*, a literary style used for nearly all official documents in this period, in which there is no verb-form to indicate the past tense. This might explain why the Rangakusha assumed that the visit had still to take place.

[6] Greene, ' Osada's Life of Takano Nagahide ', *Trans. Asiatic Soc. Japan*, XLI (Aug. 1913), pp. 421-3, 430-1. A free translation of *Yume Monogatari* is given in the same book, pp. 423-30. See also Murdoch, *History of Japan* III, 559-62.

how he had dreamt of the proposed British expedition ; of Britain's great power, her possessions in America, Africa, India and the East Indies, and especially her fleet—which Takano estimated at twenty-five thousand ships and over a million men ! The real object of the mission, the book said, was almost certainly to seek trading privileges in Japan. To drive it off would be both unfeeling, in view of its avowedly humanitarian objectives, and unwise, in view of Britain's obvious ability to resent insult. The request for trade must be refused, but safety required that it be refused politely.

Takano and Watanabe were imprisoned for their attacks on Tokugawa policy, but news of the Opium War in China led other Rangakusha to repeat the warnings they had first expressed. Suzuki Shunzan, for example, a military science expert who came from the same fief as Watanabe, began to campaign for increased defences. Takano supported him after escaping from prison in 1845.[7] Sakuma Shōzan, a samurai of the Matsushiro fief in Shinano province and later a figure of some political importance, warned that Japan would be helpless before a British attack. This attack, he thought, would come as soon as the China war had ended, since Britain would fight for trade however small its value, and had an insult to avenge in the treatment of the Morrison. This both Chinese and Dutch reports confirmed.[8]

Before long the argument became a familiar one in Japan, and it was not confined to the Rangakusha. The Wagakusha had begun by being violently anti-Chinese. In the nineteenth century, chiefly through the influence of Hirata Atsutane, the scope of their anti-foreign ideas was widened, and Hirata's considerable success as publicist and teacher did much to contribute to the hardening of traditional Japanese opposition to the opening of the ports. Here again the earlier writers saw Russia as the chief source

[7] Greene, ' Takano Nagahide ', pp. 457-9, 482. Murdoch, History of Japan, III, 563-4. Heibonsha, Dai Hyakka Jiten [Encyclopædic Dictionary], XIV, 208 (under Suzuki Shunzan).

[8] Greene, ' Takano Nagahide ', pp. 485-7. Tsuchiya, ' Bakumatsu Shishi no mita Shina Mondai ' [The China problem as seen by loyalists of the late-Tokugawa period], Kaizō, XX (July 1938), pp. 164-6.

of danger. As early as 1825, Aizawa Hakumin was writing that Russian ambitions extended both to China and Japan, and that consequently the defence of the two countries constituted a single strategic problem.[9] Others expressed similar ideas, and like the Rangakusha, in time transferred their fear and hatred to Great Britain. Satō Shin-en was a notable example. At the time when Aizawa was emphasising the importance of defence against Russia, Satō had been advocating a Japanese expedition to attack China and Manchuria. But after British strength had been so conclusively demonstrated in the years 1839 to 1842, he, too, turned his attention to the new problem. It seemed clear to him that Japan must be the next victim of British piracy and aggression. However, there remained some traces of his earlier aggressive instincts. His plans for defence included not only the building of new coast batteries in Japan proper, but also the creation of heavily-fortified outposts in the islands to the south, to act as operating bases for a new fleet of Western-style ships.[10]

Aizawa and Satō do not fit easily into any classification of the writers of the period. Both can be classified as Wagakusha, perhaps, because of their anti-Bakufu activities, but Aizawa was in origin a Confucian scholar and Satō was primarily an economist with some training in Dutch studies. Equally difficult to place is Yoshida Shōin. He was a pupil and friend of Sakuma Shōzan, a Rangakusha ; later in life he expounded expansionist views which owed much to the ideas of the two economists Honda Toshiaki[11] and Satō Shin-en ; he was at all times an ardent champion of Imperial rights. What is certain is that before the Perry treaty of 1854, Yoshida was strongly influenced by anti-foreign ideas, and especially by the danger of British attack. In 1845, when he was still only in his sixteenth year, one of his

[9] Tsuchiya, ' Bakumatsu Shishi ', pp. 159-60. Heibonsha, *Dai Hyakka Jiten*, I, 26 (under Aizawa Seishisai).

[10] Tsuchiya, ' Bakumatsu Shishi ', pp. 161-2. Heibonsha, *Dai Hyakka Jiten*, X, 547-8 (under Satō Shin-en). A characteristic passage from one of Satō's books is quoted at length in Tokutomi, *Yoshida Shōin*, pp. 56-62.

[11] Honda Toshiaki (1744-1821) ; mercantilist ; advocated development of both foreign and domestic trade on economic grounds. See Heibonsha, *Dai Hyakka Jiten*, XXIV, 31.

teachers warned him that British power, which had already engulfed India, was reaching out to China and would not stop 'until Ryūkyū is reached and Nagasaki is attacked'.[12]

The Jusha, too, despite their extreme conservatism, began to engage in discussions of foreign affairs. They had always looked to China as the source not only of their own prestige, but of all ideas in any way worthy of emulation and study. The fate of China, then, was to them a matter of grave moment. As early as 1843 Saitō Chikudō wrote a short history of the Opium War, based, apparently, on the reports of Dutch and Chinese traders. In the years that followed, the Jusha published a number of books on the subject, as well as some editions of Chinese works on world affairs—one of them, at least, in co-operation with Rangakusha. These books revealed much confusion in their thinking. The Jusha could not completely rid themselves of a long-standing hatred of Western science and of the Rangakusha who had introduced it to Japan. At the same time, a growing realisation that in the crisis which was developing, their own work might be of less value to Japan than that of their rivals, shows in their criticism of China for failing to profit from Western military techniques in her struggle with Britain. But on one thing they were quite clear, that the threat to China was by extension a threat to Japan. In 1847 Shionoya Tōin put their fears in a striking phrase. 'Seen from our standpoint,' he wrote, 'how can we know whether the mist gathering over China will not come down as frost on Japan?'[13]

Japanese scholars and pamphleteers, in fact, agreed in viewing the British attack on China as a threat to the independence of Japan. The Opium War seemed a part of Japanese history, heralding as the next stage of European expansion an attack on the country whose uncompromising

[12] Coleman, 'The Life of Shoin Yoshida', *Trans. Asiatic Soc. Japan,* XLV (1917), pp. 136-7. See also *ibid,* pp. 149-53, 159-61 ; Tokutomi, *Yoshida Shōin,* pp. 157-60, 166-8 ; Tsuchiya, 'Bakumatsu Shishi', pp. 166-7.

[13] van Gulik, 'Kakkaron, a Japanese echo of the Opium War', *Monumenta Serica,* IV (1939-40), p. 500. The same article, especially pp. 480-92, 511-6, gives a valuable survey of Jusha reactions to the Opium War generally.

attitude to foreign trade and intercourse was even more marked than that of China. And to them there seemed little chance that Japan could resist such an attack with success. They differed widely, however, in the courses of action they proposed. A few advocated the opening of the ports and the adoption of Western ideas and methods as the only sure defence against the West. Most put their faith in continued seclusion, backed by more effective coast defences.

One might expect that in such an autocracy as Tokugawa Japan, books and pamphlets would have little effect on official policy. In fact, however, the autocracy was more apparent than real. In the nineteenth century, policy was normally formulated by the Rōjū, the Council of State in Edo, and rarely, if ever, by the Shōgun himself. The Rōjū, in turn, had increasingly to take account of outside opinion. The heads of the Tokugawa branch families, especially that of Mito, were often consulted, while no policy could long be successful without the support of the *fudai daimyō*,[14] from whose ranks all important offices were filled. Even the more important of the *tozama* lords had sometimes to be appeased.

It was from these facts that the scholars derived their more immediate political importance. Many of them were themselves *samurai*, while in an aristocratic society, the writer or teacher who could support himself independently of the patronage of some great lord was the exception rather than the rule. Takano Chō-ei, for example, was befriended by Shimazu Saihin, heir to the *tozama* fief of Satsuma in Kyūshū. Sakuma's lord, Sanada of Matsushiro, was a member of the Rōjū and for a time in charge of coast defence. Satō Shin-en served in turn the lords of Tōtomi and Awa. The Jusha almost invariably held official appointments, in fiefs or directly under the Bakufu, though they seem to have been less effective than their rivals in influencing the policy of the *daimyō* and officials to whom

---

[14] *Fudai daimyō*, often described as direct vassals of the Tokugawa, were the descendants of those who had surrendered to or allied themselves with Ieyasu before the battle of Sekigahara ensured his success.

they were responsible. Saitō Chikudō and Shionoya Tōin served respectively Date of Uwajima and Mizuno Tadakuni of Echizen, both of whom were known supporters of the Rangakusha. Aizawa Hakumin, on the other hand, was *jusha* of the Mito fief, which in Tokugawa Nariaki produced the acknowledged leader of the " seclusion party ". Even Yoshida Shōin, in some ways an exception to the rule, was a *samurai* of Chōshū until he forfeited his membership of the fief in 1851.[15]

It does not follow, however, that the scholars were ever able to control Japanese policy. They could never agree on the measures needed to avert the danger they all could see, and it was in any case only the arrival of Perry in 1853 that made foreign policy an immediate and practical issue. Yet they did represent and intensify certain basic differences of Japanese opinion. These were reflected in two Bakufu decisions of 1842 and 1844.

For a time during the Opium War it seemed that the Bakufu seclusion policy might be changed. Mizuno Tadakuni was in power, supported in the Rōjū by Sanada and Hotta, and all three favoured some change in the laws. The war in China was clearly going well for Britain. At Edo's request, the Dutch reported regularly on developments there, giving details of the military forces and equipment employed.[16] One of the *Morrison* castaways had written from Canton to his countrymen at Nagasaki to warn them that Britain had not forgotten the treatment meted out to that expedition and would certainly demand satisfaction once the China war was over ; and the letter had been forwarded to the Bakufu.[17] These various influences finally took effect. In 1842 Mizuno cancelled the decree of 1825 and substituted new regulations to govern the treatment of foreign ships approaching the

[15] For the political connections of the pamphleteers and scholars see Greene, ' Takano Nagahide ', pp. 387-8, 461-3 ; Murdoch, *History of Japan*, III, 529, 557-60 ; van Gulik, ' Kakkaron ', pp. 485-7 ; and generally the entries under their names in Heibonsha, *Dai Hyakka Jiten*.

[16] The Dutch text of one questionnaire answered by the Deshima factory is given in Boxer, *Jan Compagnie in Japan*, pp. 179-81.

[17] Kobayashi, *Bakumatsu-shi*, pp. 112-3 ; Tsuchiya, ' Bakumatsu Shishi ', pp. 164-6.

coast. No longer was force to be used indiscriminately. Ships in distress, or seeking stores and water, were to be provided with such of their requirements as were absolutely essential before being ordered to depart, and were only to be fired on if they then refused to go. On the other hand, the decree stated, this was in no way to be regarded as an excuse for relaxing coast defence measures, which would, in fact, be more necessary than ever before.[18]

His action lost Mizuno the support of Tokugawa Nariaki, who soon began to press for a return to the regulations of 1825. His opposition may well have been decisive in preventing further concessions. Yet even the authority of Mito, the senior of the Tokugawa branch houses, could not drive the Bakufu officials to abandon what they thought to be the safest possible compromise, the only plan, as they saw it, that might save Japan from the fate of China. They planned to inform the world, through Dutch diplomatic channels, that while Japan still had no wish for trade, she was prepared to help ships driven to her coasts by stress of weather or lack of stores ; and this, they hoped, would avert the threatened attack, or at least postpone the crisis until coast defences had been so strengthened as to make an invasion of Japan a hazardous venture not lightly to be undertaken.[19]

Foreign opinion tended to confirm these fears of Britain. The Dutch and Chinese merchants at Nagasaki were Japan's only regular source of information on world events, and neither were likely to view with sympathy or approval Britain's growing power and influence east of Singapore. The Dutch, in particular, had long used their special position in Japan to prejudice the officials against possible competitors. The Opium War seems to have convinced them that it was only a matter of time before Britain demanded trade rights in Japan, and that the best chance of retaining some of their own influence and privileges there lay in anticipating this demand and taking the lead

---

[18] For a translation of this decree see Murdoch, *History of Japan*, III, 530.

[19] Kobayashi, *Bakumatsu-shi*, pp. 120-5 ; Murdoch, *History of Japan*, III, 462-4.

in opening Japan to world trade.[20] The Deshima *opperhoofd* was therefore ordered to inform the authorities that a special mission was being sent from Holland to discuss matters of great importance to Japan, and in the summer of 1844 the *Palembang* reached Nagasaki with a letter from the Dutch king.

The letter recapitulated some familiar arguments. It outlined the course of the Anglo-Chinese war and the settlement which had followed, attributing it, however, not to British aggression but to the need for new channels of trade, itself arising from the industrial progress and rapidly increasing population of Europe. For these same reasons a similar fate threatened Japan. There would now be more ships in Japanese waters than ever before, and clashes with them—made less likely but not completely to be prevented by the decree of 1842—might easily lead to a war in which Japan could not avoid defeat. Full safety lay only in opening her ports to trade and fostering friendly relations with the West, a policy in which the Dutch expressed themselves most willing to assist.[21]

The *Palembang* was not allowed to go beyond Nagasaki. She was dismissed with a promise that a reply would be sent through the Deshima *opperhoofd*, and the letter she brought was forwarded to Edo, where Mizuno Tadakuni was temporarily recalled to the Rōjū to handle the crisis. After months of debate an answer was drafted and sent. It admitted the logic of the Dutch king's reasoning, but rejected his advice on the grounds that seclusion was part of the ancestral laws of Japan, which could on no account be broken.[22] The decision was a triumph for Nariaki, and ended for a time the attempt to modify Bakufu policy. The ideas of the seclusion party were to remain dominant until the events of 1853 and 1854 forced, if not a change of heart,

[20] J. A. van der Chijs, *Neerlands Streven tot Openstelling van Japan voor den Wereldhandel*, pp. 14-21.

[21] For the Dutch text of this letter, with English and Japanese translations, see Greene, ' Correspondence between William II of Holland and the Shogun of Japan, A.D. 1844 ', *Trans. Asiatic Soc. Japan*, XXXIV (June 1907), pp. 104-14, 124-9.

[22] For Japanese text and English translation of the letter see Greene, ' Correspondence between William II . . . and the Shogun ', pp. 121-3, 130-1.

at least a new approach to the problem of foreign relations.

Thus in the years immediately following the Opium War, the Japanese became convinced that Britain was preparing aggressive action against Japan. The same opinion was current in some parts of Europe.[23] British records of the period, however, provide no evidence of any sudden development of interest in that country. True, the subject was brought to the attention of Her Majesty's Ministers on a number of occasions. Mr. John Copling who felt strongly about the treatment received by British ships on the Japanese coast, wrote to Lord Palmerston in April 1840 to recommend that the forces then employed in China should also be used to punish the authorities at Edo and Kagoshima (apparently for firing on the *Morrison*) and to visit Nagasaki and Hirado. At the latter places, he said, where the same hostility had not been shown, ' instead of chastisement being inflicted on the government stations and officers . . . an attempt might be made to open a commercial intercourse '.[24] His letter was sent to the Admiralty for communication to the China station, presumably because it related to the protection of British shipping, which was a naval responsibility, but no other action was taken. Undaunted by his lack of success, Copling wrote again to Palmerston in the following year on this and many other subjects connected with the China war, and then to Aberdeen in December 1842 in a last attempt to divert the forces to Japan before they were dispersed.[25] Neither letter received any special attention.

At about the same time the Admiralty, too, was urged to plan the opening of Japan. The idea was put forward by Commander John Cawley, a retired officer who had sailed with Broughton to the North Pacific and Japan in the years

[23] Not only among the Dutch. See, for example, a letter dated Trieste, 10 May 1844, reprinted in the London *Times* (3 June 1844) from the *Cologne Gazette*, claiming that preparations had already been made for a British expedition to Japan.

[24] F.O. *China Corres.*, vol. 42, Copling to Palmerston, 2 Apr. 1840. See also *ibid*, For. Off. to Adty., 11 Apr. 1840.

[25] F.O. *China Corres.*, vol. 50, Copling to Palmerston, 28 Apr. 1841 ; vol. 63, Copling to Aberdeen, 5 Dec. 1842.

1794 to 1798, and had since interested himself in the whaling grounds off the Japanese coast. No details of his scheme are available because the letter outlining it has been destroyed, but it seems to have had no more effect than those of Copling.[26]

The authors of these two plans had little influence or authority. There were, however, suggestions for an indirect approach to Japan which might have been expected to carry greater weight. In February 1840 Mr. Huttman, formerly assistant secretary to the Royal Asiatic Society, wrote to Palmerston urging the occupation of part of Taiwan as a commercial and naval station, on the grounds that it would provide easy access to the important tea- and silk-producing areas of China, as well as to new markets like Japan. He warned that there was a danger of Britain being forestalled in this by the United States, and his letter was considered sufficiently interesting to be sent to China for the information of the Plenipotentiaries.[27] The question of the European settlement in the Bonin Islands was also revived by consular authorities in the Pacific. One of them, Acting Consul Simpson, even published a pamphlet about the islands in 1843. But while there were several references to the convenience of their situation for trading with Japan, none of the correspondence, either private or official, made any concrete proposal for using the islands for such a purpose.[28]

These brief notices were neither so numerous nor so important as the references to Japan in the years 1834 to 1838. There are no comments on that country in the private papers of Russell or Aberdeen, nor in the surviving Foreign Office memoranda of Lord Palmerston. *The Times* mentioned Japan only once, in June 1844, and that only

[26] Admiralty *Digests*, IND. 12200 and 12202, digest of Cawley to Adty., 13 Dec. 1842. W. R. O'Byrne, *A Naval Biographical Dictionary* (London 1849), pp. 181-2.

[27] F.O. *China Corres.*, vol. 41, Huttman to Palmerston, 17 Feb. 1840. F.O. *China Emb. Arch.*, vol. 14, For. Off. to Plenipotentiaries, No. 3, 20 Feb. 1840.

[28] F.O. *China Emb. Arch.*, vol. 153, For. Off. to Bowring, No. 97, 24 Nov. 1853, enclosing memo. by Consul-General Miller, 20 Sept. 1843; Baker to Wyllie, Sandwich Is., 18 Oct. 1844; Simpson to Clarendon, 1 Oct. 1853 (with copy of pamphlet).

in a reprint from the *Cologne Gazette*. Neither the *Quarterly* nor the *Edinburgh Review* made any comment on policy. In fact, there is no evidence to show that by 1844 either government officials or the public had in any way changed their attitude to Japan as a result of the China war. There were a few individuals interested in the subject, as there had always been, but they had neither the influence nor the support to force action on an unwilling government. To this extent, at least, we must deny the validity of contemporary Japanese fears.

This, however, is to look only for direct evidence. Modern Japanese historians[29] have stated that the danger to their country was rather inherent in the position Britain had achieved in Asia, and in the pressure of economic factors making for expansion, than in any conscious design of commercial or territorial aggression directed against Japan. They look, in fact, to the views expressed in the Dutch letter of 1844, not to those of Japanese pamphleteers. Certainly a threat of that kind could be a very real one without being openly avowed or even consciously realised in Britain, but to prove or disprove its existence is an exceedingly difficult task. In order to probe the possibilities—and little more can be attempted—it will be necessary to examine more closely the new position Britain occupied in China as a result of the Opium War, the policies which had brought about that change, and its implications for the other lands of East Asia. Ultimately, of course, it involves an examination of the whole course of later British policy towards Japan.

One section of British opinion was certainly looking forward to increased opportunities in China and the Far East. Long before 1839, British merchants on the China coast had become convinced not only that their trade was but a fraction of what it could be, but that the policy of the Chinese government was all that stood between them and the unlimited wealth to be obtained by access to new markets in the interior and in the north. It followed from this, they

---

[29] e.g. Mutō, *Nichi-ei kōtsū-shi*, pp. 97-8 ; Kobayashi, *Bakumatsu-shi*, pp. 80-2 ; Tsuchiya, ' Bakumatsu Shishi ', pp. 156-9.

believed, that it was the duty of the British government to remove these political obstacles. It must ensure adequate protection for British subjects and property ; it must actively support the traders against both Chinese and Western rivals ; last, but by no means least, it must open the whole of China to trade. And if the policy involved Britain in a minor war, the cost of that war would be as nothing to the value of the prize won.[30]

The treaty settlement of 1842 and 1843 embodied most of the terms urged by the merchants, and a majority of them were well satisfied with the result. The fact does not necessarily mean, however, that the "old China hands" were in a position to control national policy. They had always received a certain amount of support in England, it is true, from men like Sir George Staunton, from organisations like the London East India and China Association. Once war was an accomplished fact, moreover, their influence increased. Palmerston, who had shown no great interest in the problem of China until the clash between Lin and Elliot forced action upon him, turned naturally to the experts for advice as to the terms which should be exacted from the Chinese when the war had been brought to a successful conclusion. The instructions he then drew up were carried out under the direction of his successor, Lord Aberdeen, and established a precedent for British policy which remained of importance until 1860. The British government, in fact, with some reservations, seemed to have accepted the " myth " of the China trade as expounded by the China coast merchants.[31]

The reservations, however, became of increasing importance in the years that followed. The Opium War had not produced as marked an effect in England as it had in Japan, but it had at least made large sections of the British public aware of the affairs of China for the first time. Though the age of Victorian morality had hardly begun, it seemed

[30] Pelcovits, *Old China Hands and the Foreign Office*, pp. 1-7. Morse, *International Relations*, I, 147-50, 168-9, 250-2. Costin, *Great Britain and China 1833-1860*, pp. 27-8, 31-4.

[31] Pelcovits, *Old China Hands*, pp. 4-5 ; Michie, *The Englishman in China during the Victorian Era*, I, 87-9.

to many that a war fought apparently for the opium trade was both inhuman and un-Christian. Gladstone recorded in his journal that he was 'in dread of the judgement of God upon England for our national iniquity towards China'.[32] Shaftesbury (then Lord Ashley) laid before the House of Commons petitions from the Wesleyan, Baptist and London Missionary Societies, asking that effective measures be taken to terminate British participation in the opium trade, and spoke movingly about the serious effects of the drug on the Chinese. 'Opium and the Bible', he said, 'cannot enter China together.'[33] Greville described the war as one of those quarrels 'which we ought never to have gone into', and the Radicals, both then and later, condemned on principle 'armed oppression' of a weaker people.[34]

Yet these opinions were not often allowed to outweigh political considerations. Gladstone's public actions in 1840 were dictated by tactical needs rather than by the views expressed in his journal. Shaftesbury withdrew his motion on the opium trade on being assured that it might prejudice the result of negotiations already in progress in China.[35] Even in 1856 and 1857, when a new war with China had aroused still greater and more passionate opposition, Shaftesbury's diary reveals that he supported the government, not because he thought it right, but because he wanted it to remain in power.[36]

It was, indeed, far more the age of Manchester than of morals in politics. And there were some who objected to political action in China, still more to the use of force, on the grounds that such action could only cause a disruption and diminution of trade. The East India Company had clearly been of this opinion. Sir James Graham, who served in the Cabinets of Grey, Peel, Aberdeen and Palmerston,

[32] Morley, *Life of William Ewart Gladstone* (London 1903), I, 227.
[33] *Hansard*, 3rd Ser., LXVIII, c. 389 (Commons, 4 Apr. 1843).
[34] *Greville Memoirs*, V, 126 ; S. Maccoby, *English Radicalism* 1832-1852 (London 1935), pp. 371-2. See also Morley, *Life of Richard Cobden* (London 1905), pp. 520, 658-9.
[35] Morley, *Gladstone*, I, 225-7 ; Hansard, 3rd Ser., LXVIII, cc. 461-9 (Commons, 4 Apr. 1843).
[36] J. L. and B. Hammond, *Lord Shaftesbury* (London 1925), p. 244.

expressed such views in 1831 and consistently acted on them for thirty years thereafter.[37]   Much of the criticism directed against the government in 1840 followed similar lines.[38] The Manchester school approved the commercial objects of the war, but once these had been achieved came to believe that government intervention had gone far enough.   In 1861 we find Cobden writing to the Manchester Chamber of Commerce to emphasise that any further privileges in China, such as the opening of the interior to trade, would in no way serve the interests of the British manufacturer, and would in all probability hamper trade by leading to fresh conflicts.[39]

These facts undoubtedly had an influence on Foreign Office policy.   It was not only that there was greater public interest in and knowledge of foreign affairs, and a greater disposition on the part of governments to take account of this fact.   China had become a political issue.   Graham's motion of censure in 1840 was only defeated by a small majority, while in 1857 Palmerston's defeat on the China question brought a general election.   These were primarily political manœuvres, it is true, but no Cabinet could afford to ignore considerations that might swing votes in the House,[40] especially in the confused party situation after 1847.   The " old China hands " continued to influence Foreign Office representatives in China, and this was at the root of such success as they achieved.   In London their influence waned.

These developments did not take full effect until another war had been fought with China in 1856.   In the interval, British policy was largely in the hands of Aberdeen on the one hand, of Palmerston and Clarendon on the other. Much has been made of the differences between them.

[37] C. S. Parker, *Life and Letters of Sir James Graham* (London 1907), I, 150, and II, 302-3.

[38] *Annual Register*, 82 (1840), pp. 82-104, for the debates on Graham's motion of censure.

[39] Morley, *Cobden*, pp. 845-7.

[40] See, for example, Palmerston's letter to Clarendon, 1 Mar. 1857, saying that to adopt the French proposals for Morocco and Egypt ' would revolt the moral feelings of mankind and would certainly be fatal to any English government that became a party to it '. (Maxwell, *Clarendon*, II, 300-1).

Palmerston was certainly more willing to risk a temporary disruption of trade when he conceived that national prestige or future interests required it. In making his decisions he was more ready to adopt the methods advocated by the " old China hands ", partly because " gunboat diplomacy " appealed more to his temperament, partly because his policy was first formulated in 1840, when the use of force had become inevitable and there was general agreement as to objectives. Aberdeen, by contrast, was of those who believed in the wisdom of ' not imperilling what we already possessed by striving after more '.[41]

The effect of this difference of emphasis can easily be exaggerated, however. After 1842 both men concentrated on the enforcement of existing treaty rights rather than the acquisition of new ones. It was not until the eighteen-fifties that Palmerston and Clarendon began to look to the negotiation of a new treaty as the only means of securing in fact the privileges granted on paper at Nanking. Palmerston was as ready as Aberdeen to restrain the activities of British merchants in China. Aberdeen was as determined as Palmerston not to jeopardise British interests there, and willing to use the navy to protect them if necessary. In September 1844 he told Peel that he regarded China as an exception to his usual rule against the habitual use of force to support diplomacy. European states did not need to be reminded of British might at every moment of disagreement, for they were well aware of it already. Not so the Chinese, who had only recently come into contact with it for the first time. ' They have felt our power ', he wrote, ' and they must continue to see that we are superior to other Nations if we mean to retain the ascendancy we have obtained in China '.[42] It was a sentiment which one would expect Palmerston to endorse.

Both Palmerston and Aberdeen, moreover, agreed generally on the objectives they set themselves in China. They subscribed to the China coast theory that political rather

---

[41] Michie, *The Englishman in China*, I, 163.
[42] British Museum, *Aberdeen Papers*, vol. xxvi (Add. Mss. 43064), Aberdeen to Peel, 16 Sept. 1844.

than economic obstacles were the chief barrier to the extension of British trade, and their policy was aimed at removing those obtsacles. On the other hand, they recognised that the " old China hands " were not the only group with a stake in the trade. Merchants and manufacturers in Britain, though equally anxious to see the volume of trade expanded, did not always have identical views on the methods to be employed in attaining that end, and their political influence was of some consequence to a Foreign Secretary who had to justify his policy in the House of Commons. Palmerston and Aberdeen were not equally influenced by this consideration, but both in some degree failed to press matters to extremes when many men on the China coast thought they should have done so.

Between 1842 and 1860, then, criticism on grounds of commercial advantage, and to some extent on grounds of humanity and religion, acted as a restraint on British policy in China. Similar views were expressed about British activities in Borneo and Burma. A Foreign Secretary contemplating negotiations in Japan might well anticipate the same kind of criticism at home, if his actions seemed to depend on the use or threat of force. Moreover, the problem of China and that of Japan differed markedly in one particular. The influence of the " old China hands " on the China coast itself—the point at which action had to be taken—and the willingness of the government to endorse, or at least accept, the actions of its representatives there, ensured that the threat to China remained in being for a time. There was no equivalent pressure behind proposals for opening trade with Japan. The China coast merchants were preoccupied with the difficulties of expanding their trade in China, where a beginning had been made and the opportunities seemed almost limitless. There was no reason why they should covet the little-known and (by such accounts as were available) unprofitable market to be found in Japan. They would probably have welcomed the end of Japanese seclusion, as would merchants in England. They did not, however, regard it as sufficiently important to call for public agitation. Even after 1846, when it was becoming apparent that the optimism produced by the Treaty of Nanking was not being borne out by events, they chose to demand new privileges in China rather than to seek compensation in the " closed " lands of Korea, Cochin China and Japan. In so far as action depended on merchant opinion, indeed, the Opium War, by concentrating attention more than ever on the China trade, had reduced rather than increased the possibility that Britain would use force to secure the opening of Japan.

The Dutch letter of 1844 had suggested one possible danger to Japanese seclusion quite apart from direct commercial interest. With increasing numbers of ships sailing north to the Yangtse, stress of weather might conceivably drive a few of them to the Japanese coast and so create circumstances in which a dispute might arise. Admittedly, a clash between British merchants and Japanese officials would probably have led to government intervention if the merchants were not obviously in the wrong.[43] Even so, the danger was relatively slight. The decree of 1842, if uniformly enforced in Japan, was likely to prevent any serious incident, despite Japanese hostility to Britain. Moreover, for purely geographical reasons, such misfortunes were much more likely to befall whaling vessels than merchant ships, and in the past the treatment of whalers had provoked no official protest. If the opening of Japan were to depend on some accidental dispute over the ill-treatment of British seamen, it might be indefinitely postponed.

However, if the Opium War had not materially increased British desire to interfere in Japan, it had certainly made interference more practicable. It had for the first time brought a British fleet into Chinese waters, and the need to protect British rights and interests under the Treaty of Nanking led to the creation of a permanent China squadron

[43] On 26 Dec. 1856, for example, a somewhat petulant Clarendon wrote to Lord Normanby :—' If in the remotest corner of the earth any Englishman gets a well-deserved, but uncompensated, black eye, the newspapers and parliament immediately demand an enquiry into the conduct of the bloated sinecurist in Downing Street, who has no sense of British honor '. (Maxwell, *Clarendon*, II, 135-6.)

on the East Indies station. Indeed, within a few years the China coast was regarded in London as the most important part of that station.[44] The existence of this force greatly simplified the practical task of organising an expedition to Japan. By doing so, of course, it made its organisation more likely. Moreover, the squadron proved something of a temptation to British representatives in China, diplomats, merchants and missionaries alike. They were normally more inclined to hasty action than a government in London answerable to Parliament for all its deeds, and as it took four months to get an answer from England on a question of policy, were remote enough to act on their own initiative. They tended to look on the fleet as ready support for all their actions whenever these brought them into conflict with " the natives ". It was, too, an instrument to execute their more ambitious plans for the increase of British wealth and prestige. As early as June 1844, the naval commander on the station recognised and protested against this attitude to his command, and his superiors at the Admiralty were still complaining of the same kind of difficulty four years later.[45] One can recognise in this situation a new danger to Japan. Action might be taken from Hongkong without previous reference home. That, after all, was often the pattern of events in China.

In 1845, this danger was still potential rather than actual. More immediately, however, the Royal Navy's routine surveying operations brought about the first official contact with Japan since the *Phaeton* visit of 1808.

The need for surveys of Chinese coasts and harbours, an essential aspect of the protection of commerce, had been urged by Napier in 1834.[46] It had become more urgent during naval operations in the years 1839 to 1842, and some valuable work had been done by the ships engaged,[47] but

[44] Admiralty, Secretary's Department, *Out-Letters* (Adm. 2), vol. 1605, Adty. to R/A Inglefield, 6 July 1847.
[45] Admiralty, *In-Letters* (Adm. 1), vol. 5539, R/A Cochrane to Adty., Hongkong, 13 June 1844 : *Russell Papers*, vol. 7, Auckland (Adty.) to Russell, 23 Feb. 1948.
[46] See chapter I, p. 15, and note.
[47] Admiralty, *Out-Letters*, vol. 1597, Adty. to R/A Maitland, 30 Jan. 1840 : Admiralty, *In-Letters*, vol. 5514, V/A Parker to Adty., 17 and 24 June, 26 July, 24 Aug. 1842.

much still remained to do when the peace was signed. Special surveying vessels were already at work in the East Indies and Australia. In 1843 it was decided to send another, the *Samarang*, under the command of Captain Belcher, to supplement the work being carried out by the ships of the China squadron. Belcher was to be employed, under the general direction of the Commander-in-Chief East Indies, in surveying such parts of the China coast as might be considered suitable after consultation with the Superintendent of Trade at Hongkong, and was warned that if he met with objections from Chinese officials, as seemed probable, he was in no circumstances to use force to overcome them.[48]

It was political difficulties in China, in fact, rather than any interest in Japan for its own sake, that eventually brought Belcher to Nagasaki. In July 1843, when the *Samarang* reach Hongkong, Vice Admiral Parker consulted the Superintendent about her future employment, and Pottinger at once raised objections to the surveys suggested by the Admiralty. He said they would only serve to increase 'the groundless panic' which had spread in China concerning British intentions. He readily assented, however, to an alternative plan for surveying the little-known islands to the northeast of Taiwan, to which British ships might be driven by weather,[49] and Parker accordingly transmitted this decision to Belcher.[50] Japan, too, lay northeast of Taiwan, and two years later Belcher's operations brought him there.

Belcher entered Nagasaki harbour on 6 August 1845, and requested permission through his Chinese interpreter to carry out surveys and to purchase provisions, both for this and future voyages. He denied that his visit had any other purpose.[51] In the course of general conversations

[48] Admiralty, *Out-Letters*, vol. 1600, Adty. to V/A Parker, 13 Jan. 1843 : F. O. *China Emb. Arch.*, vol. 26, For. Off. to Pottinger, No. 28, 25 Jan. 1843 and encl.
[49] F.O. *China Corres.*, vol. 68, Pottinger to For. Off., No. 94, 29 July 1843, enclosing correspondence with Parker.
[50] Admiralty, *In-Letters*, vol. 5530, Parker to Adty., 16 Nov. 1843, enclosing Parker to Belcher, 28 Oct. 1843.
[51] Belcher, *Narrative of the Voyage of H.M.S. Samarang*, II, 1-5 ; Mutō, *Nichi-ei kōtsū-shi*, pp. 548-51 (giving the Japanese record of the interrogation).

with the local officials he discussed the visits of the *Phaeton* and *Morrison* in earlier years. The first, he was told, was the cause of much of the existing feeling against Britain in Japan, while the *Morrison* had been no more than a common law-breaker. Of more significance, the officials showed great interest in Britain's recent activities in China. They even remarked (somewhat improbably) that they looked forward ' with *satisfaction* ' to the arrival of an official British mission seeking trade relations.[52] Meanwhile, they were most happy to provide him with stores for the *Samarang*, and urged him to remain at Nagasaki until they could obtain permission from Edo for future visits of the same kind. They were sure the answer would be favourable. Belcher, however, was suspicious of their friendliness, and after surveying the harbour under the guise of dredging for shells, he sailed on 10 August without waiting for the reply from Edo.[53] Orders for England reached him soon after, and his plan for a second visit came to nothing.

This visit was not the harbinger of a British diplomatic mission to Japan, though the Japanese were quick to think it so. There is no trace of any orders instructing Belcher to go there, and he himself claimed that he did so entirely at his own risk.[54] Yet, while he was careful to limit his enquiries to the subjects of stores and surveying, he seems to have had, or to have acquired, certain wider objects, which might have appeared more clearly had a second visit been possible. In 1848, when he published an account of the voyage, he expressed an ' ardent wish ' that the next visit of a British warship to Japan might obtain ' all the objects so fully anticipated upon the revisit of the *Samarang*.'[55] Here again the man on the spot was showing himself more ready to act than the government in London.

The voyage of the *Samarang* had done something more than demonstrate that Japan could no longer rely on geographical isolation as her chief protection, and that the islands of northeast Asia were becoming of interest to

[52] Belcher, *Voyage of H.M.S. Samarang*, II, 35 ; see also *ibid*, II, 7-8, 11, 14.
[53] Belcher, *Voyage of H.M.S. Samarang*, II, 7-10, 12, 17.
[54] *ibid*, II, 4.
[55] *ibid*, II, 36.

Europeans—if only as dangers to navigation. It had under-lined the importance to Japan of Britain's new position in the China seas. It was not that the Opium War had in any way increased British commercial interest in Japan. That was much more likely to become active after British merchants were established in Japanese ports, as a demand for the expansion rather than the opening of trade. It was rather that the war had caused the creation in China of consular and naval organisations which, though intended as much to control as to assist British merchants, could easily become the instruments of expansion, even aggression, should the wish or the opportunity arise. Japanese fears, therefore, were justified in one respect. Once interest was aroused—and ironically enough knowledge of those fears was to play a part in arousing it—the commercial, diplomatic and naval machinery built up to handle British relations with China could easily be turned against Japan.

Not only the machinery, but also the methods used in China could be applied to negotiations with Japan. In this connection, the fact that the Opium War and treaty settle-ment in China came some years before the first specific government plans to open Japan, is important not because it necessarily argues a causal connection between the two, but because events in China, striking enough to be "news" for the first time in Britain, conditioned British thinking about all the countries of East Asia. When finally they did give serious attention to Japanese seclusion, British statesmen, merchants and officials regarded it not as a new and separate problem, but as one exhibiting the same diffi-culties—and by implication capable of solution by the same methods—as had already been encountered in China. The attitude first became apparent in 1845, when the Foreign Office prepared secret plans for opening trade relations with Japan.

CHAPTER III

SECRET PLANS

ALTHOUGH the Opium War did not immediately raise the question of Japanese seclusion for British statesmen, it was out of the aftermath of that war that there arose the first official plans for opening trade relations with Japan, the first plans, that is, in which the Foreign Office accepted the idea of active intervention. As had also been true of proposals in the seventeenth, eighteenth and early nineteenth centuries, the initiative came from the Far East. Specifically, the issue which provided the occasion for these plans was the return to China of the island of Chusan.

Chusan had been mentioned by British merchants in Canton as early as December 1834 as a suitable centre for trade, and in October 1839, when Palmerston instructed Elliot on the conduct of operations and the terms to be exacted from China, he had ordered its occupation as a base for war, to be retained afterwards as a commercial establishment. Elliot himself regarded it as a valuable station offering access to new markets both in China and Japan.[1] Chusan was occupied in July 1840, but it proved unhealthy, and in Januray 1841, in contravention of his instructions, Elliot agreed to evacuate it in exchange for Hongkong. Palmerston did not approve of this action. He believed that even if unhealthy, Chusan should at least be retained as security until China had paid the war indemnity, and when Pottinger went out to relieve Elliot ordered him to reoccupy the island. This he did in October 1841. He found it healthier than previous experience had suggested and a useful source of provisions for the troops, but despite this improvement he agreed in the Treaty of Nanking that

[1] Costin, *Great Britain and China*, p. 71.

it should be returned to China, together with the island of Koolangsoo off the port of Amoy, once the indemnity had been paid and arrangements completed for opening the new treaty ports to trade. By a subsequent agreement, this second condition was dropped.[2]

Beginning in 1844, there were several attempts to persuade the British government to retain the island on one pretext or another. J. F. Davis, who succeeded Pottinger as Plenipotentiary and Superintendent, wanted to return Koolangsoo when the last instalment of the indemnity had been paid, but keep Chusan as a pledge that China would fulfil her treaty obligations to admit Europeans to the city of Canton—one of the earliest disputes to arise out of the peace settlement.[3] Though he later withdrew the suggestion under Aberdeen's criticism, Davis had at least based his argument on the terms of the Treaty of Nanking. Others were not so legally inclined. Montgomery Martin, Colonial Treasurer in the Hongkong administration, had a high opinion of the commercial possibilities of Chusan and a poor one of Hongkong. In October 1844 he wrote to Davis to urge the retention of Chusan, emphasising its value as a base from which to open trade with northern China and Japan. Davis rather unwillingly forwarded the report to Lord Aberdeen. He took care, however, to dissociate himself from the views it contained, especially the acid criticisms of Hongkong.[4] Meanwhile, Martin sent another copy direct to Sir Robert Peel in London, where his proposals were backed up by a letter from the East India and China Association, which showed some interest in the possibility of opening trade with Japan.[5]

Dr. Gutzlaff, Chinese Secretary to the Superintendency, agreed with Martin's assessment of the importance of Chusan. Thence, he said, ' with the enterprize which has always marked British Traders, they would . . . find their

[2] Costin, *Great Britain and China*, pp. 83-90, 95-7, 101.

[3] *ibid*, pp. 115-6, 122-5.

[4] F.O. *China Corres.*, vol. 89, Davis to Aberdeen, Separate, 28 Oct. 1844, enclosing Martin's report.

[5] F.O. *China Corres.*, vol. 91, Martin to Peel, 14 Nov. 1844 ; vol. 104, London E. India and China Assoc. to Aberdeen, 17 Feb. 1845.

way to Japan, and open there a valuable commerce'. But he did not feel that Britain could with justice make any claim to the island. In view of rumours of French designs on Chusan, however, he thought that while the island must be returned, it would be as well to ensure by agreement with China that it would never be ceded to any other foreign power. This proposal Davis heartily endorsed, as being much more respectable than ' the flighty, baseless, and impracticable lucubrations ' of Montgomery Martin.[6]

In the East the press took up the debate. The *China Mail*, published in Hongkong and hence inclined to urge the claims of that colony, made frequent attacks on Martin and on the *Friend of India* which supported his plans.[7] At home the government was not to be convinced that the value of Chusan could justify a breach of treaty. Peel commented that Martin seemed determined to keep the island ' by any means, honest or dishonest—and I suspect would rather prefer the latter '.[8] However, Aberdeen dared not altogether ignore the rumours that France was preparing to occupy Chusan as soon as the British forces had been evacuated, though he regarded them as no more than a pretext to ensure its retention as a base. He therefore determined to be wary. He agreed with Peel that the island would have to be restored, but added that Davis must first exact from China some such guarantee as Gutzlaff had suggested. To make the result still more certain, he informed the French ambassador in London that Davis would also be instructed to use force, if necessary, to prevent its seizure in contravention of the Anglo-Chinese agreement.[9] On these terms Chusan was evacuated in July 1846.

Japan had been mentioned several times during these debates and discussions. Martin's letters, beginning in October 1844, had been based partly on the belief that trade with Japan was a desirable object, and none of his

[6] F.O. *China Corres.*, vol. 101, Davis to For. Off., No. 151, 15 Oct. 1845, and Gutzlaff's letter enclosed.
[7] e.g. *China Mail*, 12 Nov. and 11 Dec. 1845.
[8] *Aberdeen Papers*, vol. XXVI (Add. Mss. 43064), Peel to Aberdeen, 25 Aug. 1845.
[9] *Aberdeen Papers*, vol. XXVII (Add. Mss. 43065), Peel to Aberdeen, 20 Oct. 1845 ; Aberdeen to Peel, 21 and 28 Oct. 1845.

opponents had seen fit to contradict him on the point. Moreover, two other incidents early in 1845 kept the subject in Davis's mind. The British consul at the new treaty port of Ningpo had interfered officially in January to prevent the Chinese from returning a Japanese castaway to his own country, and had later found the man employment at Chusan. His action had been taken entirely on humanitarian grounds, without thought of trade, and was censured as politically unwise by both Davis and Aberdeen,[10] but none the less may have served to remind his superiors of commercial possibilities. A more direct reminder came from Foochow, another of the new treaty ports. There G. T. Lay, an interpreter in Chinese who had been investigating trade prospects, discovered that Foochow was the port through which the Chinese conducted trade with the Loochoo islands, and thus indirectly with Japan, and that British goods were commonly sought by the merchants for that purpose. Moreover, after some study of the Japanese language he thought it possible, from similarities in dialect, that the Foochow district was the original home of the Japanese people. Certainly it seemed very likely that it was a point from which trade relations could readily be established with them. Davis thought this report was a little sanguine, in which view he was subsequently confirmed by the dispatches of the new consul, Rutherford Alcock, but forwarded it to Aberdeen none the less.[11]

Directly and indirectly, references to Japan were becoming quite common, and it is not surprising, therefore, that it should have occurred to Davis that an attempt might be made to open communication with that country. In May 1845 he wrote a secret letter to Lord Aberdeen. He pointed out that when the last instalment of the indemnity had been paid, probably early in 1846, Chusan would be evacuated, an event which would require the use of a number of transports and part of the navy's China squadron, as

[10] F.O. *China Corres.*, vol. 98, Davis to For. Off., No. 48, 26 Mar. 1845, and encls. ; vol. 96, For. Off. to Davis, No. 61, 8 Aug. 1845.

[11] F.O. *China Corres.*, vol. 97, Davis to For. Off., No. 11, 15 Jan. 1845, encl. Lay to Davis, Foochow, 17 Dec. 1844 ; vol. 99, Davis to For. Off., No. 73, 16 May 1845 ; vol. 100, Davis to For. Off., No. 119, 8 Aug. 1845.

well as affording an excuse for his own presence there. This force, once assembled, would provide the materials of ' a splendid and imposing mission '. It could easily be diverted temporarily to Edo, only a few days' sail from Chusan, and there used to open negotiations for a commercial treaty, an object which Davis regarded as ' second only in importance to a Treaty of Commerce with China '. He argued that such a mission would involve little expense or risk :—

> ' The crisis appears to me most peculiarly favourable to the success of this important experiment ; and even in the improbable event of failure we can do no possible injury to our " relations " with Japan, when in fact none whatever exist. The Japanese Government is perfectly well informed as to the results of the late contest with China near its own door, and at the same time that it has witnessed our irrestible success, the lapse of nearly four years, and the restoration of Chusan itself, will have demonstrated that our good faith is not inferior to our power.
> I can scarcely imagine the possibility of its doing otherwise than at once seeing the policy of consenting to a Treaty of Commerce, based in substance on the Treaty of Nanking, and introduced to its notice through the medium of an imposing mission, such as the opportunity in question will afford without any additional expense whatever, except perhaps a few presents. . . . '[12]

Gutzlaff knew the Japanese language and could obtain the assistance of several Japanese natives then in China. Davis himself claimed considerable knowledge of Japan, which he thought would make him a clear choice to head the mission. Finally, he stressed that in order to ensure success strict secrecy must be maintained and adequate naval support provided, asking that the Admiralty be instructed to place a suitable force at the Superintendent's disposal when the time came to carry out the plan.

The references to Gutzlaff suggest that the Chinese Secretary may well have been the source of much of Davis's information. Certainly he had very similar ideas and a few

[12] F.O. *China Corres.*, vol. 99, Davis to Aberdeen, Separate and Secret, Hongkong, 6 May 1845.

months later produced a plan of his own even wider in scope.[13] Gutzlaff, too, felt that the defeat of China, to whom all peoples of the Far East were in the habit of looking with awe and respect, would make success probable in Japan if only Britain were to act while the memory of it was still fresh. Japan, he said, feared British attack, and that fear might be put to good use in breaking down the prejudices of the Japanese government—the people and even some of the feudal lords, especially Satsuma, were already anxious for trade. Moreover, the Japanese admired courage and this would breed respect for Britain. The ' liberal ' example set by China would also play its part in bringing about a favourable decision. But Gutzlaff did not confine his plans to Japan. He advocated negotiations with Korea, too, as well as with Siam and Cochin China, envisaging a commercial mission, with himself as interpreter, which would make a grand tour of the Pacific seaboard of Asia. Davis forwarded his report to the Foreign Office, expressing general agreement with the proposals it contained and emphasising that Gutzlaff had no knowledge of the plans which the Superintendent had suggested in May.[14]

It was Lord Aberdeen, Foreign Secretary since September 1841, who had to decide what action, if any, should be taken on these recommendations. He had, of course, been subject to some of the same influences as Davis, for the Foochow and Ningpo correspondence had all been sent home in addition to Martin's reports, while the intervention of the London East India and China Association must have carried more weight than any of these. Martin came back to England in 1845 and continued to bombard the Foreign Office, the Board of Trade and the Prime Minister with letters.[15] Increasingly he concerned himself with the opening of Japan, and early in 1846 offered his services as a

[13] F.O. *China Corres.*, vol. 100, Gutzlaff memo. of 12 July 1845 in Davis to Aberdeen, Sep. and Confid., 1 Aug. 1845.

[14] F.O. *China Corres.*, vol. 100, Davis to Aberdeen, Sep. and Confidential, 1 Aug. 1845.

[15] See, for example, F.O. *China Corres.*, vol. 107, Martin to Aberdeen, 12 Nov. 1845; *Aberdeen Papers*, vol. XXVI (Add. Mss. 43064), Peel to Aberdeen, 25 Aug. 1845; Bd. Trade, *Minutes*, vol. 55, minutes of 29 Aug. 1846.

'commercial envoy' for that purpose, though without success.[16] Yet although he managed to air his views in the Press both in England and in India,[17] one is forced to recognise that his campaign did not constitute public pressure on an important scale and cannot be given credit for Aberdeen's decision.

Aberdeen was in some ways predisposed to favour such a plan as Davis had suggested and the arguments he had advanced to support it. The Peel government was anxious to further British trade and improve commercial relations with other countries—Lord Ripon at the Board of Trade had put their policy in general terms when he stated that Her Majesty's Government were 'very desirous of availing themselves of any opportunity of opening new markets for all important Articles of our Manufactures by commercial arrangements with foreign powers upon principles of mutual advantage'.[18] This, of course, did not refer to Japan, where considerably greater difficulties might be expected than in the negotiations undertaken with France, Holland and Brazil. But Davis had pointed out that the risks were small, and it is significant that it was precisely this point that was emphasised in the summary of his letter found in Aberdeen's private papers.[19] Indeed, the so-called " weakness " of Aberdeen's policy—in China, at least—was little more than a determination to preserve trade relations undisturbed.[20] This emphasis on commercial interests naturally led him to approve the objectives, if not the methods proposed by Davis.

Even the methods were not entirely alien to his ideas. He was not averse to having a strong naval force on the China coast to support British policy, for when Pottinger and Davis protested against the reduction of the squadron in the summer of 1844 it was strengthened by the Admiralty

[16] F.O. *China Corres.*, vol. 117, Martin to Aberdeen, 3 Feb. 1846; Aberdeen to Martin, 12 Feb. 1846.
[17] London *Times*, 28 Aug., 2 and 8 Sept. 1846. *China Mail*, 11 Dec. 1845, quoting Indian press articles.
[18] Bd. Trade, *Minutes*, vol. 50, Ripon minute of 23 July 1842.
[19] *Aberdeen Papers*, vol. CXXIV (Add. Mss. 43162), f. 69.
[20] This appears clearly in Aberdeen to Davis, 8 Aug. 1845 (quoted in Morse, *International Relations*, 1, 374) and 24 Apr. 1846 (*ibid*, I, 375-6).

at Aberdeen's request.[21] This was in spite of a protest from Rear Admiral Cochrane, commanding the East Indies station, that such an increase was neither desirable nor necessary, and would only encourage consular officials in their constant appeals to the sanction of force when refused redress for imaginary grievances.[22] Aberdeen himself admitted that such a tendency existed, and that he did not approve of it.[23] On the other hand, he went so far as to state on one occasion that he considered China a special case, a proper field for the display of military strength during negotiations, the only part of the world in which he wished to maintain ' a greater force than might at first sight have appeared to be necessary '.[24]

Aberdeen, then, replied to Davis in terms of cautious approval. He fully concurred in the importance of opening this immense new field to British commerce, an importance which justified him, he thought, in accepting the risks involved ' more readily than might perhaps . . . be deemed consistent with strict political prudence '. Somewhat illogically, he added that he did so the more willingly because failure, as Davis had observed, ' could scarcely draw along with it any serious national damage '. The time and manner of the attempt were to be left to the Superintendent's discretion, but Aberdeen was not altogether happy about 'the naval pomp and parade ' which Davis seemed to think necessary. It might arouse more fear and jealousy than respect. He thought it as well, therefore, to give the Japanese government previous notice of the expedition, and of its peaceful intentions, in order to avoid any unnecessary clash that might jeopardise the success of the negotiations.

That portion of the Foreign Secretary's dispatch in which he discussed the terms to be secured, demonstrates

[21] *Aberdeen Papers*, vol. XXVI (Add. Mss. 43064), Aberdeen to Peel, 17 Oct. 1844. Admiralty, *Out-Letters*, vol. 1603, Adty. to R/A Cochrane, No. 188, 30 Nov. 1844.

[22] Admiralty, *In-Letters*, vol. 5539, Cochrane to Adty., No. 6, Hongkong, 13 June 1844.

[23] *Aberdeen Papers*, vol. XXVII (Add. Mss. 43065), Aberdeen to Peel, 28 Oct. 1845.

[24] *Aberdeen Papers*, vol. XXVI (Add. Mss. 43064), Aberdeen to Peel, 16 Sept. 1844.

clearly not only how little the Foreign Office knew about Japan, but also how much it was influenced by the history of British relations with China. It is therefore worth quoting at length :—

'At this stage of the business, and practically un-informed as we are with respect to Japan, it will be unnecessary, not so say impossible, for me to give you any specific directions as to the precise points of the negotiation, or the mode of conducting it. The general object will of course be to establish relations of amity and commerce with Japan ; and if the counterpart of our Treaties with China, with such modifications as local cir-cumstances may require, could be accomplished, such a consummation would appear to answer for the present every object which Her Majesty's Government have in view.

'Should you be able to effect an entrance into Japan, and find the Government more amenable than we can at present venture very confidently to anticipate, you would of course endeavour to expand as far as possible the advantages secured to us by our Treaties with China, by prevailing on the Japanese Government to open not Five but all the Great Ports of the Empire to our trade, and also secure to British subjects the free exercise of their religion wherever they may think it fit to establish themselves.

'Were it deemed possible you might also propose the establishment of permanent political relations with Japan by the fixed residence of an accredited British Diplomatic Agent at the Court. . . .

'You will therefore understand that you are to use your own discretion in endeavouring by your best exertions to give effect to your own suggestions ; that you are not to seek exclusive advantages of any description, political, commercial or religious, for Great Britain ; that you are not to admit any act or expression on the part of the Japanese Government implying superiority on their part or inferiority on ours ; but that both parties are to negoti-ate and constantly to treat each other on a footing of perfect equality ; that you are not to commit your Govern-ment to any measure, such for instance as the prevention of smuggling on the Coasts of Japan, which may entail expense or responsibility on them without any correspond-ing advantage ; and finally that you are to seek to lay

on the broad basis of justice and liberality the foundations
of our future relations with Japan, and to endeavour to
impress both the People and the Government with a sense
of our national good faith and integrity at least as much
as with that of our Power.'[25]

The questions of national equality, religious toleration,
smuggling and diplomatic representation mentioned here,
were precisely those already causing difficulties in British
relations with China. In drawing thus on British experience
in China, in viewing possible relations with Japan in the
light of that experience, Aberdeen set an example which
was followed by his successors when they drafted instructions on the subject to their representatives in the East,
and which was reflected in the terms of the treaty ultimately
negotiated by Elgin in 1858.

The caution embodied in the Foreign Secretary's dispatch
was less extreme than some of the wording suggests. Davis
was not ordered to avoid recourse to arms in all circumstances—as Belcher had been, for example—nor to abandon
altogether the use of 'naval pomp and parade'. He was
simply to avoid giving provocation to the Japanese. Indeed,
Aberdeen insisted that the detailed conduct of the mission
was left to the Superintendent's discretion. He was even
willing to provide the naval escort he had requested, and
instructed the Admiralty to issue orders to Rear Admiral
Cochrane, the commander on the station, which would leave
Davis as far as possible a free hand.[26]

As in other details, Aberdeen adhered closely to Davis's
suggestions in maintaining the strictest secrecy about the
plans. Davis had written his dispatch in his own hand to
prevent its contents becoming known to his subordinates.
Similarly, Aberdeen at first decided to send no full powers
for negotiations with Japan, not only because they would
probably be unnecessary in a country which knew nothing
of European diplomatic usage, but also because there was
a danger that information might leak out if too many departments were given access to it.[27] Nor was he content with

[25] F.O. *China Corres.*, vol. 96, Aberdeen to Davis, Separate and Secret,
8 Aug. 1845.
[26] F.O. *China Corres.*, vol. 106, For. Off. to Adty., Most Secret, 8 Aug. 1845.

marking his letter to the Admiralty " Most Secret ". He added a paragraph emphasising that the utmost care should be taken to prevent any suspicion of the existence of these plans from becoming public. It appears that even the Board of Trade was not informed in writing until after the government had fallen and Palmerston had succeeded Aberdeen in July 1846.[28]

Though later somewhat relaxed, this secrecy was still being enforced when Aberdeen determined, on the basis of Gutzlaff's recommendations, to add Cochin China to the list of countries with which Davis was empowered to treat. It was designed, of course, to minimise the chance of foreign competition. When the India Board, which had been informed only of the plans for Cochin China, asked to what extent it was intended by " secrecy " to prevent disclosure of the correspondence to the Court of Directors, the Foreign Office replied that the use of the term meant that it was desired ' to keep the whole subject of our projected negotiations in the Far East as secret as might be practicable. . . . The truth is, we do not wish it to be known in other countries what plans are concocting here for expanding our commerce and influence in the East '.[29]

Aberdeen's dispatch of 8 August reached Davis in October 1845 and he at once wrote a reply outlining his future plans. He repeated his belief that the time was ripe for such a venture, adducing as additional evidence the friendliness shown towards the *Samarang*[30] to show that the Japanese were no longer so rigid as before in their interpretation of the seclusion laws. He had taken the naval Commander-in-Chief into his confidence, and they were agreed that the voyage could not be undertaken until

---

[27] F.O. *China Corres.*, vol. 96, Aberdeen to Davis, Separate and Secret, 8 Aug. 1845. The full power was sent a few weeks later—vol. 96, same to same, 19 Sept. 1845.

[28] The first extant letter is F.O. *China Corres.*, vol. 118, For. Off. to Bd. Trade, 29 Aug. 1846.

[29] F.O. *China Corres.*, vol. 107, For. Off. to India Bd., 28 Nov. 1845. See also vol. 107, India Bd. to For. Off., 28 Nov. 1845 ; vol. 108, Aberdeen to Davis, Sep. and Secret, 18 Mar. 1846.

[30] See chapter II, pp. 51–3.

April 1846, by which time the monsoon would have changed and the indemnity been paid. As to the manner of approach, Davis conceded Aberdeen's point that the unannounced arrival of a large force might alarm the Japanese. He proposed, therefore, to send a steamer about one week ahead of the main body with a letter explaining its peaceful and friendly intentions. But he was not willing to reduce the size of the force. ' I do not perceive ', he wrote, ' any advantage (but the reverse) in presenting ourselves near the Japanese Capital in such a shape as might lead to our being despised, or perhaps insulted. The appearance of a respectable force is probably the best mode of securing a hearing. . . .'[31] Davis, it is clear, was not content to be a mere supplicant for trade and went further than Aberdeen in his reliance on the gunboat as an instrument of diplomacy—a fact later of much importance.

The plan was, then, to visit Japan immediately after the evacuation of Chusan. In fact, it was never carried out. The evacuation itself was postponed until July 1846, and in the interval a number of factors operated to deter Davis from continuing with the Japan project.

The first of these factors was the rivalry of other Western powers. The French were beginning to take an interest in the Loochoo Islands and had requested trading privileges there, so far without success.[32] The Americans were planning to negotiate directly with Japan. The American mission, which had been urged on the President by Congress early in 1845, was at first entrusted to Everett, the new U.S. commissioner to China, but Everett fell ill on his way out from America and transferred his instructions and credentials for Japan to Commodore James Biddle, in whose flagship he was taking passage. Biddle reached Macao in December 1845, and Davis soon heard of his plans. He first reported on them in March 1846, when Biddle was at Hongkong, and a few weeks later he obtained fuller information through Gutzlaff, who agreed to translate Biddle's full

---

[31] F.O. *China Corres.*, vol. 107, Davis to Aberdeen, Separate and Secret, Hongkong, 27 Oct. 1845.
[32] Murdoch, *History of Japan*, III, 533-6; Kobayashi, *Bakumatsu-shi*, pp. 116-8.

power—though he refused to lend the commodore either of his two Japanese assistants to act as interpreter to the expedition.[33]

At this stage, as his dispatches show, Davis was not much disturbed by the thought of competition, either American or French. He believed, indeed, that Biddle's experience in Japan would be useful in guiding the British negotiations, and showed no sign of changing his opinion in May 1846, when he reported that both Biddle and Cecille, commander of the French squadron, had left China for Japan.[34]

It was only the question of naval strength, in fact, that made these events significant to British plans for Japan. Late in 1845 Cochrane, with Admiralty approval, had decided to divert part of his squadron to Borneo to make an attack on the pirate strongholds which threatened the shipping lanes in south-east Asia, and to support the Sultan in his efforts to maintain friendly relations with Great Britain.[35] The task proved longer and more difficult than he expected. The Chusan expedition was held up waiting for Cochrane to return from the south, and by June 1846 Davis was complaining that more ships were being withdrawn from the China coast, further weakening what he already thought to be an inadequate force there. Only a frigate and three brigs remained, not enough to fulfil the treaty stipulation that a British warship be stationed permanently at each of the open ports.[36] His protest was upheld by Palmerston and the Admiralty, but little could be done. Naval weakness was not confined to the East Indies station. It was due not to lack of ships, but to Parliamentary estimates too small to permit the manning of such as were available, and it was already said to be

[33] F.O. *China Corres.*, vol. 110, Davis to For. Off., No. 44, 22 Mar. 1846; vol. 111, Davis to Aberdeen, Separate and Secret, 10 Apr. 1846. The Japanese working for Gützlaff were two of the *Morrison* castaways, Kyūkichi and Iwakichi.

[34] F.O. *China Corres.*, vol. 112, Davis to Aberdeen, Separate and Secret, 24 May 1846.

[35] Admiralty, *Out-Letters*, vol. 1603, Adty. to R/A Cochrane, No. 148, 7 Oct. 1845, and No. 170, 24 Nov. 1845.

[36] F.O. *China Corres.*, vol. 112, Davis to Aberdeen, Sep. and Secret, 24 May 1846; Davis to For. Off., No. 85, 23 June 1846.

handicapping the new government in its conduct of foreign relations in many parts of the world.[37]

In June Davis determined to proceed with the evacuation of Chusan as soon as the transports were ready and without waiting for Cochrane. This would make his force much less impressive, but he still planned to visit Japan ' should time and circumstances render the same advisable '.[38] It was after his arrival at Chusan, as he reported to Aberdeen on his return, that he changed his mind and decided to postpone the Japan expedition to a more suitable opportunity. He had already been disturbed by the lack of naval support and Cochrane's failure to return in time. At Chusan he received information (which later proved to be false) that Biddle and Cecille were to join forces for negotiating with Japan, and this news was decisive. Between them the French and American commanders could probably muster five ships, two of them large, a much greater force than Davis could hope to raise on the China coast ; and to follow them in such circumstances, it seemed to him, would be to lose dignity. He chose rather to await the result of their visit, as by waiting until the following spring he could benefit by their experience and at the same time give Cochrane the opportunity of gathering a more sizable force. If they succeeded, then he would succeed if his mission looked as powerful. If they failed, the Japanese would be less inclined to add to their enemies by quarrelling with a strong British squadron. There were other reasons, too. Failure in Japan would lower British prestige in China, where fresh disputes had just broken out over the right of entry to Canton, and it would be better for others to fail if any must. Moreover, he said, ' we have acquired in the East generally a character for encroachment, and if the French and Americans should for once be willing to share this with us, the participation is calculated to do us no harm '.[39]

[37] *Russell Papers*, vol. 5, Auckland to Russell, 8 Sept. 1846 ; Minto to Russell, 10 Sept. 1846.
[38] F.O. *China Corres.*, vol. 112, Davis to For. Off., No. 85, 23 June, 1846. See also F.O. *China Emb. Arch.*, vol. 59, Davis to Capt. Talbot, No. 101, 20 June, 1846.
[39] F.O. *China Corres.*, vol. 113, Davis to Aberdeen, Separate and Secret, Hongkong, 6 Aug. 1846.

In the event, both French and American visits to Japan proved fruitless. Cecille visited Loochoo in June 1846 to press the French request for a trade agreement—which was refused—and went thence to Nagasaki to show the flag. He was treated with the customary incivility and left after only forty-eight hours. Biddle reached Edo Bay in the following month and announced that he had come to settle the terms on which American ships might use Japanese ports if the Japanese were willing to open them. Seven days later he received a formal refusal of his request, couched in the most disrespectful terms. His anxiety to avoid conflict—enjoined on him by the instructions of his government—led to one incident which the Japanese interpreted as acceptance of a gratuitous insult, and did much to weaken the effect originally produced by the obvious power of his ships. Its ineffectiveness did much to determine the methods used by later foreign visitors to Japan.

Davis heard only a garbled version of Cecille's visit to Nagasaki,[40] but he had complete and accurate information about the American failure.[41] The manner as well as the fact of that failure had considerable effect on his own decisions. In August 1846, as we have seen, he had announced his intention of postponing the Japan negotiations until the following spring. By the end of the year that postponement had become indefinite. In fact, Davis may have abandoned the idea of a Japan treaty altogether, for he never revived the plan. Nor did he make any further reference to the possibility that American failure might make Japan less inclined to offend a British negotiator. Disputes at Canton, which required the Superintendent's immediate return to Hongkong from Chusan in July 1846, had undoubtedly played a part in preventing him from visiting Japan in the summer, and one is tempted to look to British relations with China for an explanation of

[40] F.O. *China Corres.*, vol. 114, Davis to Palmerston, Separate and Secret, 15 Oct. 1846; vol. 115, Davis to For. Oft., No. 185, 28 Dec. 1846.
[41] F.O. *China Corres.*, vol. 114, Davis to Palmerston, Separate and Secret, 15 Oct. 1846; vol. 134, R./A Seymour to Adty., 20 Dec. 1846 in Adty. to For. Off., 13 Mar. 1847.

this continued postponement. Yet Davis himself offered no such explanation, and the disputes at Canton did not reach crisis proportions until March 1847, by which time the decision about Japan had already been taken. Important as they were later to become, conflicts in China were not the chief cause of postponing the Japan mission in the autumn of 1846. Davis was willing enough to leave the China coast to conduct negotiations elsewhere. Instead of Japan, however, he turned his attention to the plans for opening trade with Cochin China, which had been drawn up at Gutzlaff's suggestion in the previous year. In November 1846 he wrote to the new Foreign Secretary, Lord Palmerston, to announce his intention of going to Cochin China in the spring, a project which he considered ' much more likely to be attended by success than the mission to Japan, in which the Americans have lately so entirely failed '.[42]

Lord Palmerston approved both Davis's decisions and the reasons given for them.[43] Aberdeen had shown himself willing to leave the execution of the plan to the Superintendent's discretion, though he might have demurred at the reasons given for postponement. Palmerston, on the other hand, was much more susceptible to the arguments Davis used. When, in the summer of 1846, Davis reported his decisions to postpone the Japan expedition because he could not raise enough force to match the French and American missions, he was appealing—though the dispatch was addressed to Lord Aberdeen—to all Palmerston's national prejudice. Like Davis, Palmerston was prepared to act only if naval support were available on an adequate scale. This would continue to be impossible until the Foreign Office or the Admiralty decided that the Japan mission was important enough to be given priority over some of the other duties required of the China squadron. There seemed no immediate prospect of any such decision.

Nor was there likely to be much opposition to the abandon-

[42] F.O. *China Corres.*, vol. 115, Davis to Palmerston, Separate and Secret, 24 Nov. 1846.
[43] F.O. *China Corres.*, vol. 108, For. Off. to Davis, No. 43, 10 Dec. 1846; vol. 121, Palmerston to Davis, Separate and Secret, 25 Jan. 1847.

ment of the scheme. A number of newspapers had reported that plans were being made, but none knew any details and few actively supported the idea. Such agitation as there was can be traced to Montgomery Martin, whose hopes rested on ' an amicable commercial mission ' rather than on diplomatic negotiations backed by a powerful squadron.[44] The *Edinburgh Review* remained silent, while the *Quarterly* was as hostile as ever to the use of force. It agreed that there would be advantages in an open communication with Japan if the ports were opened by the Japanese themselves, or privileges were granted to a commercial envoy. But if, as seemed more likely, the Japanese feared and hated Britain enough to refuse all friendly overtures, then, it said, ' we know not by what law of nations we can insist on a reversal in our favour of the code of an empire which never itself indulged in acts of aggression. We doubt, indeed, whether either menace or violence could lead to any result more satisfactory than they would deserve. . . . '[45]

Despite the efforts of a few individuals who remained interested in the extension of British trade and influence to Japan, the plans abandoned in 1846 were not revived until 1852. The naval force continued smaller than either Palmerston or Davis desired. In the spring and summer of 1847, at Foreign Office insistence, Rear Admiral Inglefield was ordered to keep the China squadron at full strength, even at the cost of leaving inadequate reserves on the rest of the East Indies station,[46] but this was a mere palliative so long as reinforcements could not be sent from home. The European situation, especially the danger of a break with France, made this impossible, and Davis continued to complain.[47] At the same time, relations with China were increasing the work of the squadron and engaging most of

[44] F.O. *China Corres.*, vol. 118, Martin to Palmerston, 26 and 28 Aug. 1846: London *Times*, 28 Aug., 2 and 8 Sept. 1846: London *Daily News*, 18 Dec. 1846 (reprinted in *China Mail*, 8 Apr. 1847).

[45] *Quarterly Review*, LXXVIII (June 1846), pp. 21-2.

[46] Admiralty, *Out-Letters*, vol. 1605, Adty. to Inglefield, No. 94, 30 Apr. 1847, and No. 136, 6 July 1847.

[47] F.O. *China Corres.*, vol. 140, Davis to For. Off., No. 27, 12 Feb. 1848, and No. 38, 26 Feb. 1848: F.O. *China Emb. Arch.*, vol. 69, Davis to Capt. McQuhæ, Canton, 13 and 17 Dec. 1847.

the Superintendent's attention. Britain claimed that her treaties gave British subjects the right to enter the city as well as the port of Canton. This the Chinese consistently denied. The anti-foreign feelings of the local population and the provocative behaviour of some of the British merchants led to occasional acts of violence, one of which had been responsible for bringing Davis hurrying back from Chusan in July 1846. In March 1847, as a result of orders from Palmerston that he was to take a firm line at Canton, Davis resorted to the use of force. This interpretation of his instructions brought an immediate rebuke from the Foreign Secretary ; but while open hostilities were thereafter avoided, disputes continued at intervals in 1848 and 1849.[48]

Taken together, the two factors of naval weakness and conflict with China seem sufficient explanation of the continued postponement of the Japan project in these years. Indeed, the fact that no attempt was made to utilise the occasional periods of quiet in China as an opportunity for opening negotiations with Japan, whereas Davis found time to visit Cochin China in 1847, suggests that of the two the naval problem was the more important. The naval weakness was relative, of course, not absolute. It depended on two assumptions : first, that only a powerful and impressive mission could succeed in Japan ; second, that the object was not of that importance which would justify diverting ships from other duties. Both assumptions sometimes came under attack,[49] but responsible officials were not easily persuaded to abandon them.

It was the energy of Davis which had led to the plan for opening Japan, and it was his decision to postpone it that governed the later actions of the Foreign Office. Palmerston, like Aberdeen, was willing to trust to the Superintendent's discretion and fuller knowledge. At no time did he show any inclination to take the initiative in

[48] For the disputes over Canton see Morse, *International Relations*, I, 376-91 ; Costin, *Great Britain and China*, pp. 125-33.

[49] Montgomery Martin, for example, attacked the first. The *China Mail* (e.g. in its issues of 27 Aug. 1846, 10 Oct. 1850 and especially 2 Mar. 1854) commented acidly on the second.

the matter.   Once the voyage had been postponed, he was satisfied with keeping the way open for it to take place at some future date.   In February 1847, for example, when the Dutch minister in London informed him that the Japanese had decided to notify the various countries of the West, through Dutch diplomatic channels, of their resolution to keep their ports closed to all but Dutch and Chinese merchants, Palmerston refused to accept such intervention. He declined to be bound by representations from any other agency than the Japanese government itself, though he did not admit the existence of any British plans for negotiating with it.[50]

It was quite in accord with this attitude that Palmerston should provide S. G. Bonham with discretionary powers to negotiate with Cochin China[51] and Japan when appointing him to succeed Davis early in 1848.   Bonham received instructions to encourage trade with Japan through the treaty ports north of Canton, but was not specifically ordered to visit that country.   The initiative for such a move must come, if at all, from the Superintendent of Trade.   'As regards Japan and Cochin China ', the dispatch ran, ' . . . you may be guided by the opinion you may form in China as to the probable advantage to be derived from an attempt at negotiation with the Governments of those Countries.   You will always bear in mind, that Her Majesty's Government, if they should enter into relations with those Countries, desire nothing more than what is required for free commercial intercourse on mutually advantageous terms ; they seek no political influence . . . and have no desire to acquire territory in either of those Countries. . . . '[52]

The substitution of Bonham for Davis materially reduced the possibility that the Japan plans would be revived.   In accordance with what had now become accepted practice, the Foreign Office left it to Bonham to decide not only

[50] The Japanese decision dated from 1843, and the Dutch explained that they had not communicated it before because there had not previously seemed any prospect of British action.   See F.O. *China Emb. Arch.*, vol. 68, For. Off. to Davis, No. 29, 22 Feb.   1847, enclosing :—Count Schimmelpennick to Palmerston, 19 Feb. 1847 ; Palmerston to Schimmelpennick, 22 Feb. 1847.

[51] Davis had failed in his attempt to secure a treaty with Cochin China in 1847.

[52] F.O. *China Corres.*, vol. 138, For. Off. to Bonham, No. 1, 11 Jan. 1848.

when but whether any attempt should be made to put them into effect. It was unlikely, therefore, that the Russell government[53] would take any further steps unless stimulated into activity by outside pressure of some kind, either in the form of foreign rivalry or of fresh plans proposed at home or in China. While the Board of Trade, to quote Russell's words, ' would give up anything to promote trade ',[54] and the Cabinet as a whole was convinced of the importance of commercial relations with other countries, the government still did not accept the view that ' all considerations of a higher nature . . . be sacrificed to the pushing of our manufactures by any means into every possible corner of the Globe '.[55] Indeed, the conduct of foreign relations entailed rather the solution of immediate and practical problems than the application, irrespective of circumstances, of a number of abstract principles—a view to which Russell himself subscribed[56]—and no Foreign Secretary was likely, unprompted, to create work for himself by planning missions to a country as remote as Japan, in which the prospects for British trade were to say the least doubtful. Palmerston himself had shown no enthusiasm for the Japan plans. In June 1847, moreover, he had learned something of the failure of the seventeenth-century Hirado factory,[57] and this knowledge, combined with frequent references in dispatches and elsewhere to the marked drop in Dutch trade with that country, armed him against too ready a belief in the prophecies of the few enthusiasts who saw in Japan a vast new market for British goods.

Bonham, as Superintendent of Trade, was in the best

[53] The Russell government remained in power until February 1852, though Palmerston resigned and was succeeded at the Foreign Office by Granville in Dec. 1851.

[54] *Russell Papers*, vol. 8, Russell to Baring, 15 Oct. 1849, with reference to the Newfoundland fisheries problem.

[55] *Granville Papers*, vol. 18, Granville to Russell, 12 Jan. 1852, in a general statement of British foreign policy drawn up at the Queen's request.

[56] *Granville Papers*, vol. 18, Russell to Granville, 29 Dec. 1851, when informing him of the Queen's wish that a foreign policy " programme" be drawn up.

[57] See F.O. *China Corres.*, vol. 135, India Bd. to For. Off., 18 June 1847, with extracts from the East India Co. records, pointing out that the generous privileges of which Montgomery Martin spoke had been revoked by Hidetada in 1616.

position to convince the Foreign Office of the need for action. Davis, his predecessor, had had an author's interest in the project, but had been held back by the conviction that a display of force was necessary to success.[58] Bonham seems to have lacked even the initial interest. He was a cautious man, nearing the age of retirement. His experience lay not in trade or diplomacy but in the administration of East India Company territories in southeast Asia, and he was much occupied with his duties as Governor of Hong-kong.[59] Even though Japan was sometimes brought to his notice, it was to no effect. Dr. Gutzlaff, the Chinese Secretary, who had been interpreter to the *Morrison* expedition, still hoped that something would be done and occasionally referred to the subject in his letters. In 1849 he persuaded Bonham to grant an increase of salary to Kyūkichi, one of the *Morrison* castaways employed in the Superintendency, on the grounds that his services would be invaluable in the event of an expedition to Japan.[60] Wade, another of the China establishment's interpreters, translated part of a Chinese book dealing with Japan.[61] Harry Parkes, later to be British minister in Tōkyō, began to learn the Japanese language while interpreter at Shanghai, and encouraged by the Foreign Office's promise that his pay would be increased as a reward for success, continued his studies for some years despite the illiteracy of his teacher and lack of time and books.[62] But there is no evidence that any of these

[58] Davis's attitude was not particular to Japan. In 1847, for example, he congratulated Capt. La Pierre, commander of the French squadron on the China coast, on the sinking of five Cochin Chinese war-junks which dared to oppose him, in terms which reveal much of his views on the " diplomatic " methods to be used in East Asia :—' C'est ainsi qu'on est quelquefois obligé d'exiger le respect des peuples demi-sauvages envers les Nations civilisées de l'Occident. On commence par détruire à coups de Canon les barricades de la barbarie ; puis s'ensuivent la Religion, le Commerce, avec leurs résultats '. (F.O. *China Emb. Arch.*, vol. 69, Davis to Capt. La Pierre, Hongkong, 26 Apr. 1847.)

[59] F.O. *China Corres.*, vol. 143, Bonham to For. Off., No. 35, 24 May 1848.

[60] F.O. *China Corres.*, vol. 153, Bonham to For. Off., No. 15, 2 Feb. 1849, and enclosures : F.O. *China Emb. Arch.*, vol. 97, Bonham to Gutzlaff, No. 10, 3 Feb. 1849.

[61] The translation contained little new information, but gave a fairly accurate account of the relationship between Emperor and Shōgun. It was forwarded to London in Bonham to For. Off., No. 103, 28 Sept. 1850 (F.O. *China Emb. Arch.*, vol. 107).

men attempted to persuade either Bonham or Palmerston to put an end to Japanese seclusion.

About a year after Bonham's arrival at Hongkong, a second British surveying ship paid a visit to Japan. In May 1849 H.M.S. *Mariner* was ordered to survey the Edo Bay area and sailed from Shanghai after engaging Otokichi, another of the *Morrison* castaways, as interpreter.[63] The last days of May and the first week of June were spent in surveying Sagami Bay and the harbours of Uraga and Shimoda, but the Japanese officials were urgent in their protests and their requests for her departure, and on 7 June she left Japan for China without having obtained permission for any more extended surveys.[64] Since the instructions to the *Mariner* have not been found, it is not clear whether the visit had any ulterior motives, but certainly Commander Matheson had no diplomatic duties. The Foreign Office had no advance knowledge of the visit.[65] Bonham claimed that he only ' heard by accident ' after the *Mariner* returned to Shanghai[66] and reported the matter in case it should be taken up by ' the Mercantile Interests ' at home. He did not think Matheson's report of much value—no opportunity had been given for the consular service to be represented on board—for it served only to show that there was little prospect of the Japanese receiving a diplomatic mission ' should H.M. Government have any intention of sending one '.[67] He obviously had no intention of reviving the scheme on his own initiative.

The *Mariner*'s voyage did not represent, nor did it lead

[62] F.O. *China Corres.*, vcl. 129, Davis to For. Off., No. 159, 27 Aug. 1847 and encl. ; vol. 138, For. Off. to Bonham, No. 29, 19 Apr. 1848 ; vol. 159, Bonham to For. Off., No. 173, 14 Dec. 1849 ; vol. 182, Parkes to Hammond (permanent Under-Sec.), 14 July 1851.

[63] Halloran, *Wae Yang Jin*, p. 74. For Otokichi's earlier history see chapter I, pp. 21-7.

[64] For an account of the visit see Halloran, *Wae Yang Jin*, pp. 78-93, and a summary of Matheson's report in F.O. *China Corres.*, vol. 156, Bonham to Addington, 26 July 1849.

[65] F.O. *China Corres.*, vol. 162, Adty. to For. Off., 23 June 1849, enclosing R/A Collier's report (of 17 Apr. 1849) on future movements of ships on the China station, made no reference to sending the *Mariner* to Japan, and Admiralty approval was only given after the event (Admiralty, *Out-Letters*, vol. 1608, Adty. to Collier, No. 208, 2 Nov. 1849).

[66] F.O. *China Corres.*, vol. 156, Bonham to Addington, 26 July 1849.

[67] *ibid.*

to, action by any of the responsible officials in London or in China. But if neither Superintendent nor Foreign Office were willing to revive old plans or make new ones, there were private citizens who took a more active interest in Japan. Between 1849 and 1853 there were two attempts to bring pressure to bear on the British government, attempts which differed both in their origin and in their objectives. The first was made by a missionary, the second by Montgomery Martin.

The Loochoo Naval Mission was founded by officers who had at various times visited the Loochoo Islands in the course of their duties. In 1845 they decided to send a medical missionary there, not only because it was a likely field for the propagation of Christianity, but also because a foothold in the Loochoos might make it possible to introduce Christianity into Japan, or at least enable a missionary to learn enough of the Japanese language and customs to be ready for the first opportunity of entering that country.[68] The man chosen for this task was Dr. Bettelheim, a Hungarian Jew by birth, who arrived with his family at Napa, chief port of the islands, in the spring of 1846. From the beginning he proved a problem to the Superintendency at Hongkong. Though actually controlled by Japan through the Satsuma fief of southern Kyūshū, the islands were nominally subject to Chinese suzerainty, and the Chinese soon protested to Davis against Bettelheim's presence there and visits by British warships. Davis, with Foreign Office approval, refused to accept responsibility for the missionary's activities and maintained the right of British warships ' to proceed wherever their friendly objects or intentions may carry them '.[69] But his successor was soon to find that the doctor's own demands for protection could cause more trouble than Chinese protests.

In February 1849 a British ship was wrecked in the Loochoos and her master appealed to Rutherford Alcock, consul at Shanghai, for assistance in bringing away her crew

[68] F.O. *China Corres.*, vol. 106, H. Clifford (Hon. Sec., Loochoo Naval Mission) to For. Off., 28 Aug. 1845, and encl.
[69] F.O. *China Corres.*, vol. 123, Davis to For. Off., No. 13, 28 Jan. 1847, vol. 121, For. Off. to Davis. No. 45, 25 Mar. 1847.

and whatever could be salvaged from the wreck. In March
H.M.S. *Mariner* was sent to the islands, taking with her
Vice-Consul Robertson, who with Matheson, the *Mariner*'s
commander, soon found himself involved in Bettelheim's
disputes with the islanders. On 7 March, after doing all
that was possible at the wreck, they received a letter from
Bettelheim requesting their assistance. At the same time
the Loochoo officials asked that the missionary be taken
away. The *Mariner* proceeded to Napa, where Bettelheim
met her to complain of his treatment, chiefly of restrictions
on his contacts with the islanders and a number of other
petty annoyances. He refused the passage to Shanghai
offered him by Commander Matheson. Instead he asked
for Matheson's intervention with the local officials. The
latter, however, repeated their request for his removal,
arguing that his maintenance was a heavy burden on the resources of so small and poor a country, and when Matheson
pointed out that they had not complained of any illegal acts
on Bettelheim's part to justify his removal, they gave him a
letter for the British government which reiterated the arguments advanced during the discussion. Bettelheim, in his
turn, entrusted Matheson with a petition to Parliament asking that naval vessels might occasionally visit the islands to
give him protection.[70]

In his report of the voyage, Robertson emphasised that
by writing to the British government the island officials had
created an opportunity for further intercourse. In particular they had made possible an indirect approach to the
valuable trade of Japan. ' Loochoo is in itself a nothing ',
he wrote, ' . . . but its connection and communication
with Japan is of so important a character, as to warrant a
belief that in the event of an arrangement for the residence
of Foreigners . . . Napa would become the mart of Japan
for foriegn as it is now for home Trade, offering as it does
a " Neutral Ground " which the Japanese may not be unwilling to take advantage of, and opening a new and
important feature in our relations with that distant and

[70] Halloran, *Wae Yang Jin*, pp. 10-2, 23-30. F.O. *China Corres.*, vol. 155,
Bonham to For. Off., No. 58, 4 May 1849, encl. Robertson's report of 19 Mar.
1849.

sealed part of the world'. Gutzlaff, to whom Bonham referred for advice, supported Robertson's optimistic views and urged support for Bettelheim in his 'advanced post toward the Japanese Empire', but the cautious Bonham contented himself with forwarding the papers to the Foreign Office and asking for instructions.[71] Less than three weeks later he reported that Commander Glynn of U.S.S. *Preble* had visited Napa and received another request for Bettelheim's removal, which had also been urged on him by the Japanese at Nagasaki.[72]

Before Bonham's dispatch reached London the Foreign Office had already heard of the *Mariner*'s visit to Loochoo and had asked the Admiralty to arrange for occasional visits to the islands.[73] Robertson's report, however, seemed to indicate that more might be achieved without much difficulty. In August, therefore, it was decided to try to open trade with the Loochoos. A letter was drafted in reply to that of the Napa officials, thanking them for their help to British seamen and recommending Bettelheim to their protection. In almost childish English, it explained that Britain and Loochoo each produced commodities of value to the other, which could be exchanged to the advantage of both, and expressed the hope that the Loochoo authorities would send a friendly reply permitting trade to be carried on.[74] This letter was sent to Bonham, and acting on the instructions which accompanied it, he arranged for a warship to deliver it to Napa and at the same time show Bettelheim such attention as would 'raise him in the estimation of the Loochoo authorities'. He took care, nevertheless, not to give the doctor the impression that he could use this naval support for his own ends.[75]

[71] F.O. *China Corres.*, vol. 155, Bonham to For. Off., No. 58, 4 May 1849, and enclosed reports from Robertson and Gutzlaff.
[72] F.O. *China Corres.*, vol. 155, Bonham to For. Off., No. 75, 24 May 1849.
[73] F.O. *China Corres.*, vol. 162, For Off. to Adty., 23 June 1849. Bonham's dispatch was not received until 24 July.
[74] F.O. *China Corres.*, vol. 160, draft, For. Off. to Authorities of Loochoo, 10 Aug. 1849.
[75] F.O. *China Corres.*, vol. 159, Bonham to For. Off., No. 168, 27 Nov. 1849. F.O. *China Emb. Arch.*, vol. 97, Bonham to Capt. Massie (S.O. Hongkong), No. 121, 20 Nov. 1849; Bonham to Bettelheim, No. 122, 21 Nov. 1849. Bonham's letter to Bettelheim originally offered him the warship's support for 'any Service which you may request', but he altered this in draft to read 'any Service . . . of which your lonely position may make you stand in need'.

A reply was received from Loochoo early in 1850, identical in its arguments with that made to the French request for trade in 1846.[76] It rejected the offer of trade on the grounds that far from having a surplus of goods for export, the islands had barely enough for their own needs and had found it exceedingly difficult to supply food and stores to the few ships which had visited Loochoo so far. Moreover, it said, the laws of Japan were severe in their prohibition of trade, and if the islanders broke them they might find themselves cut off from that country, on which they depended for many necessities. Finally, the letter catalogued once again the objections to Bettelheim's presence. Forwarding it to London, Bonham added on his own account that Bettelheim had been able to gain no information which might confirm or refute the argument against trade, nor indeed ' to advance the interests of Commerce or to propagate the Christian Religion in any way whatever '. However, he was in no personal danger, except such as arose through his own lack of discretion, and had been advised to act with moderation.[77]

Palmerston, like Bonham, showed no further inclination to press the matter of trade or of a possible connection with Japan. During the next two years his attitude to Bettelheim was simply that as a British subject abroad he was entitled to his government's support, a policy on which he insisted in other, more famous, cases, despite opposition in the Cabinet. In July 1850, at his request, fresh instructions were sent by the Admiralty to ensure the occasional visit of a warship to Napa.[78] In the autumn H.M.S. *Reynard* called there and was given another petition asking for

[76] For the reply to France see Murdoch, *History of Japan*, III, 533-6. Murdoch here and Kobayashi (*Bakumatsu-shi*, pp. 118-9) maintain that Satsuma later got secret permission from the Bakufu to open trade through Loochoo, but did nothing because the French request was not renewed. This refusal of the British request suggests that not lack of opportunity but Japanese opposition—from Tokugawa Nariaki of Mito, for example—may have been the real reason for doing nothing.

[77] F.O. *China Corres.*, vol. 165, Bonham to For. Off., No. 14, 9 Feb. 1850, enclosing the Loochoo reply, dated 28 Dec. 1849.

[78] F.O. *China Corres.*, vol. 173, For. Off. to Clifford (Loochoo Naval Mission), 2 July 1850; For. Off. to Adty., same date. Admiralty, *Out-Letters*, vol. 1609, Adty. to R/A Austen, No. 70, 4 July 1850.

Bettelheim's removal,[79] which provoked Palmerston into an angry reply implying that unless the missionary received better treatment the visits of British warships might become less friendly.[80]

Bonham found some difficulty in forwarding these letters. After an unsuccessful attempt to send them by junk from Foochow, he finally arranged for a warship to take them early in 1852. T. T. Meadows, one of the interpreters in Chinese, was to deliver them, in order to ensure that the object of the mission was clearly understood by the islanders and not distorted by Bettelheim, who had acted as interpreter on previous occasions[81]—an arrangement which spoke ill for Bonham's faith in the missionary's straightforwardness ! Meadows' report was hostile to Bettelheim. It described him as imprudent and dictatorial and warned that he would undoubtedly obtain ' a virtual dictatorship in the principality ' unless the Foreign Office were particularly cautious as to the manner in which it supported him[82]

Granville, continuing the policy laid down by Palmerston, wrote to Loochoo in January 1852 to commend the better treatment Bettelheim was apparently receiving,[83] but showed no other interest. Bettelheim, however, had not yet given up hope of interesting the government in his single-handed crusade against Japanese seclusion. In September 1852 he wrote personally to Palmerston, now out of office, to appeal in almost lyrical terms for his support—' one more jewel there is, a Koh-i-noor, waiting to be enamelled in the crown

[79] F.O. *China Emb. Arch.*, vol. 110, Bonham to Cdr. Cracroft (H.M.S. *Reynard*), No. 76, 10 Sept. 1850. F.O. *China Corres.*, vol. 170, Bonham to For. Off., No. 122, 29 Oct. 1850 (received London 19 Dec. 1850) ; vol. 183, Adty. to For. Off., 13 Jan. 1851.

[80] F.O. *China Corres.*, vol. 182, drafts, For. Off. to Loochoo, 2 Jan. and 11 Feb. 1851. The first, written on receipt of Bonham's dispatch, was mild in tone, but the second, after receipt of the Admiralty letter, was more threatening.

[81] See chiefly F.O. *China Emb. Arch.*, vol. 124, Bonham to Cdr. Ellman, Separate, 17 Nov. 1851 ; vol. 140, Bonham to Bettelheim, No. 6, 12 Jan. 1852. F.O. *China Corres.*, vol. 187, Bonham to For. Oft., No. 3, 12 Jan. 1852.

[82] F.O. *China Corres.*, vol. 188, Meadows to Bonham, 26 Feb. 1852, in Bonham to For. Off., No. 34, 9 Mar. 1852.

[83] F.O. *Miscellanea, Ser. II*, vol. 23, Addington minute of 1 Jan. 1852. F.O. *China Corres.*, vol. 195, draft, For. Off. to Loochoo, 17 Jan. 1852. This letter was eventually sent by junk from Foochow.

of your imperishable glory, the *Emancipation of Japan* '.[84] The accompanying petition to Parliament argued in more sober style. The Japanese prohibition of trade, said Bettelheim, could best be broken down by obtaining a promise of religious toleration, for the two ideas were closely linked in the Japanese mind ; in fact, ' the political position of Loochoo is so particularly favourable for doing it good and so prominently fit for any undertaking regarding Japan that it would be doubly neglecting a special providence not to attempt both at once '.

Bowring, now Superintendent of Trade, was unmoved by this special pleading. He took the opportunity to observe that Bettelheim's purpose seemed to be ' to engage Her Majesty's Government in a Missionary Crusade ' and rebuked Bettelheim himself for his presumption.[85] Palmerston sent the letters to Clarendon, but the new Foreign Secretary took no action. Indeed, there was no further attempt to support or encourage Bettelheim in any way.

So far as they concerned plans for opening Japan, Bettelheim's efforts to arouse interest had been singularly unsuccessful. Bonham had been indifferent, Bowring openly contemptuous. Palmerston, after a brief flicker of interest in trade, had concentrated on what he felt to be the more important task, the support of a British subject in a remote and hostile country. His successors had been reluctant to take action even for that end. No public interest had been aroused, nor had other missionary societies attempted to follow the doctor's example, and though Bettelheim continued to live at Napa, his later work met with little more success—despite which fact the Japanese ultimately erected a monument in tribute to him.

Another enthusiast who tried to bring pressure to bear on the government used methods better calculated to gain his ends. Montgomery Martin had first become interested in the Japan trade through his attempt to secure the retention of Chusan as a British naval and commercial station.

[84] F.O. *China Corres.*, vol. 195, Bettelheim to Palmerston, Napa, 19 Sept. 1852.

[85] F.O. *China Corres.*, vol. 199, Bowring to For. Off., No. 14, 21 Jan. 1853. F.O. *China Emb. Arch.*, vol. 154, Bowring to Bettelheim, 22 Jan. 1853.

In the years 1845 to 1847 he had made great efforts to interest the Foreign Office, the Board of Trade and Parliament in his plans. He had written to *The Times*, had interviews with Aberdeen and Palmerston at the Foreign Office, with Dalhousie and Clarendon at the Board of Trade, but all to no effect.[86] Plans to negotiate with Japan were then already in existence, though Martin did not know it.

At the beginning of 1849, since nothing had been done meanwhile, Martin re-opened the subject in a correspondence with the Board of Trade. He recommended ' a tentative commercial mission ' with credentials from the Board of Trade rather than a full-scale diplomatic embassy. Moreover, he preferred that it be carried out by a single well-equipped but unarmed ship, visiting Korea, Cochin China and Siam as well as Japan. In Japan, he said, it should request a return to the privileges of 1613—Martin believed them still to be in force—emphasising the peaceful character of Britain's previous relations with Japan and the purely commercial nature of her interest in China. Letters from the Queen must be provided, of course, but used only in the last resort. Every care must be taken that there be no hint of a connection with the East India Company, whose territorial expansion was ' well known and dreaded ', nor with the Superintendency at Hongkong, which was still generally regarded in the countries bordering China as being connected with the Company.[87]

Labouchere at the Board of Trade was impressed by the importance of opening commercial relations with these countries, and by the support given to the scheme by Sir Henry Ellis, formerly a member of the Amherst embassy to China and of the Board of Control. He looked up the papers concerning the 1845 plans and consulted Palmerston, suggesting that more information would be required before deciding whether such an attempt would have a better chance of success than ' a mission of a more ostentatious

---

[86] See above pp. 56-8 and F.O. *China Corres.*, vol. 161, Martin to Palmerston, 22 Mar. 1849.
[87] F.O. *China Corres.*, vol. 161, Martin memo. of 5 Jan. 1849 in Bd. Trade to For. Off., 10 Jan. 1849.

character '.[88]   Martin also wrote to the Foreign Secretary.
He argued that much might be gained while little could
be lost by the course he proposed, and urged the importance
of forestalling foreign rivals, especially the Americans, and
of strengthening Britain's position in the East against what
seemed an inevitable attack.[89]   Since no reply was forthcoming in the next few weeks, he wrote again on 16 March.
He pointed out that in getting the Board of Trade to take
the initiative in the matter, he had been following the advice
given him by Palmerston in 1847, and was now anxious
for a definite decision on his plans.[90]   The reply he received
a few days later was disappointing.   The Foreign Office
clerks had done some research into Japan's natural resources[91] and the results had suggested that trade with Japan
would not be as valuable as Martin thought.   On 20 March
the permanent undersecretary wrote to him to say that
Palmerston believed the proposal to be one ' of much importance and requiring very mature consideration ', but was
not immediately willing to recommend that action be taken
on it.[92]

Faced with this refusal, Martin decided that political
pressure might succeed where private argument had failed.
He had already arranged to visit the chief cities of northern
England to interest manufacturers in his plans, and now
determined,[93] with Board of Trade consent, to continue with
this tour.   He did more than make enquiries of the manufacturers, however.   From the beginning of April, a steady
flow of memorials from the commercial organisations of the
north began to reach the Foreign Office and Board of Trade,
marking the stages of Martin's itinerary.   All of them
recommended that 'a tentative commercial mission' be sent

[88] F.O. *China Corres.*, vol. 161, Bd. Trade to For. Off., 10 Jan. 1849;
also Labouchere to Eddisbury, 5 Jan. 1849.

[89] F.O. *China Corres.*, vol. 161, Martin to Palmerston, 3 and 7 Feb. 1849;
Bd. Trade to For. Off., 7 Feb. 1849.

[90] F.O. *China Corres.*, vol. 161, Martin to Palmerston, 16 Mar. 1849.

[91] F.O. *China Corres.*, vol. 161, For. Off. memo. on Japan trade, 17 Jan.
1849 (based on the accounts of Kaempfer, Siebold and Thunberg)

[92] F.O. *China Corres.*, vol. 161, For. Off. to Martin, 20 Mar. 1849.

[93] F.O. *China Corres.*, vol. 161, Martin to Palmerston, 22 Mar. 1849.

to Japan, Korea, Cochin China and Siam ; most recapitulated Martin's previous arguments, often word for word ; some mentioned Martin by name and one, that from the Manchester Commercial Association, dispensed with detail and argument on the grounds that Martin had already expounded them to Lord Palmerston.[94]   There can be no doubt, in fact, whence came the inspiration for this sudden expression of mercantile opinion. Probably for that reason, Palmerston refused to be impressed by it. To all the petitioners he sent the same discouraging reply, that ' the matters to which your memorial relates are of much importance and requiring very mature consideration, and that Her Majesty's Government have not yet seen their way sufficiently clear to have been able to come to any decision on the subject '. In fact, nothing was to be done. Martin had achieved no more by an indirect than by a direct approach. Nor was any further attempt made to urge the scheme's adoption, and it is a measure of how artificial was the interest Martin aroused that none of the chambers of commerce or other organisations involved chose to press the matter at the time or, as far as can be discovered, ever raised the subject again.

Despite the memorials of 1849, British merchants were not interested in Japan. Most of them were convinced that in China there lay a vast unexplored source of trade and riches from which they were barred only by political difficulties, by the policy of an obstructionist Chinese government. Hence they felt justified in calling on the British government to support them, even to the point of war, in their efforts to secure access to that fabulous—and largely

---

[94] The petitions to the Foreign Office were :—
F.O. *China Corres.*, vol. 161, Merchants and Manufacturers of Halifax of 12 Apr. 1849 (reply, 17 Apr.) ; Merchants of Huddersfield, undated (reply, 18 Apr.) ; Manchester Chamber of Commerce of 27 Apr. (reply, 30 Apr.) ; Manchester Commercial Association of 28 Apr. (reply, 4 May) :
Vol. 162, Sheffield Company of Cutlers of 5 May (reply, 11 May) ; Borough of Bradford of 21 May (reply, 23 May) ; Merchants of Birmingham, undated (reply, 11 June).
Those from Halifax, Huddersfield, Manchester Chamber of Commerce, Sheffield and Birmingham were also sent to the Board of Trade (see Bd. Trade, *Minutes*, vol. 58, minutes of 14 and 30 Apr., 15 May, 16 June 1849).

mythical—market. Until 1858, at least, the Foreign Office also believed in the potentialities of the China trade. Neither merchants nor statesmen had the same ideas about Japan. Though ardently propagated by a few individuals, the " myth " of the Japan trade had not caught the imagination of the merchants generally, whether because they were preoccupied with China or because such evidence as was available did not support extravagant hopes. The Foreign Office was equally indifferent. Bettelheim and Martin, for all their efforts, had failed to persuade Palmerston to take action, and that in a matter which one might have expected to arouse his interest. It is true that the Foreign Office had recognised, and continued to recognise, that the opening of Japan was desirable in principle, but it is also true that it had relatively full information on Japan's resources and past trade, nearly all of it unfavourable to commercial prospects. Although it is not a point on which direct evidence is available, this seems to provide the most logical explanation of the government's inaction.

So far the initiative for action had rested with the Superintendent of Trade. Davis had proposed the plans in 1845 and Davis had postponed their execution in the following year. When his successor proved reluctant to revive them, the Foreign Office made no attempt to force action upon him, despite the efforts of Bettelheim and Martin to arouse its interest. Indeed, by 1852 the project seemed to be not so much postponed as abandoned. When Lord Malmesbury succeeded Granville and the Foreign Office prepared a list of matters pending in the department for the new Minister, reference was made to the negotiations which were to be opened with Siam, but not to those with Japan.[95] Clearly, some new stimulus would be needed to revive them.

---

[95] *Granville Papers*, vol. 20, State of Business, Foreign Office, 25 Feb. 1852. The same is true of a similar statement, also in this volume, drawn up when Palmerston handed over to Granville in December 1851.

CHAPTER IV

THE PERRY EXPEDITION : 1852–1854

THE year 1852 saw the appearance of a new factor that was to have considerable influence on official British policy towards Japan. This had so far, as we have seen, been based on the assumption that the anticipated difficulty and expense of coercing Japan into treaty relations more than outweighed the advantages to be gained, an attitude in marked contrast to that revealed in China. Such was not the attitude of the Americans, however. Since their expansion into the northwest territories of the American continent, Japan had become for them an intermediate point on the route to China, and penetration of its markets would not —as it would for Britain—involve movement beyond an existing trading area that was already sufficiently remote. Moreover, in their need for coaling stations and ports of refuge on the long Pacific crossing, they had an immediate and practical reason for taking the initiative in opening Japan. The fact that they did so was viewed with complacency by the British government. British action, it believed, had already eased American difficulties in China. It would in some sense redress the balance, therefore, if American initiative in Japan broke down the policy of seclusion and thereby made it easier for Britain to establish trade relations. Such a result seemed both probable and desirable.

By the beginning of 1852 it was becoming generally known that the United States planned to send an expedition to secure a treaty with Japan. Speculation about the mission's nature and exact objects was soon widespread. The *China Mail* of Hongkong, which despite its feud with Montgomery Martin had long favoured the dispatch of a

British mission to Japan, was among the first to report the American plan. In October 1851 it printed an article from the New York *Journal of Commerce* announcing (somewhat prematurely) that Commodore Aulick had already sailed to make the attempt.[1] Thereafter, until news of Perry's success in 1854, it carried frequent (and often contradictory) reports culled from the European, Indian and American press. The chief topic of discussion was whether Perry would have authority to use force, whether he would find it necessary to do so, and above all, whether he would be justified in using it. Most of the Indian papers quoted by the *China Mail* thought—perhaps hoped—that he would not rely only on persuasion to gain his ends. This was an attitude to which the *China Mail* itself objected most strongly.[2] It could see no *casus belli* in the exaggerated stories about the treatment of shipwrecked sailors, nor any justice in using Japanese castaways for such selfish political ends, thereby subjecting them to considerable personal danger on their return to Japan.[3] Admittedly it was difficult, if not impossible, to see how success could be achieved without the use of force. Nevertheless, it said, no nation had the right to force trade on another, and ' the vindication of such proceedings . . . ought to rest on better grounds than any of the excuses and political sophisms hitherto put forward '.[4]

In Britain, *Bentley's Miscellany* held views similar to those of the *China Mail,* and expressed them in an article which also criticised British policy in India and China.[5] Other magazine articles, on the other hand, agreed that the United States had a right to interfere, though they did not openly advocate the use of force.[6] *The Times* occasionally printed American newspaper reports asserting Perry's intention of resorting to cannon if no other argument prevailed, while its American correspondent, apparently on the grounds that

[1] *China Mail,* 23 Oct. 1851.
[2] e.g. *China Mail,* 13 May and 17 June 1852.
[3] *China Mail,* 18 Nov. 1852. It had been suggested that Perry might make the return of Japanese castaways the excuse for his visit.
[4] *China Mail,* 17 June 1852.
[5] *Bentley's Miscellany,* XXXI (1852), pp. 545-52.
[6] e.g. *Lawson's Merchants' Magazine,* I, 1 (May 1852).

the Anglo-Saxons were a master-race and had a duty to bring ' besotted Oriental nations . . . into the ranks of civilization ', went so far as to predict that the United States would ' shortly enact the same gunpowder drama England played in '42 with China, and . . . do it with less moderation '.[7] This was not an avowed editorial policy, however. It was left to the *Edinburgh Review* to defend such views, albeit more soberly expressed. In October 1852 it outlined recent Western contacts with Japan and recommended the Japanese to grant Perry's requests, since they could not hope to resist his modern armaments. It continued : ' The compulsory seclusion of the Japanese is a wrong not only to themselves, but to the civilised world . . . The Japanese undoubtedly have an exclusive right to the possession of their territory ; but they must not abuse that right to the extent of debarring all other nations from a participation in its riches and virtues. The only secure title to property, whether it be a hovel or an empire, is, that the exclusive possession of one is for the benefit of all '.[8] One wonders whether the *Review* would have been equally willing to apply such a principle to British domestic politics.

It is clear that the Perry expedition aroused a good deal of public interest in Britain and her overseas possessions. The frequency of articles in *The Times* is an approximate guide, if not to public opinion, at least to what the editors thought was interesting to their readers. In 1846 and 1847, when Martin was first urging his plans in England, there were altogether three references to Japan in that paper. In the next four years there were none at all. In 1852 the number rose to eleven. This is not an impressive total, it is true, if one were to compare it, for example, with the number of references to China, but it is nevertheless a sign of wider interest, especially when taken in conjunction with the fairly frequent magazine articles written about the American mission. On the other hand, we must be careful not to assume that this interest was necessarily an influence

---

[7] London *Times*, 8 Apr. 1852. See also issues of 19 and 20 Apr. 1852, 18 May 1854.

[8] *Edinburgh Review*, XCVI, 196 (Oct. 1852), p. 383.

on British policy. Only the *China Mail* thought fit to urge the British government to follow the American example. There was no concerted campaign to that end, and the widely differing views expressed in other articles sharply reduced the effect of the whole. Indeed, in formulating its policy towards the expedition the Foreign Office was subject to no significant outside pressure.

We have already seen that Commodore Biddle's attempt to establish contact with Japan in 1846[9] had not served to prompt Britain into emulation. On the contrary, it contributed to the abandonment of existing plans by adding one more reason for making the British mission an imposing one, requiring a force for which the necessary warships were not available. Biddle's failure, again, tended to confirm the Superintendent and the Foreign Office in their belief that nothing could be done in Japan without adequate naval support. Their reaction to other American and Russian attempts prior to the Perry expedition was equally cautious.

Early in 1849 Commander Glynn of U.S.S. *Preble* left Hongkong for Japan. His ostensible purpose was to secure the release of fifteen seamen from the American whaler *Lagoda* who were known to be prisoners of the Japanese, but Bonham knew that more was intended. Gutzlaff had agreed to translate the letters carried by the commander, and these showed that in addition to the release of the seamen Glynn planned to seek permission to establish an American consular agent in Japan, and obtain from the Japanese the promise of some place or island near Edo for use as a coaling station on the proposed new steamship route between San Francisco and Shanghai. Reporting this to Palmerston, Bonham said he expected Glynn to take 'strenuous steps' to attain his ends, but made no suggestion that he might follow the American's example. Like Gutzlaff, he apparently believed that Britain would share in any privileges Glynn obtained.[10]

Palmerston made no comment on this report, though he

[9] See chapter III, pp. 66-9.
[10] F.O. *China Corres.*, vol. 153, Bonham to For. Off., No. 20, 14 Feb. 1849, encl. copies of Glynn's letters, and enclosure Gutzlaff to Bonham, 11 Feb. 1852.

forwarded it to the Board of Trade, nor on Bonham's later dispatch which outlined the results of the visit. Glynn obtained the release of the American seamen but failed in his other objects, and his anger at the treatment he received at Nagasaki led Bonham to expect that the United States would send a more powerful expedition to Japan to demand explanations and satisfaction. Still, the mission had produced some interesting information. H. N. Lay, son of a British consul in China, had gone on the voyage as interpreter and reported to Bonham on his return that the Japanese 'started back with terror' at every mention of Britain. The released prisoners, according to Gutzlaff who interrogated them, said that Japan anticipated attack by Britain, and despite a hesitant faith that they would be protected by the winds on 'praying to the idols', feared a fate like that even then being suffered by China.[11] Judging by their failure to comment on this, Bonham and Palmerston had no immediate intention of giving substance to these fears.

Since these reports of the *Preble* visit, arriving in London immediately after Martin's attempt to organise 'a tentative commercial mission', failed to move the Foreign Office to action, it was not likely that Russian plans would do so. In the autumn of 1852 the Russian minister in London informed Malmesbury that his government hoped to enter into commercial relations with Japan. It therefore intended to send Admiral Poutiatine to the Pacific to secure a treaty and at the same time keep an eye on Perry's movements, and was informing the British government of the plan in the belief that it held similar views on American activities in that area. Malmesbury's only reaction was to instruct Bowring to give Poutiatine every assistance.[12] This was consistent with the Foreign Office attitude to the Biddle and Glynn attempts. It was equally consistent with the

[11] F.O. *China Corres.*, vol. 155, Bonham to For. Off., No. 74, 23 May 1849, encl. reports from Lay and Gutzlaff, both dated 22 May 1849.
[12] F.O. *China Emb. Arch.*, vol. 139, For. Off. to Bowring, No. 56, 5 Oct. 1852, encl. copy of de Seniavine to Brunnow, 29 Aug./10 Sept. 1852. Poutiatine was no more successful than Biddle and Glynn: see Eckel, 'A Russian Expedition to Japan in 1852', *Pac NW Quarterly*, XXXIV, 2 (Apr. 1943), pp. 159-67.

policy which Malmesbury had by this time formulated towards the Perry expedition.

The subject of this new expedition was first raised officially by Dr. John Bowring, British consul at Canton, who was acting as Superintendent of Trade in 1852 during Bonham's absence in London on sick leave. Bowring had been appointed to Canton in 1847 by Lord Palmerston, and was unlike Bonham in many ways. Where Bonham was cautious, Bowring was adventurous, even rash. His background lay in trade (in the West Country woollen industry) and politics. He was a friend of Cobden and Jeremy Bentham and had been Member of Parliament for Bolton for several years, in addition to performing a number of commercial missions for the Board of Trade in Europe and the Middle East. He was, in fact, in every way more likely than Bonham to press for a British mission to Japan.

As Bowring's promotion was only temporary, he was not given quite the same authority as Bonham. It was necessary for him to have powers to negotiate with China, for they might be needed at any time, but the instructions and full powers for Japan were not transferred to him.[13] Consequently he was unable to take any immediate action when he learnt that Perry was gathering a large squadron in readiness to go to that country. In May 1852 he reported to the Foreign Office such facts as he had been able to obtain and urged that the possibility of opening commercial relations with Japan must be ' a matter of much interest to Great Britain '. In the circumstances, he suggested, it would be as well that he be provided with the necessary authority and instructions to negotiate with Japan and authorised ' under certain contingencies ' to use them.[14]

Lord Malmesbury, who had been Foreign Secretary since the end of February, had already been urged by a private correspondent to follow or forestall the Americans in Japan for fear that Britain should lose her markets in the East to American competitors. He had returned only a formal

---

[13] F.O. *China Corres.*, vol. 186, For. Off. to Bowring, No. 1, 19 Jan. 1852.
[14] F.O. *China Corres.*, vol. 189, Bowring to For. Off., No. 26, 18 May 1852.

acknowledgement to the letter, adding non-committally that that the government was ' much occupied with the question of the advancement of British commercial interests in Siam and the neighbouring countries '.[15]   Bowring's dispatch, which arrived in July 1852, required a more specific answer. It was not, however, the one Bowring hoped to receive. He was ordered to report on the progress and results of the American expedition, but was given no power to negotiate because Bonham already had it and would probably return to duty before any action was needed.   Malmesbury cer- tainly had no intention of competing with Perry.   ' Her Majesty's Government ', he wrote, ' would be glad to see the trade with Japan open ; but they think it better to leave it to the Government of the United States to make the experiment ; and if that experiment is successful, Her Majesty's Government can take advantage of its success '.[16]

What was implied in this dispatch was more openly stated by Malmesbury in his instructions to Bonham in December 1852, when the latter was about to return to China.   The government had still not decided what to do about Japan. Bonham was told that he must continue to collect inform- ation and report to the Foreign Office anything that would help it to determine the course to be pursued by Britain in the event either of Perry's success or of his failure.   More- over, though he had been given full authority to negotiate with Japan, there seemed no reason to anticipate such urgency as would prevent him first referring home for further instructions.   Meanwhile he should make his actions conform to the view that ' as the Government of the United States, though nearly as much interested as this Country in the opening of the Trade with China, kept aloof while the British operations which resulted in that arrangement were in progress, so Her Majesty's Government should equally maintain an expectant position in regard to the proposed operations of the United States against Japan '.[17]   The Foreign Office, far from regarding American action as

[15] F.O. *China Corres.*, vol. 196, R. Sprye to Malmesbury, 6 Apr. 1852 ; For. Off. to Sprye, 15 Apr. 1852.
[16] F.O. *China Corres.*, vol. 186, For. Off. to Bowring, No. 30, 21 July 1852.
[17] F.O. *China Corres.*, vol. 186, For. Off. to Bonham, No. 29, 16 Dec. 1852.

cause for disquiet, expected to profit by it. Japan was clearly not important enough to justify international competition. Indeed, the wording of the dispatch in general showed that to Malmesbury the opening of Japan was at least as important for its possible effect on the policy of the Chinese government as for the immediate commercial advantages it might bring in Japan itself.

Bowring and Bonham continued to report on the progress of the American expedition throughout 1852, 1853 and the early part of 1854. Bowring had begun with a fairly accurate account of Perry's objects before receiving Malmesbury's instructions. He gave it as a prevalent opinion that the Japanese, relying on the rivalries of the Powers, would resist by force of arms if faced by only a single aggressor, but would open their ports peacefully, albeit reluctantly, in face of joint action.[18] His report on Japan's trade[19] contained little that was new and nothing to suggest that its value existed in fact rather than in prospect. Bonham's reports, as one would expect, were largely factual. However, on Perry's return from his first visit to Japan in 1853, Bonham interpreted the six months' grace given to the Japanese as a sign that the Commodore, having no authority to use force and realising that without it he could accomplish nothing, had 'prudently left the matter in abeyance' until he could obtain fresh instructions.[20] Reports such as this were not likely to change British policy.

From December 1852 these reports were being received by a new government. Aberdeen was Prime Minister, Palmerston Home Secretary and Russell Foreign Secretary, though the latter was succeeded at the Foreign Office by Clarendon in February 1853. Clarendon had a difficult task. Aberdeen, Russell and Palmerston all continued to take an interest in foreign affairs, but did not always agree either among themselves or with Clarendon. In Europe, disputes with Russia over Turkey engaged more and more of his attention, while he was hoping that in China the

---

[18] F.O. *China Corres.*, vol. 192, Bowring to For. Off., No. 99, 18 Aug. 1852.
[19] F.O. *China Corres.*, vol. 194, Bowring to For. Off., No. 176, 24 Dec. 1852.
[20] F.O. *China Corres.*, vol. 204, Bonham to For. Off., No. 85, 9 Aug. 1853.

T'aip'ing Rebellion might 'be turned to the best account' for increasing British privileges.[21]   In fact, so great was the 'scramble and pressure' at the office, he told Russell, that it sometimes prevented things being done 'with the reflexion they require '.[22]

Clarendon, with so much to engage his attention, made no attempt to revise Malmesbury's instructions about the Japan expedition.   The only new question he raised in 1853 was that of Perry's move to establish a coaling station in the Bonin Islands, a point not covered in the instructions issued by Malmesbury but approached very much in the spirit of Malmesbury's policy.   As early as April 1853 the Admiralty had informed the Foreign Office that the Americans were planning to acquire an island base in Chinese or Japanese waters.[23]   Nothing more happened about this until October, when Alexander Simpson, formerly a British consul in the Pacific, wrote to Clarendon to call attention to a press report that Perry had purchased a site for a coaling station in the Bonins and point out that these islands were properly British territory.[24]   Two weeks later a dispatch confirming the news was received from Bonham.   He, too, believed the islands to be British, and had so informed Perry.   However, as Perry himself said, the fact would not invalidate the purchase of land there, and Bonham suggested that the British government had best make a formal occupation of the group if it wished to retain its rights.   His own opinion was that they were too barren to support a large population and possession of them would not be any great advantage.[25]

The Admiralty confirmed that Beechey had claimed the Bonins for Britain in 1827 and the Colonial Office produced a collection of papers relating to the discussions of 1834, but neither expressed any opinion about future policy.   The

[21] F.O. *Miscellanea, Ser. II*, vol. 23, Clarendon to Addington, private, 8 May 1853.   Malmesbury had expressed a similar hope in F.O. *China Corres.*, vol. 186, For. Off. to Bonham, No. 29, 16 Dec. 1852.

[22] *Russell Papers*, vol. 11, Clarendon to Russell, 24 Sept. 1853.

[23] F.O. *China Corres.*, vol. 207, Adty. to For. Off., 15 Apr. 1853.

[24] F.O. *China Corres.*, vol. 209, Simpson to Clarendon, 1 Oct. 1853.

[25] F.O. *China Corres.*, vol. 204, Bonham to For. Off., Separate, 17 Aug. 1853.

Foreign Office sent the papers to Bonham in case they should be of value in any negotiations he might undertake with Japan, and told him that Britain was not at that time prepared to enforce her rights in the islands, though she might wish to do so should any other country try to develop a permanent settlement there.[26] Bonham showed Simpson's letter to Perry. The commodore doubted the validity of the British claim, but said that it mattered little who had sovreignty over the islands so long as they remained open to all as a harbour of refuge for shipping. In this view both the Foreign Office and Colonial Office concurred,[27] having no wish to create new difficulties in Pacific waters.

It was January 1854 before Clarendon, at the instigation of Bowring,[28] gave serious thought to the question of Japan. Bonham had decided to retire and Bowring, then on leave in England, was to be appointed to succeed him. Addington, permanent under-secretary at the Foreign Office since 1842, drew up at Clarendon's request a memorandum outlining the instructions it would be necessary to give the new Superintendent. Despite his earlier misgivings about Bowring's suitability for the post,[29] Addington thought that now the die was cast, Bowring must be given the full confidence of the government and commissioned to go to Siam and Japan as well as to Peking. There was scope for his energy in those places even though it would be necessary to restrain ' his excess of vitality and zeal '. In China, the under-secretary believed, joint action with France and the United States would be the best course, but in Japan British policy should wait on the result of Perry's visit. If he succeeded, then Bowring should be sent ' properly accompanied by Ships of War ' to obtain privileges similar to

[26] F.O. *China Corres.*, vol. 198, For. Off. to Bonham, No. 97, 24 Nov. 1853.
[27] F.O. *China Corres.*, vol. 212, Bonham to For. Off., No. 4, 4 Jan. 1854, encl. correspondence with Perry ; vol. 220, For. Off. to Col. Off., 7 Mar. 1854 ; vol. 221, Col. Off. to For. Off., 11 Apr. 1854. See also F.O. *United States Corres. Ser. II* (F.O. 5), vol 590, For. Off. to Crampton (Washington), 17 Apr. 1854.
[28] *Clarendon Papers* (Bodleian Library), C vol. 8, ff. 416-7, Bowring to Clarendon, Batavia, 26 Mar. 1853 ; ff. 425-6, same to same, London, 24 Aug. 1853.
[29] *Clarendon Papers*, C vol. 8, ff. 428-9, Addington memo. of 26 Aug. 1853, remarking that if Bowring were appointed he would ' probably be over the Great Wall before we had time to look around us '.

those granted America. If he failed, 'it might be better to wait awhile '. With these sentiments Clarendon agreed.[30]

The instructions to Bowring, as finally approved in February 1854, emphasised that trade with China was the object to which the Superintendent's attention 'must be most particularly directed' and that Bowring must not on any account leave China to carry on negotiations elsewhere unless he felt sure that British interests would not suffer by his absence—an order which from the beginning weighted the scales against a visit to Japan. Subject to that proviso, he was authorised to take any suitable opportunity of opening commercial relations with Siam, Cochin China and Japan. Of these, he was told, Japan offered unquestionably the most important opening for trade. He was to be guided by the results of the American expedition and to open negotiations if he saw 'a reasonable probability' of success, but the exact terms he should try to obtain were left to his own judgment and local knowledge. There, were, however, a few points on which the Foreign Office would insist :—

> ' But in any Treaty you may conclude wou will be careful to provide for British Jurisdiction over British Subjects —for the interpretation of the terms of the Treaty by the British version—for the power of revision at the expiration of a stated time—and for participation in all the benefits which now or hereafter may be conceded by the Japanese Government to Foreign Nations. It will be necessary also, as far as possible, to stipulate for religious privileges.'[31]

The China " treaty-pattern " is here very apparent. The Foreign Office was still thinking of Japan in terms of British relations with China. In 1845 Aberdeen had instructed Davis to concentrate in Japan on those matters—opium smuggling, national equality and diplomatic representation at the capital—which were then, or just had been, engaging his attention in China. Similarly in 1854, when he was about to open negotiations for treaty revision in China and

[30] F.O. *Miscellanea, Ser. II*, vol. 24, Addington minute of 12 Jan. 1854 ; Clarendon minute of same aate.

[31] F.O. *China Corres.*, vol. 210, For. Off. to Bowring, No. 3, 13 Feb. 1854.

after considerable difficulties about the interpretation of existing treaties with that country, Lord Clarendon too seemed automatically to assume that the same kind of problem would arise in Japan.

These instructions did not represent any important change in the policy laid down by Malmesbury in the previous two years. British interest did not stem from an attempt to emulate or forestall the Americans. Clarendon was most anxious to co-operate with the United States in the task of treaty revision in China,[32] and from the fact that he communicated a copy of Bowring's new instructions to the American government,[33] one can assume that he would have welcomed United States co-operation in Japan as well. At the least he wished to avoid Anglo-American rivalry there. Addington's memorandum, we have seen, urged that British action be conditional on American success, and in its final form this idea was implicit in the dispatch to Bowring.

Bowring himself was at first perfectly willing to see ' a reasonable probability ' of success in Japan. But he soon found difficulties of his own. In April 1854 he heard that Perry had succeeded in getting Japanese agreement to terms based on China's treaties with the West, and although the American convention had still to be signed he began to make plans to leave Hongkong. He would have gone at once to Japan, he said, had there been ships available to escort him. For the moment, there were not, however, and he felt it unwise to go without ' a respectable armament ', a force such as that to which Perry attributed his own success. Moreover, on so important an occasion Great Britain must not be shabbily represented '.[34] A month later these difficulties had been overcome and he was almost ready to

[32] F.O. *United States Corres.*, vol. 561, For. Off. to Crampton, No. 28, 20 May 1853; same to same, No. 49, 30 June 1853 : vol. 565, Crampton to For. Off., No. 122, 13 June 1853.

[33] F.O. *United States Corres.*, vol. 590, For. Off. to Crampton, No. 38, 24 Feb. 1854, enclosing also copies of Foreign Office correspondence with France on the subject of co-operation in China.

[34] F.O. *China Corres.*, vol. 213, Bowring to For. Off., No. 3, 18 Apr. 1854. See also *Clarendon Papers*, C vol. 19, ff. 402-5, Bowring to Clarendon, 27 Apr. 1854.

sail. Sir James Stirling, Commander-in-Chief on the China station, had agreed to provide the ships and offer passages to representatives of the three principal British commercial firms in China. Of these, Mr. Beale of Dent and Company at Shanghai had already accepted.[35] There was nothing urgent to keep Bowring in China, since negotiations with the Chinese had broken down, so he decided to transfer the Superintendency to Shanghai after the arrival of the mail and proceed thence to Japan.[36]

While Bowring was waiting for the mail at Hongkong, the first news of Perry's success reached London.[37] Edmund Hammond, Addington's successor as permanent under-secretary, at once drafted a letter to the Admiralty to inform them that Bowring had already received instructions to go to Japan when opportunity offered ; that Perry's success afforded that opportunity ; and that Stirling, if he had not already done so, should be ordered to provide as large a force as he could spare, since the size of the American and Russian squadrons in Japanese waters made desirable ' a certain degree of pomp '. This did not mean that the government wished to use force. On the contrary, said Hammond, ' the Admiral will . . . abstain from any act of hostility against Japan unless forced to have recourse to it, for self-defence ; he will not blockade, or intercept the communications of the Japanese ; but he will make it clearly understood that any forebearance which he may show in resenting injury will be only temporary and until he can report to and receive orders from his Government '.[38] Clarendon agreed in general with this draft but apparently did not approve of the use of threats made ineffective by the necessity of referring to London. He struck out most of the last paragraph, amending it to read ' unless forced to have recourse to it for self-defence or for the punishment

[35] The others invited were Jardine Matheson and Co., Lindsey and Co.

[36] F.O. *China Corres.*, vol. 213, Bowring to For. Off., No. 46, 24 May 1854.

[37] F.O. *China Corres.*, vol. 212, Bonham to For. Off., No. 54, 5 Apr. 1854, reporting that Perry had succeeded but giving no details of his treaty except that it was probably modelled on the British treaty with China, reached the Foreign Office on 30 May 1854. Bowring's dispatches arrived some weeks later.

[38] F.O. *Miscellanea, Ser. II*, vol. 24, Hammond minute of 4 June 1854.

of insult ', thereby giving the admiral greater freedom of action, since he presumably had the power to determine what constituted self-defence or insult. There was also a point which Hammond had neglected. The French wished to join Britain in negotiations with Japan and Clarendon thought it ' on every account desirable to comply with their wish '.[39] The amended draft was accordingly held up for a few days until the necessary arrangements had been made with Paris, but on 8 June it was sent to the Admiralty and a copy forwarded to Bowring with instructions to co-operate with the French plenipotentiary on the visit to Japan.[40]

The Admiralty made difficulties, however. War had broken out with Russia earlier in the year, and although the conflict was likely to be largely European, the Foreign Office and Board of Trade had asked that Stirling be ordered to protect British shipping from the Russian Pacific squadron based on Siberia and Kamchatka. The Admiralty now asked whether the fresh orders about Japan were to supersede those already given Stirling in accordance with this previous request.[41] Clarendon wasted no time in revising his instructions. He had never considered the conclusion of a commercial treaty with Japan to be sufficiently important to justify the slightest risk to the British position in China, and had certainly never intended that it be attempted at the expense of the protection of British shipping in time of war. To the Admiralty he confirmed that the capture of the Russian squadron was the first and most important task. To Bowring and the French government he wrote that he saw no immediate prospect of Stirling being able to go to Japan.[42] As a result of this decision, the Admiralty sent to Stirling a copy of the Foreign Office letter of 8 June, but warned him at the same time that his first duty was to

[39] *ibid*, Clarendon minute of same date.

[40] F.O. *China Corres.*, vol. 221, For. Off. to Adty., 8 June 1854. F.O. *China Emb. Arch.*, vol. 169, For. Off. to Bowring, No. 69, 8 June 1854, enclosing correspondence with Paris.

[41] F.O. *China Corres.*, vol. 221, Adty. to For. Off., 9 June 1854.

[42] F.O. *Miscellanea, Ser. II*, vol. 24, Clarendon minute of 10 June 1854. F.O. *China Corres.*, vol. 220, For. Off. to Bowring, No. 83, 20 June 1854; vol. 221, For. Off. to Adty., 24 June 1854.

watch and if possible attack the Russian squadron. All other objects must be considered as subsidiary to this, and the Japan mission must only be undertaken 'when there shall no longer be any danger . . . to Her Majesty's possessions or to British Trade '.[43]

Bowring and Stirling had meanwhile come to much the same conclusion. Standing instructions for the East Indies station emphasised that the China coast was to be considered the most important part of that station and that 'the first and paramount duty ' of the squadron was the protection of British lives and property there.[44] In the spring of 1854 there appeared to be a number of potential threats to those lives and property. One arose from the T'aip'ing Rebellion which had broken out in south China in 1850, for by the end of 1853 the rebel forces had advanced down the Yangtse to the neighbourhood of Shanghai, and fighting had taken place in and near that city. Since the British settlement was threatened, the China squadron had to be prepared to protect it. To this was added the danger of hostilities with Russia, and in the early months of 1854 both Stirling and Bowring kept anxious watch on the movements of Poutiatine's ships.[45]

News of the outbreak of war reached China at the beginning of June, by the very mail for which Bowring was waiting before leaving for Shanghai and Japan. It had a decisive effect on his immediate plans. He still had to go to Shanghai, for the T'aip'ing crisis demanded his presence there, but Stirling no longer felt able to provide ships for the Japan mission and it had to be abandoned. It was a decision which both regretted the less since they had by then received fuller information about the Perry treaty. Far from being the equivalent of the British treaties with China,

[43] F.O. *China Corres.*, vol. 222, Adty. to Stirling, No. 103, 28 June 1854 in Adty. to For. Off., 3 July 1854.

[44] Admiralty, *Supplementary* (Adm. 13), vol. 4, Standing Instructions, E. Indies Station, 17 Jan. 1853, transferred to Stirling when he assumed command in 1854 (see Adty. to Stirling, 16 Feb. 1854, also in this volume).

[45] Admiralty, *In-Letters*, vol. 5629, Stirling to Adty., 15 and 29 Apr. 1854. F.O. *China Corres.*, vol. 213, Bowring to For. Off., No. 13, 20 Apr. and No. 23, 3 May 1854. *Clarendon Papers*, C vol. 19, f. 442, Bowring to Clarendon, *Winchester* at sea, 27 May 1854.

they thought, it was of little commercial value and had been granted with the utmost reluctance by the Japanese. The latter claimed to have no goods to exchange, a statement many of the American officers felt to be substantially correct. The outlook was not encouraging and the necessity of postponing the mission, Bowring said, would at least give the Foreign Office time to consider the provisions of the Perry treaty and issue any fresh instructions that might be necessary.[46]

Bowring informed the French minister, de Bourboulon, that he had abandoned the plan to go to Japan. In September he decided to attempt the apparently easier task of negotiating with Siam, taking with him the presents which had originally been intended for that country, but which he had more recently proposed to use in Japan.[47] Clarendon's approval of his decision to postpone the Japan expedition arrived a few weeks later.[48]

Once again British policy towards Japan had been subordinated to other and more pressing interests. The plans of 1854 did not differ in any important respect from those made in 1845. They were not the result of any strong conviction—trade with Japan was still not thought to warrant any great risk or expense. Nor were they the result of any desire to compete with the Americans. The new British plans were made not when Perry's expedition was announced but at the time of Bowring's appointment, and took effect only on news of Perry's success. The fact is significant. The Foreign Office saw American action in Japan not as a model of what should be done but as a guide to how easily results might be achieved. Thus Biddle's failure contributed to the postponement of Davis's plans ; Perry's success to the adoption of Bowring's.

In 1854, however, British policy was still ham-strung by the theory of " gunboat diplomacy ". The plans of 1845

[46] F.O. *China Corres.*, vol. 214, Bowring to For. Off., No. 59, Shanghai, 15 June 1854. For Stirling's views see F.O. *China Corres.*, vol. 222, Adty. to For. Off., 7 Sept. 1854 : Admiralty, *In-Letters*, vol. 5629, Stirling to Adty., No. 44, 30 June 1854.
[47] F.O. *China Corres.*, vol. 215, Bowring to For. Off., No. 113, 22 Aug. 1854 ; vol. 216, Bowring to For. Off., No. 137, 8 Sept. 1854.
[48] F.O. *China Corres.*, vol. 211, For. Off. to Bowring, No. 124, 20 Sept. 1854.

had been abandoned because it proved impossible, in view of the China squadron's other commitments, to raise the imposing naval force which Davis thought indispensable. The Foreign Office under Clarendon was equally convinced that nothing less than an honour guard of warships would enable a British diplomat to succeed in negotiations with Japan. The T'aip'ing Rebellion and the Crimean War, both bringing new threats to British lives and shipping in China, made it first difficult and then impossible to detach a squadron for the purpose. The mission was again postponed. In theory this postponement was until the spring of 1855. In practice, less than three months after the decision had been made, Sir James Stirling, Commander-in-Chief of the East Indies station, took matters into his own hands.

If Perry's treaty had made the Japan project seem feasible to the British government, his appearance at Uraga precipitated a crisis in Japan. Discussions of foreign policy were shifted thereby from the merely theoretical to the urgent and practical. The issue was no longer what to do about the potential threat from Britain, if and when it should materialise, but what answer to give to an American demand for treaty relations which had already materialised, and which had been made, moreover, by a plenipotentiary backed by a powerful squadron. The decisions taken on this subject in Japan during the winter of 1853-4 belong properly to the story of Japanese-American relations. None the less, they are also of importance to us here in that they conditioned later Japanese policy towards Great Britain. It it necessary, therefore, before considering the origin and course of Stirling's negotiations, to devote some space to a discussion of those decisions and of the political background in Japan.

The chief responsibility for the formulation of Bakufu policy rested with the Rōjū, a group of five or six experienced administrators appointed from among the ranks of the *fudai daimyō* and together constituting the Tokugawa Council of State. By 1852, when the Japanese first learned from Deshima of the projected American expedition, Abe

Masahiro had become acknowledged head of that body. Almost equally influential, however, was Tokugawa Nariaki of Mito, former head of one of the three senior Tokugawa branch families and an unyielding opponent of any attempt to relax the seclusion laws. Nariaki had quarrelled with Mizuno Tadakuni over the edict of 1842, which modified the treatment to be accorded foreign ships visiting the Japanese coast, and had subsequently been forced to resign headship of his fief to his son. But his influence with the feudal lords remained strong. Abe realised this, and recognised that a permanent breach with the Mito house would seriously weaken the political position of the Bakufu. He was, therefore, anxious to reach an understanding with Nariaki on all major issues.

Perry's arrival in 1853 made foreign policy the most urgent issue of them all. It was, moreover, the one on which Abe and Nariaki were least likely to agree. Abe knew—and explained to Nariaki—that the Bakufu was too weak, militarily and economically, to adopt any policy that might lead to war. War could end only in crushing defeat for Japan. Nariaki, on the other hand, had long held that, however weak Japan might be, the opening of the ports and the beginning of foreign trade would serve only to weaken her still more, to make it ever easier for the foreign barbarian to acquire and consolidate a position of domination. The remedy, he thought, lay not in surrender but in re-armament. And his belief could not be shaken by any arguments Abe was able to advance.[49]

Abe's problem was a difficult one. Japan was in no state to resist foreign attack. At the same time, the Bakufu was in no position to act independently of feudal opinion generally. The forces of opposition, long sectional and therefore comparatively harmless, were beginning to come together in a common loyalty to the Emperor. Foreign policy, a subject which evoked heated argument everywhere,

---

[49] For the conflict of opinion between Abe and Nariaki see :—Kobayashi, *Bakumatsu-shi*, pp. 162-3, 169-74 ; Omori, *Dai Nihon Zenshi* [Complete History of Japan], III, 704-6 ; Akao, ' Perry torai zengo ni okeru taigai kokumin shisō no kōsatsu (A Study of Popular Thought in Regard to Foreigners at the Time of Perry's Arrival) ', *Shirin*, XXII (1937), pp. 531-5.

might easily become the focus of disputes which would jeopardise at once the power of the Tokugawa and the safety of Japan. On both counts, the widest possible agreement on policy was indispensable.

As a first step, Abe accepted the letter brought by Perry in the autumn of 1853. The commodore was to return for his reply early in 1854, but the respite, Abe hoped, would enable him to effect a working compromise with Nariaki and his supporters. He decided, therefore, to circulate copies of the American letter among the *daimyō* and officials, and seek advice as to the answer he should make to its demands. This was in itself a confession of weakness, but he seems to have hoped that the replies to this appeal would have enough in common to suggest a policy capable both of placating the Americans and of gaining the support of a majority among the feudal lords. In this he was not altogether disappointed. The replies did, indeed, have much in common, though on balance they did not make his task much easier.

In answering the circular, Nariaki showed himself unwavering in his views despite the confidential information on Japan's defences and finance with which he had been provided. He repeated his belief that trade had no value to Japan. To open the ports, he said, would be to increase the national danger, to invite the same fate that had befallen China. It might even bring revolt at home. On the other hand, a programme of intensive defence preparations, including the purchase and manufacture of Western-style ships and guns, coupled with an announcement that Japan would resist any attempted foreign encroachment, would raise morale and increase the popularity of the government, thereby removing one danger and minimising the other.[50]

In opposition to Nariaki stood two men of considerable importance. One of them, Hotta Bitchū-no-kami, formerly one of the Rōjū and colleague of Mizuno Tadakuni, had long urged relaxation of the seclusion laws.[51] His advocacy

---

[50] *Dai Nihon Komonjo—Bakumatsu Gaikoku Kankei Monjo* [Old Japanese Documents—Documents on late-Tokugawa Foreign Relations], I, 509-22, Nariaki to Bakufu, 14 Aug. 1853.
[51] Satoh, *Lord Hotta, the Pioneer Diplomat of Japan*, pp. 20-31.

of concessions was therefore to be expected. The other was Ii Naosuke, head of the largest and most important of the *fudai* fiefs. Since it was on the *fudai* that the Bakufu traditionally relied for political and military support, the opinions of Naosuke were bound to carry great weight. His first letter, however, was non-committal, emphasising the need for defence preparations and the proscription of Christianity.[52] It represented a compromise between the views of Naosuke and those of his chief retainers. Abe, who had reason to doubt its sincerity, promptly requested a more detailed and personal statement, and this, when it came, revealed that Naosuke, who had for some time been one of the *daimyō* responsible for the Edo Bay defences, was well aware of the practical impossibility of resisting Western demands by force of arms. He recommended that ports should be opened to provide the coal, stores and other assistance required by American ships, and that the Japanese themselves should engage in trade overseas. Such a course would satisfy the foreigners' wish for trade while limiting their visits to Japan. It would also make available to the Bakufu the profits to be derived from foreign trade, a matter of some moment to a nearly bankrupt government. Above all, it would provide the means of creating and training a powerful navy, which in turn would enable Japan to close her ports again, if she chose to do so, with a reasonable prospect of success.[53]

It is clear that Nariaki and Naosuke, however conflicting their recommendations, were aiming at a common goal. Both saw in foreign encroachment a serious threat to the safety of Japan. Both were concerned to avert the danger. They were engaged, therefore, in seeking practical measures to achieve that end, not in an academic discussion of the *pros* and *cons* of opening trade. Because each assessed the situation differently, they agreed as to ends, differed sharply as to means. Nariaki saw greatest danger in permitting

[52] Satoh, *Agitated Japan : the life of Baron Ii Kamon-no-kami Naosuke*, pp. 43-6 ; Akimoto, *Lord Ii Naosuke and New Japan*, pp. 84-8 ; *Bakumatsu Gaikoku Kankei Monjo*, II, 74-6, Ii Naosuke to Bakufu, 12 Sept. 1853.
[53] *Bakumatsu Gaikoku Kankei Monjo*, II, 255-9, Ii Naosuke to Bakufu, 1 Oct. 1853. There is a translation of this letter in Gubbins, *Progress of Japan*, pp. 285-8.

foreigners to secure an initial foothold in Japan, and was willing to risk immediate conflict to avoid it. Naosuke, on the other hand, could forsee nothing but defeat in any early clash with the Western Powers. He therefore proposed a plan which would give Japan breathing-space, time to prepare for a war that was to come, and would at the same time provide her with the most effective means of making the necessary preparations for that war.

Japan's essentially " anti-foreign " approach to the problem of relations with the West is typified in the views of these two men. It underlies the policies of both, contrasting as they were. Despite this fundamental similarity, however, the recommendations made by Naosuke and Nariaki represent opposite extremes in the choice before *daimyō* and officials in 1853. In this, both spoke for minorities. It was long the accepted view that feudal opinion generally sided with Nariaki, and if this is taken to mean that most of those consulted were opposed to the opening of trade, it is true enough. But it is also an over-simplification. Some 59 of the letters expressing *daimyō* opinions still survive. Inobe Shigeo has pointed out[54] that of these 19 can be classified as supporting the opening of the ports in greater or less degree, while 25 were for refusal of the American request. Two expressed no opinion. The remaining 13 urged that Japan should avoid any action that might lead to war, and if one adds these to the 19 who favoured concession, there results a small majority against Nariaki on the vital question of armed resistance. Inobe makes the point still clearer by certain re-arrangements in classification. By concentrating on the immediate issue, the suggestions put forward for replying to the American request, rather than on the general or ultimate objectives specified by the *daimyō*, he is able to reclassify the letters of several whose long-term policy was expulsion of the foreigner, but who recognised that this was not practicable at once and urged that in the meantime the Rōjū should either open the

[54] Inobe, ' Perry torai no sai ni okeru kokuron no kisū (The National Opinion provoked by the Arrival of American Expedition of Commodore M. C. Perry to Japan) ', *Shirin*, XIII (1928), especially table pp. 348-50 and comments thereon pp. 350-4. See also Akao, *op. cit.*, pp. 545-54.

ports temporarily or take other steps to avert war. By this means the totals become 25 for opening the ports, 19 for avoiding conflict and only 15 for outright rejection of Perry's demands. Few were prepared to join Naosuke in urging trade as the long-range solution to the problem of defence, but the policy of peace, even if it entailed concessions, was widely preferred to that of war.

This analysis, however, is based on the known views of something less than one-fifth of the *daimyō*. Moreover, it takes no account of the differences in power and influence among the *daimyō* themselves. These naturally varied with a number of factors—personal ability, political and family ties with the Tokugawa, military resources—of which only size of fief, as represented by its assessed rice revenue, can be readily classified for statistical purposes. Size of fief, therefore, is chosen as the criterion for a more detailed examination of some of the opinions included in the numerical analysis given above.

If one excludes the Shōgun's personal domains, there were at this period only 18 fiefs with revenues rated at or above 250,000 *koku* a year.[55] These included all three of the Go-sanke (the senior Tokugawa branch houses of Owari, Kii and Mito) ; two of the Go-kamon (the Matsudaira houses related to the Tokugawa but not in the line of succession to the shōgunate) ; one of the *fudai daimyō* ; and 12 of the *tozama daimyō*. Among the replies to Abe's request for advice, 12 from these 18 fiefs are still extant. Two of the *tozama*, Ikeda of the Tottori fief and Kuroda of Fukuoka, recommended the opening of ports to trade. With them can be grouped Ikeda of Okayama fief, who thought trade undesirable but unavoidable, and the *fudai* Ii Naosuke, who urged that Japanese should themselves trade overseas. A further five were agreed that Japan should avoid immediate war. Shimazu of Satsuma wanted the Rōjū to avoid giving any definite reply for some years, until Japan had re-armed to the point where refusal could be safely made. Two more *tozama*, Hosogawa of Kumamoto and

[55] See the table of fief revenues for 1860 given in Shiba, K., *Nihon Rekishi Chizu* [Historical Atlas of Japan], rev. ed., Tōkyō 1927, tables pp. 41-52.

Date of Sendai, urged that trade be refused but war avoided, in which view they were supported by the Tokugawa house of Owari. The Mito branch, of which Nariaki's son was titular head, went a little farther in arguing that the time so gained must be used for preparations leading to ultimate expulsion of the foreigner. Of the remaining three letters, that from Nabeshima of the Saga fief was for immediate and outright expulsion. Matsudaira Echizen-no-kami of Fukui, one of the Go-kamon, and Mōri, the *tozama* lord of Chōshū, both recommended (somewhat ambiguously) that the Rōjū refuse the request for trade and concentrate its attention on defence.[56]

The greatest of the feudal lords, then, were divided very much as Inobe's analysis would lead one to expect—and not according to their political relations with the Bakufu. The seven *tozama* mentioned here, for example, had been, and were again to be, opponents of the Tokugawa in domestic politics. Yet they were far from agreement among themselves on the question of foreign affairs. The concerted attempt to use foreign policy as a political weapon against the Bakufu belongs to later years.

Similar differences of opinion are apparent among the Bakufu officials who normally had direct influence in the formulation of policy. The *ō-metsuke* and *metsuke*, whose function it was to watch for intrigue, disaffection or mal-administration among *daimyō* and officials, argued that the final answer to Perry must be a refusal of his demands, but that it must be delayed for a time in order to avoid war. There were dissentients, however. The *kaibō-kakari metsuke*[57] were more specific about the ultimate objective, in that they accepted the delay only because it would make possible preparations for expelling the foreigners by force of arms. Most of the other senior officials answered jointly in a letter which recommended that trade be permitted for a time, to

---

[56] See Inobe, *op. cit.*, pp. 346-54; Akao, *op. cit.*, pp. 545-54. The letters are to be found in volumes I and II of *Bakumatsu Gaikoku Kankei Monjo*.

[57] Officials entrusted with supervision of defence (and usually this implied also foreign affairs) were identified by the prefix *kaibō-kakari*, lit. " in charge of sea defence ".

I

be followed by the closing of the ports once rearmament had been completed.[58]

It is clear that most of the *daimyō* and officials believed that, to the West, trade was no more than an excuse for territorial expansion ; that it had no value in itself ; and that it should therefore be forbidden if at all possible. The real point at issue, however, was not whether seclusion was desirable, but whether it was practicable. Abe was sure that concessions of some kind must be made if Japan were to avoid a catastrophic war. The answers to his circular indicated that Naosuke and his followers would support such a policy, though they seemed to go further than Abe would wish. Only a small group, albeit a powerful one, insisted on bringing matters to a head at once. The majority took a middle ground, and would in all probability support a policy of limited concessions if they could be convinced that the alternative was war. Japanese foreign policy, there-fore, would be negative. It would resist foreign demands, but not to the point of war.

The first evidence of Abe's choice appeared late in 1853 when the Russian admiral Poutiatine came to seek treaty relations with Japan. His request for a treaty was refused on the grounds that national opinion would not permit alteration of the laws, however necessary it might seem, and he was told that several years must pass before Japan could be brought to accept such a change.[59] Poutiatine made no attempt to force reversal of this decision, and his peaceful departure gave the Rōjū new hope.

Perry proved much more obstinate. The Rōjū hoped that when he returned in 1854 it would be possible to avoid giving any definite answer to his request and still maintain friendly relations with him.[60] This was not one policy but

---

[58] Inobe, *op. cit.*, pp. 354-6 ; *Bakumatsu Gaikoku Kankei Monjo*, I, 603-12, II, 27-30. The joint letter was signed by 8 men, comprising 5 *jisha-bugyō* (responsible for supervision of shrines and temples) ; 2 *machi-bugyō* (respon-sible for the administration of the city of Edo) ; and 1 *kanjō-bugyō* ("finance magistrates", normally responsible for the administration and revenue of the Tokugawa estates, but often in this period appointed as *kaibō-kakari*). Some senior officials, it appears, answered individually as *daimyō*.

[59] Kobayashi, *Bakumatsu-shi*, pp. 193-5.

[60] Inobe, *op. cit.*, pp. 355-6.

two—and they proved irreconcilable. Perry soon convinced Abe that he must choose between a treaty and a declaration of war, and it was inevitable that he should choose the former. But every effort was made to keep concessions to the minimum consistent with peace. In the result, Perry's convention opened Shimoda and Hakodate as ports of refuge for American ships, provided for the protection of American subjects and the appointment of a consul, but did practically nothing to facilitate trade. It was widely criticised both in Europe and America as a small return for the expenditure of much time and money. But it was still more unpopular in Japan. The agreement confessedly represented a defeat for Bakufu policy, not a change in it, and was officially branded as the least that would have served to ward off a threatened attack.[61] Certainly it was not intended to prepare the way for more extended relations with the West. Within a few months fresh instructions were issued to the Nagasaki officials, reasserting and re-emphasising the laws which forbade Christianity and prevented Japanese from going overseas. Indeed, military forces were put at their disposal to ensure that foreigners as well as Japanese observed them.[62]

These events did not augur well for the success of any British negotiations in Japan. The Opium War and British actions in India had been cited in several of the *daimyō* letters of 1853, while it had even been suggested that by granting privileges to Russia and America, Japan might be able to obtain their help in resisting British attack.[63] It is true that there were indications in the orders issued by the Bakufu that privileges similar to those granted Perry might be extended to other countries if they sent envoys to demand them.[64] But that was no more than safety required. It did not mean that Stirling would be any more welcome a

---

[61] *Bakumatsu Gaikoku Kankei Monjo*, VI, 73-4, Rōjū to ōmetsuke and metsuke, 5 May 1854.

[62] *Bakumatsu Gaikoku Kankei Monjo*, VII, 163-4, Shōgun to Nagasaki bugyō, 24 Aug. 1854 ; VII, 164-6, Rōjū to Nagasaki bugyō, 24 Aug. 1854.

[63] Inobe, *op. cit.*, pp. 353-4, 360-2 ; *Bakumatsu Gaikoku Kankei Monjo*. I, 566-78, II, 213-30.

[64] *Bakumatsu Gaikoku Kankei Monjo*, V, 294-6 ; VI, 192.

visitor than Perry had been, or that he would receive any spontaneous offer of such a treaty, still less the kind of agreement envisaged by Bowring and the Foreign Office. Indeed he was not likely to obtain even the same terms as Perry unless he was prepared to demand rather than to solicit them.

CHAPTER V

THE STIRLING CONVENTION : 1854–1855

THE outbreak of war with Russia in 1854 and the continued success of the T'aip'ing rebels had led Sir John Bowring, with the knowledge and concurrence of the naval Commander-in-Chief, to postpone for a time his plans for visiting Japan. Yet in the months of September and October of the same year, Sir James Stirling was at Nagasaki engaged in negotiating with the officials there. It is true that Stirling's objectives differed radically from those Bowring had been instructed to secure ; that his results were disappointing to almost everybody except himself ; and that he negotiated without the authority, or even the knowledge of the Foreign Office. None the less, he concluded the first formal Anglo-Japanese agreement of the nineteenth century. For that reason, and because his negotiations seem in some respects to conflict with the pattern of British policy that has so far emerged, they must be examined in detail.

Just as it had been chiefly the Crimean War which had led Bowring to postpone his plans for Japan, so it was the war which gave Stirling occasion for visiting that country. The Russian squadron which he sought was known to be in the vicinity of Japan, perhaps sheltering in a Japanese port. This was in itself sufficient reason for a visit. Moreover, in any operations directed against the Russian bases in Kamchatka and the Sea of Okhotsk, the use of Japanese harbours, if only to obtain fuel and stores, would be of immense value to British warships. Such facilities could only be secured by permission of the Japanese government, and one might reasonably argue that negotiations to obtain them fell within the scope of Stirling's duties.

Stirling claimed in his report that this was his only

reason for negotiating with the Nagasaki officials.[1] We must ask, however, whether the evidence supports this claim, for the convention he secured is very similar to that concluded by Perry, who went with very different motives. Did Stirling also hope to secure commercial privileges? Some of his officers thought he did, and their views have often been repeated since.[2] Certainly he knew that a commercial treaty had been planned. Though he was careful to point out that he did not receive Admiralty instructions about taking Bowring to Japan until after the convention was signed,[3] his close co-operation with Bowring earlier in the year[4] invalidates any claim of total ignorance. On the other hand, his dispatches, both before and after the convention, consistently demonstrate his lack of interest in trade. Like Bowring, he held that Perry's treaty had no commercial value, that it had accomplished no very great result and that the British expedition had best be postponed to a more favourable moment. He added, however, that Perry probably achieved all that was possible in the circumstances and that such an agreement might lead eventually to further concessions.[5] Stirling advanced the same defence of his own convention. The wording of his official report suggests that to him, at least, trade was an ultimate rather than an immediate object of British relations with Japan.[6] Robertson, in charge of the Superintendency at Hongkong during Bowring's absence in Shanghai, quoted the admiral's opinion as being ' that at present the effecting a commercial treaty with Japan would be impossible, and that foreign nations must be content to break ground, first of all, with the admission of a friendly intercourse '.[7] In

[1] Parliamentary Papers 1856, vol. LXI (Cd. 2077), pp. 219-20, Stirling to Adty., No. 71, 26 Oct. 1854.
[2] Tronson, *Personal Narrative of a Voyage to Japan . . . in H.M.S. Barracouta*, p. 8. *China Mail*, 22 Mar. 1855, quoting a letter from an officer of the squadron. The most recent statement of this view is in Eckel, ' The Crimean War and Japan ', *Far Eastern Quarterly*, III, 2 (Feb. 1944), p. 111.
[3] F.O. *China Corres.*, vol. 217, Stirling to Bowring, 16 Nov. 1854. Admiralty, *In-Letters*, vol. 5657, Stirling to Graham, private, 27 Oct. 1854.
[4] See chapter IV, pp. 98-102.
[5] Admiralty, *In-Letters*, vol. 5629, Stirling to Adty., No. 44, 30 June 1854.
[6] Parl. Papers 1856, vol. LXI (Cd. 2077), pp. 219-20, Stirling to Adty., No. 71, 26 Oct. 1854.
[7] F.O. *China Corres.*, vol. 216, Robertson to Hammond, No. 53, 28 Oct. 1854.

a private letter to the First Lord, Stirling even claimed that Japan was 'far more important in a Political than in a Commercial sense'.[8]

If Stirling's testimony were the only evidence available, it could, perhaps, be dismissed as the defence of a man who had failed to obtain trading privileges and anticipated criticism on that account. But the story of the negotiations bears out his statements. At no time did he attempt to insert commercial clauses either in the convention of 1854 or in the exposition of its terms drawn up at the exchange of ratifications in 1855.

Stirling arrived at Nagasaki on 7 September 1854 with his flagship H.M.S. *Winchester* and three other ships, and at once communicated with the local *bugyō*[9] He had already provided himself with an interpreter for this purpose. Stirling could not make use of any of the consular interpreters who had been learning Japanese, because his was not a diplomatic mission, but there were several Japanese castaways in China who spoke some English and might therefore serve instead. Three of these had been on the *Morrison* in 1837 and had since been in British service. The two most intelligent had worked in Gutzlaff's office at Hongkong, but one was dead[10] and the other had resigned from government service in 1852.[11] The third, Otokichi, had settled at Shanghai. He had acted as interpreter to

[8] Admiralty, *In-Letters*, vol. 5657, Stirling to Graham, private, 27 Oct. 1854.

[9] The *bugyō* was the official appointed by the Bakufu to control the administration of Nagasaki and the foreign trade conducted there. The 1854 negotiations between Stirling and the *bugyō* have been described in G. Fox, 'The Anglo-Japanese Convention of 1854', *Pacific Hist. Rev.*, X, 4 (Dec. 1941), pp. 413-20, an article based largely on Admiralty sources and containing useful bibliographical information. The chief British sources are to be found in a Foreign Office Confidential Print (in Admiralty, *In-Letters*, vol. 5640), which contains all the papers from Stirling's report given in Parl. Papers 1856, vol. LXI (Cd. 2014 and 2077), pp. 209-35, and in addition some passages and papers omitted from Parl. Papers, especially a Diary of Negotiations kept by the Admiral's Secretary, Capt. M. J. Currie (hereafter cited as Admiralty, *In-Letters*, vol. 5640, Diary of Negs.).

[10] According to the statement made to Japanese officials at Hakodate by Rikimatsu, a castaway who also worked at Hongkong until employed as interpreter to Cdre. Elliot's squadron in 1854-5. See *Bakumatsu Gaikoku Kankei Monjo*, X, 70-2, Japanese minutes of meetings between Elliot and Hakodate *bugyō*, 28 Apr.–2 May 1855.

[11] F.O. *China Corres.*, vol. 190, Bowring to For. Off., No. 47, 18 June 1852.

the *Mariner* in 1849 and was subsequently hired as gate-keeper to Mr. Beale of Dent and Company, the merchant who accepted Stirling's offer to accompany the Japan expedition early in 1854 when it was expected that Bowring would undertake it.[12]   Since Stirling was at Shanghai when planning his own later visit, it was natural enough that he should engage Otokichi.   Unfortunately, Otokichi was not well qualified for his task.   He could read and write *kana*, the phonetic script of Japanese, but not the more difficult *kanji* used by officials.   Thus although copies in *kana* were sometimes provided for his benefit,[13] he was of little help in translating the letters and other papers exchanged between Stirling and the *bugyō*.

The Japanese at Nagasaki were no better equipped for communicating in English.   Their official interpreters had begun the study of that language early in the nineteenth century and attained some proficiency in it, but thereafter they had worked largely at Edo and interest at Nagasaki had waned.[14]   By the time of Stirling's arrival the officials there were forced to admit that they had no means of writing in English and could therefore give only verbal replies to his letters.[15]   However, Donker Curtius, the Dutch Super-intendent at Deshima, knew English well enough to trans-late the admiral's letters into Dutch, and this made it possible for the Dutch-speaking interpreters attached to the *bugyō*'s Office to translate them into Japanese.   This method was normally used during the negotiations.[16]

Yet the Japanese interpreters, according to foreign ob-servers of the next few years,[17] were not entirely reliable

[12] See chapter IV, p. 99. Tronson, *Voyage to Japan*, p. 15. *Bakumatsu Gaikoku Kankei Monjo*, VII, 506–10, Nagasaki bugyō to Rōjū, 22 Oct. 1854, summarising Otokichi's own account of his career.

[13] Admiralty, *In-Letters*, vol. 5640, Diary of Negs., 13 and 18 Sept., 15 Oct. 1854.

[14] Sakamaki, ' Japan and the United States ', pp. 87–9, 104–7.

[15] Parl. Papers 1856, vol. LXI (Cd. 2077), p. 221, extract from Diary of Negs., 9 Sept. 1854.

[16] Admiralty, *In Letters*, vol. 5640, Diary of Negs., 14 Sept. and 13 Oct. 1854.   The Japanese translations in *Bakumatsu Gaikoku Kankei Monjo* are all marked as having been translated into Dutch by Curtius.

[17] e.g. Alcock, *Capital of the Tycoon*, I, 101-2. Harris, *The Complete Journal of Townshend Harris*, pp. 352, 374-5, 490.

even when using Dutch, the western language which they knew best. Their vocabulary, doubtless efficient enough for normal purposes, was archaic and included few of the terms used in treaties and diplomatic negotiations. Those at Edo had made serious errors in translating the Bakufu reply to Perry in 1853,[18] so it is not surprising that there should have been mistakes in both translating and interpreting during Stirling's negotiations in 1854. Certainly Otokichi was not likely to prevent them. As it transpired, the mistakes made were important enough to alter the whole course of the negotiations, and they began with Stirling's first communication to the *bugyō*.

Immediately on his arrival, Stirling sent ashore a letter addressed to the Governor of Nagasaki, the title by which he knew the *bugyō*. It informed him officially of the outbreak of war with Russia, which was being conducted vigorously and with success, and added a warning about Russian designs on Japan. In carrying on the war in the China seas, it stated, British squadrons would have frequent occasion to visit the coasts and ports of Japan ' in order to prevent the Russian ships of war and their prizes from making use of those ports, to the detriment of the interests of Great Britain and her allies '. Britain had no desire to give offence to Japan, however. This made it essential that Stirling be informed ' of the views and intentions of the Japanese Government with respect to the admission into its ports of the ships of war of the belligerent parties in the present contest ', and he consequently asked the *bugyō* to inform him of Japanese policy in the matter, ' not only in reference to the port of Nagasaki, but also in regard to all other ports and places within the Japanese territory '.[19]

European diplomats might have thought this highhanded, but would probably have recognised that Stirling sought something like a declaration of " benevolent neutrality ". To Japanese officials such a conception, based as it was on European usage of which they were ignorant,

---

[18] Omori, *Dai Nihon Zenshi*, III, 700-1.

[19] The important paragraphs of this letter (Stirling to Gov. Nagasaki, 7 Sept. 1854) appear in Parl. Papers 1856, vol. LXI (Cd. 2077), pp. 220–1.

would have been puzzling enough in its simplest form. In fact they were never given the opportunity of understanding it. By the time it had been translated first into Dutch and then into Japanese, the letter had acquired a new and very different meaning. The Japanese version[20] was not a request for information about Japanese policy. It stated rather that Stirling intended to make use of Japanese ports in prosecuting the war against Russia and had come to seek —perhaps even " demand "—the Japanese government's permission to do so. It even distorted his wish to avoid any act ' which may justly give offence ' to Japan into a veiled threat that war might follow should his request be refused.[21] The translation was a vague document, it is true, and open to several constructions. But their later correspondence on the subject leaves no room for doubt that the *bugyō* and the Rōjū took it to be a request for the immediate opening of all Japanese ports to British ships.

The Rōjū had been warned by the Dutch during the summer first that Bowring, then that Stirling, was coming to negotiate.[22] No special instructions had been issued as a result of this information, however. The Nagasaki *bugyō* had standing orders on the subject of foreign relations which permitted him to settle only matters of detail on his own responsibility. Major points were normally referred to the appropriate *ōsetsu-kakari*,[23] an official specially charged with

[20] *Bakumatsu Gaikoku Kankei Monjo*, VII, 214-7. A more accurate translation (origin unspecified) appears in Japan, Gaimushō Chōsa-bu [Foreign Office Research Section], *Nichi-ei Gaikō-shi* [History of Anglo-Japanese Relations], I, 35-7.

[21] The translation of this letter is discussed in more detail in my article ' The language problem in the Anglo-Japanese negotiations of 1854', *Bulletin School of Oriental and African Studies*, XIII, 3 (1950).

[22] *Bakumatsu Gaikoku Kankei Monjo*, VII, 39-63, Curtius to Bakufu, 30 July 1854; VII, 147-50, report brought by Dutch ship, 1854, 7th month (25 July–23 Aug.).

[23] *Bakumatsu Gaikoku Kankei Monjo*, VI, 511, Rōjū to Nagasaki, Uraga and Shimoda bugyō, 1854, 6th month (25 June–24 July). Before 1859 the Bakufu established no special department to handle foreign affairs, and the Rōjū appointed a special commission to conduct negotiations with each Western envoy who came to seek a treaty. Members of these commissions retained the title of their normal administrative office (e.g. *ōmetsuke, kanjō-bugyō*) prefixed by the name of the Western country concerned and the phrase *ōsetsu-kakari* (literally " in charge of reception "). Thus the *Russia ōsetsu-kakari kanjō-bugyō* was the *kanjō-bugyō* responsible for discussions with Poutiatine.

the conduct of negotiations, but no *ōsetsu-kakari* had been appointed to negotiate with Britain and the *bugyō* accordingly applied direct to the Rōjū for instructions as to what reply he should make to Stirling.

On 9 September the *bugyō* forwarded a translation of Stirling's letter to Edo, together with some observations of his own on the difficult situation it had caused. To grant such privileges to Britain, he said, might endanger Japan's relations with Russia. On the other hand, a flat refusal might provoke Stirling into using force. In this dilemma there seemed only one possible course, to offer Stirling the use of one or two ports—Nagasaki and Hakodate, perhaps, since both were already being used by foreigners—in the hope that this would be enough to avert conflict.[24]

The Rōjū were equally quick to see the danger of offending Russia. On 21 September, only fourteen days after the date of Stirling's letter, instructions were sent from Edo to the *bugyō* and *metsuke* at Nagasaki appointing them to conduct the negotiations. They were to refuse Stirling's request in its existing form on the grounds that to grant it would be to break faith with Russia and other friendly countries, thereby, perhaps, arousing their active hostility. Every effort was to be made to get him to withdraw or modify his demands. He could be granted the use of Nagasaki and Hakodate for the provision of wood, water and other supplies and for effecting repairs ; if he pressed the point, then Shimoda could be opened for the same purposes. On no account were any other concessions to be made.[25]

The Rōjū's instructions eventually formed the basis of Stirling's convention, but they were, of course, largely irrelevant to the subject of his letter. There was to be much discussion before he could be brought to consider them. Meanwhile, at Nagasaki, he was growing impatient at the delay. On 27 September he informed the *bugyō* that he had waited twenty days for an answer to his letter, and since

[24] *Bakumatsu Gaikoku Kankei Monjo*, VII, 247-50, Nagasaki bugyō to Rōjū, 9 Sept. 1854.

[25] *Bakumatsu Gaikoku Kankei Monjo*, VII, 250-3, Rōjū to Nagasaki bugyō, 21 Sept. 1854.

none had been forthcoming, now proposed to go to Edo and demand one from the government there. The prospect greatly alarmed the *bugyō*, who begged him to remain another ten days and offered as a reward for compliance better facilities for the recreation of the seamen and for the purchase of stores.[26]   Stirling agreed with some show of reluctance.   He took the opportunity of reiterating that his purpose was quite unlike that of previous visitors to Japan. They, he said, were ' mendicants soliciting some relaxation in the laws ', while he came ' asking for nothing and unwilling to accept anything but an answer to a question arising out of the war '.[27]   The message, of which there is no trace in the Japanese records, does not seem to have influenced the actions or opinions of the *bugyō*.

On 3 October arrangements were made for the admiral to land next day for his first meeting with the *bugyō*, Mizuno Chikugo-no-kami.   Otokichi, at the request of the Japanese, and under Mizuno's personal guarantee of safe conduct, was to be interpreter.   In this capacity, too, he left much to be desired.   His English seems to have been no better than that of Rikimatsu, interpreter to Commodore Elliot's squadron, of whom it was said that he ' rendered the substance of all conversations in such patches and shreds that it was an exercise of ingenuity to sew them together '.[28] However good his Japanese, it is quite certain that Otokichi succeeded in perpetuating the mistaken idea of Stirling's purpose which the Japanese had already acquired from the translation of his original letter.

The most important mistakes in interpreting were made during the meeting of 4 October.   Once the polite preliminaries were over, Mizuno invited Stirling to make a general statement of his views about the arrangement he had come to effect.   The moderate tone of Stirling's answer surprised

---

[26] Parl. Papers 1856, vol. LXI (Cd. 2077), pp. 221-2, Stirling to Gov. Nagasaki, 27 Sept. 1854 ; extract from Diary of Negs., 28 Sept. 1854. *Bakumatsu Gaikoku Kankei Monjo*, VII, 338-42, Nagasaki bugyō to Rōjū, 28 Sept. 1854.

[27] Admiralty, *In-Letters*, vol. 5640, Diary of Negs., 30 Sept. 1854.

[28] Whittingham, *Notes on the late Expedition against the Russian Settlements in Eastern Siberia*, pp. 228-9.

him, so much so that he said he saw 'some little difference' between this oral statement and the meaning of the
letter as it had been translated to him. At his request, the
admiral went into greater detail. According to Captain
Currie's summary of the speech, he said that 'in wartime
neither the ships of Russia nor of England should be allowed
to come into the ports of Japan to refit and supply themselves with stores, to enable them to go out and capture
the merchant-ships of their enemy'. So long as the Russians
were not allowed to use Japanese ports for such purposes,
Stirling was prepared to forbid his own ships to do so,
though he insisted on their right to visit Japan to ensure
that the Russians were not in fact so using its ports.[29]

This record is a summary not a verbatim report, but it
was read by Stirling before being forwarded to the Admiralty
and we can assume that it represented accurately the substance of what he said. Otokichi, however, was as little
at home with the English of diplomatic usage as were the
other Japanese. The speech as he translated it, and as it
appeared in the Japanese record of the interview,[30] was very
different in meaning. Minor discrepancies between the two
versions were such as could occur in any two independent
summaries of a given speech—and we cannot assume that
Currie was necessarily accurate in detail—but there were
major errors in the Japanese which can only be accounted
for as the result of faulty interpreting. Stirling had
attempted a simple (and slightly biassed) definition of what
was forbidden to belligerents in neutral ports in time of
war. That is to say, he had insisted that use of Japanese
ports for refitting, storing ship and harbouring prizes must
be denied to *both* Russian *and* British ships. In this statement lay the crux of the matter. As Otokichi translated
it, the ban applied only to actual fighting in Japanese ports.
He represented Stirling as claiming the right to exercise all
the other privileges he had listed—those relating to stores,
repairs and prizes—and as demanding, in effect, a treaty

[29] Admiralty, *In-Letters*, vol. 5640, Diary of Negs., 4 Oct. 1854.
[30] *Bakumatsu Galhoku Kankei Monjo*, VII, 379-80, Japanese minutes of
conference, 4 Oct. 1854.

which would grant them to Britain to the exclusion of Russia.[31]

Had Stirling's speech reached the *bugyō* in its original form, it would have confirmed his suspicion that the letter had been mistranslated. It might well have led him to withhold Edo's offer to open Hakodate and Nagasaki, since he knew it to have been authorised with the greatest reluctance. As it was, Otokichi's version of the speech substantially confirmed the Japanese translation of Stirling's letter and left the *bugyō* in no doubt that Britain sought the use of all Japanese ports for her operations against the Russians. He therefore explained that only one or two ports could be opened for the purposes mentioned because suitable facilities did not exist at them all. It was a reply which followed logically enough in the Japanese record, but made nonsense to Stirling. The latter, however, saw where the difficulty lay. He said he had explained himself ' as well as could be done through imperfect interpretation ',[32] and offered to write another letter in an attempt to make his ideas clear. This offer was accepted and the meeting broke up for the day.

Next day, in pursuance of his promise, Stirling sent ashore a written statement of his views. At the close of the 4 October meeting, Mizuno had revealed that he had been officially empowered to treat, a fact which he had studiously concealed—and at one point even denied—during the foregoing discussions. Stirling therefore put his new letter into the form of a draft convention. In summary, its provisions were as follows :—

Article   I.—The warships of Great Britain and her opponents in this and future wars are to be excluded from Japanese ports and waters except as herein provided.

Article II.—The warships of Britain and other Treaty Powers are to be admitted to Nagasaki and two other ports, but in time of war are not to effect repairs, obtain supplies of munitions, bring in prizes or remain over fourteen days.

[31] See my article ' The language problem in the Anglo-Japanese negotiations of 1854 ', *B.S.O. and A.S.*, XIII, 3 (1950).
[32] Admiralty, *In-Letters*, vol. 5640, Diary of Negs., 4 Oct. 1854.

Article III.—If the ships of one beligerent contravene Article II, the other may demand their expulsion.

Article IV.—British ships in Japan are to observe port regulations, but are to be entitled to equal privileges with those of any other friendly nation.

Article V.—This agreement is to be in force until 1 September 1855, and may then be ' extended, modified or wholly annulled ' as agreed between the representatives of the two signatories.[33]

This document was Stirling's third attempt to explain his wishes, and in English it makes them abundantly clear. Yet it made no apparent difference to the *bugyō*'s policy. Responsibility for this seems to rest once again with the translators, though less certainly so than before. Article II embodied the point on which previous misunderstandings had centred, and in the existing Japanese translation[34] Article II contains one all-important mistake. The negative is omitted from the second part of the article, with the result that it reads so as to permit ships to make repairs, obtain supplies and harbour prizes in Japanese ports, instead of forbidding these activities as did the English text. In Japanese the change requires only the omission of a single character, and taken in isolation this could easily be dismissed as a clerical error, not necessarily a contemporary one. But taken in conjunction with the *bugyō*'s reply and the mistakes that had already been made, it seems more likely that the change was due either to mistranslation, or to a deliberate attempt on the part of the translator to " correct " the document to conform with the ideas already credited to Stirling.

Stirling received a reply to this draft on 9 October, when he went ashore for his second conference with Mizuno. The reply stated that the admiral was understood to seek harbours in which his ships could effect repairs and obtain supplies, and that Nagasaki and Hakodate would therefore

[33] Admiralty, *In-Letters*, vol. 5640, Diary of Negs., 5 Oct. 1854.
[34] *Bakumatsu Gaikoku Kankei Monjo*, VII, 386-90, translation of Stirling's draft convention of 5 Oct. 1854.

be opened for these purposes. They were not, however, to be used for war in any way. Fighting was not to be permitted in them, nor could the *bugyō* ' entertain any matters relating to questions of war '. He could not agree to the proposal to treat all nations alike, since intercourse of long standing created a natural bias in favour of some—presumably a reference to the Dutch and Chinese who had long traded at Nagasaki. Finally, he objected strongly to the idea that the convention might be altered again at the end of a year.[35]

When Stirling had been given time to peruse this reply, discussion of it began. Mizuno repeated in the conference-room most of the points he had made in writing, emphasising his determination not to ' meddle with war '. He made it plain that he was prepared to open Hakodate and Nagasaki to both warships and merchantmen—Stirling throughout had referred only to warships—and that while the ports were only to be used to obtain essential supplies, the Japanese would not distinguish between emergencies caused by stress of weather and those arising from naval warfare. Faced with this offer, Stirling abandoned his attempts to persuade the Japanese that he sought a strictly military arrangement. He decided to accept Mizuno's reply as a basis for discussion, and the rest of the conference was spent in working out the details of a convention.

There were no new difficulties. It was quickly agreed that Nagasaki and Hakodate were to be opened on the conditions already suggested, the former at once, the latter after fifty days. No other ports were to be used except in cases of extreme distress. At both open ports Japanese laws and regulations must be observed, but masters would have jurisdiction over their own seamen. Mizuno asked that British ships be provided with written evidence of nationality, Stirling that a clause be added guaranteeing Britain use of any ports opened to other foreign countries in the future. After some discussion they agreed that the convention, once signed, should be final, subject only to

[35] *Bakumatsu Gaikoku Kankei Monjo,* VII, 408-10, Nagasaki bugyō to Stirling, 9 Oct. 1854. Parl. Papers 1856, vol. LXI (Cd. 2077), pp. 222-3, extract from Diary of Negs., 9 Oct. 1854.

ratification, and by late afternoon, when the meeting ended, the convention had assumed in outline a form acceptable to both parties.[36]

The agreement was still oral, however, and had yet to be committed to paper. To speed up this process and supplement existing arrangements for interpreting, Stirling had recourse to a member of the flagship's crew who spoke a little Dutch and could thus, with Otokichi's help, check some of the work of the Japanese translators. By this means a number of minor errors were corrected.

The *bugyō* was first to prepare a draft convention on the new lines, and this was received and translated aboard the flagship on 11 October. It omitted the most-favoured-nation clause which Stirling had proposed, and amplified the arrangements about port regulations by providing that any serious infringement would lead to the closing of the ports, but was otherwise in accordance with the decisions taken two days before. The officials who brought it stated that Mizuno was not authorised to make any further concessions. Subject to Edo approval, however, he was willing to accept an additional article permitting Britain to use all ports that might be opened in future. Stirling accordingly promised to prepare a new draft by the following day, incorporating such an article but otherwise holding as closely as translation would permit to the Japanese proposal.[37]

Stirling's fresh draft, dated 12 October, contained six articles. Article I provided for the opening of Hakodate and Nagasaki for repairs and supplies ; Article II for the dates at which they were to be opened and for the observance of port regulations by all British ships. Article III forbade the use of any other Japanese ports except by ships in distress. Article IV laid it down that British ships would conform to Japanese laws and that seamen breaking those laws were to be punished by their own captains (without any mention of closing the ports). Article V was a most-favoured-nation clause, though the existing privileges of

---

[36] Admiralty, *In-Letters*, vol. 5640, Diary of Negs., 9 Oct. 1854. *Bakumatsu Gaikoku Kankei Monjo*, VII, 410-8, Japanese minutes of conference, 9 Oct. 1854.
[37] Admiralty, *In-Letters*, vol. 5640, Diary of Negs, 11 Oct. 1854.

Dutch and Chinese were specifically excluded from its operation, while the final article provided that ratifications were to be exchanged at Nagasaki within twelve months of the signing of the convention. In an accompanying letter, Stirling emphasised that the last article was normal European usage and that the most-favoured-nation clause must be included because ' an English officer must not sign, and his Government would not ratify, any engagement whatever which would place British subjects in Japan in a worse position than Americans, or those of any other nations '.[38]

There were still a few changes to be made. Next day Japanese officials came off to the *Winchester* to arrange a meeting ashore for 14 October and to discuss Stirling's draft. At their insistence, Article I was made more specific by detailing the purposes for which the two ports were to be opened—' effecting repairs, and obtaining fresh water, provisions and other supplies of any sort they may require for the use of the ships '—and in Article III it was made clearer that only immediate danger would justify entry to any other Japanese port. Finally, the *bugyō*'s " penalty clause " was re-inserted into Article IV, providing that the ports would be closed if captains or ' high officers ' broke the laws.[39]

On the morning of 14 October Stirling went ashore for the final meeting. He found the *bugyō* still a little unhappy about the wording of the convention. Mizuno objected that Stirling's version of Article I would permit ships to obtain supplies almost without restriction, whereas his own intention was to limit them to real necessities. The English text was eventually changed to read ' supplies . . . they may absolutely want ' instead of ' they may require ' A similar difficulty over Article III was explained satisfactorily as a simple difference of idiom between the two languages. Articles IV, V and VI were accepted unchanged, but Mizuno wanted to add a sentence to the latter which would prevent changes being made in the arrangement by future

[38] Admiralty, *In-Letters*, vol. 5640, Diary of Negs., 12 Oct. 1854. *Bakumatsu Gaikoku Kankei Monjo*, VII, 425-7, gives the translations of Stirling's letter and draft.
[39] Admiralty, *In-Letters*, vol. 5640, Diary of Negs., 13 Oct. 1854.

visitors. Stirling suggested a plain statement that there-after the convention would not be altered, but this did not quite meet the objection. Eventually they agreed to add a new Article VII, stating that once the convention was ratified, ' no high officer coming to Japan shall alter it '.[40] This later caused much criticism in Britain, as many people assumed that it blocked any future negotiations on the subject of treaty revision. In fact, the English phrase ' no high officer ' was no more than the interpreter's translation of a Japanese word[41] meaning ' commander of a warship ', and Mizuno's intention, therefore was not so much to make the agreement perpetual as to make it binding on all British ships, including those not under Stirling's command.

The convention was drawn up and signed the same day, Stirling signing the English text, Mizuno and the *metsuke* Nagai Iwa-no-Jō signing the Japanese. The two documents were not identical. The arrangement of articles in the Japanese text differed slightly from that in Stirling's version, nor were they numbered, which made them more difficult to identify. In the last article, the Japanese word *senshō* did not have quite the same connotation as the English ' no high officer '. But the most important difference lay in Article V, which had been passed over without discussion at the final meeting. Stirling's copy entitled British ships to equal treatment with those of other countries in ports then open or thereafter to be opened, only excepting the privileges already enjoyed by the Dutch and Chinese. Mizuno's copy, on the other hand, omitted all reference to Dutch and Chinese and to ports already open, so that it limited British participation to future privileges conceded by Japan to other countries.[42] As was to be expected, this later proved a source of dispute.

[40] Admiralty, *In-Letters*, vol. 5640, Diary of Negs., 14 Oct. 1854. *Bakumatsu Gaikoku Kankei Monjo*, VII, 430-9, Japanese minutes of conference, 14 Oct. 1854. The English text of the convention is given as Appendix A, pp. 205-6.

[41] *Senshō*. The characters are Ueda *Daijiten* (American edit.), numbers 9675 and 2425.

[42] Appendix A, pp. 205-6, gives the English text of the convention and shows the differences in meaning between that and the Japanese version. The Japanese text in *Bakumatsu Gaikoku Kankei Monjo*, VII, 439-41, corresponds with the copy given to Stirling, to be found in Foreign Office, *Protocols of Treaties, Japan*, I (F.O. 93/49-1).

Stirling had already agreed to make arrangements to provide British ships visiting Japan with some form of written identification—though in this connection he had consistently used the term 'merchant ships', while the Japanese intended warships to be included. Before leaving Nagasaki, he asked for and obtained a copy of the port regulations his ships were to observe under the terms of the convention, though he was referred to Hakodate for any that might be in force at that port. The Nagasaki regulations consisted largely of prohibitions. Ships on arrival were to anchor in the outer harbour and await instructions ; they were to fire no guns in harbour, nor send away boats for surveying or other purposes ; no foreigner was to land on any of the islands, engage in trading or communicate with private boats ; finally, all business was to be conducted through the officials. In an accompanying letter, the *bugyō* enjoined observance of these rules, adding that all wood, water, food and other supplies needed by ships must be requisitioned through his office, not bought in the town. However, he promised that if a ship made a long stay, arrangements would be made for her crew to exercise on one of the islands in the harbour.[43]

The fact that Stirling accepted these regulations without question[44] is additional evidence that he had no intention of arranging trade. Indeed, the whole story of the negotiations demonstrates that he went to Nagasaki in 1854 simply to negotiate an agreement which would assist his operations against the Russian squadron. That the convention in its final form differed in many respects from that which he had planned was due chiefly to the work of the interpreters. Stirling's preliminary request for information was distorted into a demand for the opening of all Japanese ports. On the basis of that distortion the Rōjū drew up instructions for its negotiator, instructions to which the *bugyō* firmly adhered, ignorant of—or perhaps even choosing to

---

[43] Admiralty, *In-Letters*, vol. 5640, Diary of Negs., 18 Oct. 1854. *Bakumatsu Gaikoku Kankei Monjo*, VII, 455-8, Nagasaki bugyō to Stirling, 18 Oct. 1854, encl. Port Regulations.

[44] Parl. Papers 1856, vol. LXI (Cd. 2077), p. 225, Stirling to Gov. Nagasaki, 19 Oct. 1854.

ignore—the admiral's attempts to introduce other issues into the discussions. It is true, of course, that the Japanese expected Stirling to demand terms at least equal to those obtained by Perry. This preconceived idea, combined with ignorance of European diplomatic usage, undoubtedly contributed to the mistakes of the translators, but it is clear that their linguistic knowledge was not adequate to the task of translating documents as they found them, rather than as they expected them to be. Otokichi, Stirling's own interpreter, probably laboured under the same misapprehensions about the purpose of the expedition, and was certainly no better equipped to correct them.

At the meeting of 9 October, when he received the Japanese counter-proposal, Stirling realised[45] that the Japanese were willing to go further than he had asked in the matter of opening ports. Considering their whole attitude sufficient guarantee against Russian use of their ports—which he could in any case prevent by force once Nagasaki and Hakodate were open to him—he decided to negotiate on the basis they proposed. He was well satisfied with the result. Not only did the convention open two ports for British use, he reported to the Admiralty, but also, 'although it makes no sort of provision for commercial intercourse, it affords the means of cultivating a friendly understanding with the Government and People of an extensive Empire, whose Neutrality in War and Friendship at all times, are matters of vital importance to British Interests in the Adjacent Seas '.[46] The Japanese, if not equally satisfied, were at least thankful at having reduced what they believed to have been Stirling's demands. They had opened not all, but only two of their ports, and that under the strictest regulations.

Stirling was almost alone in his enthusiasm for the convention. Despite widespread criticism of it,[47] however, the

[45] According to his own statements. See Parl. Papers 1856, vol. LXI (Cd. 2077), pp. 219-20, Stirling to Adty., No. 71, 26 Oct. 1854; F.O. *China Corres.*, vol. 216, Robertson to Hammond, No. 53, 28 Oct. 1854.

[46] Parl. Papers 1856, vol. LXı (Cd. 2077), pp. 219-20, Stirling to Adty., No. 71, 26 Oct. 1854.

[47] British reactions to the convention are treated in more detail in chapter VI, pp. 145-51.

Foreign Office decided to ratify, and the ratifications were sent to Stirling in January 1855 to be exchanged at Nagasaki by himself or Commodore Elliot, with instructions to do everything possible to ensure that the English and Japanese texts agreed.[48] The question of identification documents for British ships was referred to the Admiralty and Board of Trade. They decided that merchant ships could show their registers, specially stamped with the royal arms, and that warships needed no special identification ; and in May Stirling was instructed to deliver copies of the registers to Japan and make suitable explanations about naval vessels.[49]

While he thus had sound reasons for revisiting Japan and had every intention of doing so, the admiral still had no power to conduct formal diplomatic negotiations. Nor did he much wish to do so. He knew, of course, that his convention was being severely criticised. Bowring had written to him that ' the terms of the Convention and the Harbour regulations attached thereto are such, as it would have been impossible for me to have accepted under the instructions I have received from Her Majesty's Government '.[50] The *China Mail* was, and remained, consistently hostile.[51] This Stirling had expected, since he had made no provision for trade. More important to him was the fact that Japanese ports were being used by his ships as bases for operations against the Russians and that during 1855 the resources of those ports, and especially of Hakodate, were being steadily developed to that end.[52] It was difficulties arising in this connection that Stirling wished to go back and adjust, not questions of trade.

The Japanese were determined to keep strictly to the

[48] Parl. Papers 1856, vol. LXI (Cd. 2077), p. 226, For. Off. to Adty.,26 Dec. 1854 ; pp. 226-7, same to same, 25 Jan. 1855 ; pp. 227-8, Adty. to For. Off., 27 Jan. 1855.
[49] Parl. Papers 1856, vol. LXI (Cd. 2077), pp. 228-9, For. Off. to Adty., 22 May 1855.
[50] F.O. *China Emb. Arch.*, vol. 167, Bowring to Stirling, No. 120, 27 Nov. 1854.
[51] e.g. *China Mail*, 2 Nov. 1854, 9 Aug. 1855.
[52] Admiralty, *In-Letters*, vol. 5657, Stirling to Adty., No. 42, 15 Apr. 1855 ; No. 55, 2 July 1855 ; No. 74, 1 Oct. 1855. Eckel, ' The Crimean War and Japan ', pp. 117-8.

letter of the treaties they had made. In February 1855 the Rōjū issued a statement denying rumours current in Japan that the Americans were to be allowed to trade at Nagasaki. As late as September of that year they were publicly affirming a hope that it might eventually be possible to revoke the agreements already concluded,[53] and although this was strictly propaganda for internal consumption, the actions of the officials at the treaty ports were carefully regulated to avoid contradicting it. At Shimoda, visited chiefly by American ships, the *bugyō* produced two sets of port regulations. One, as severe as those handed to Stirling at Nagasaki, was for the ships of countries to whom the port was open. The other, no more than a direct order to depart, was to be handed to all other ships. The arrangement was modified slightly some weeks later, but chiefly to introduce regulations applicable to ships of non-Treaty Powers which came on official business, not to relax the restrictions on trade or intercourse.[54]

At Hakodate, much used by the British squadron in 1855, conditions were at first no better. After the conclusion of the United States treaty, the Hakodate *bugyō* had been notified that the port was to be opened. He was instructed to refer any disputes to Edo and warned to be strict in his supervision of foreign visitors, especially in enforcing the laws prohibiting trade and Christianity. In the following spring he was ordered to extend the same treatment to the British.[55] This he did, but the visits of so impressive an array of British warships during the summer, and the constant protests of their commanders, seem to have worn down his resistance. By the early autumn, British visitors to the port were commenting that, although their treatment still left much to be desired, it was at least

---

[53] *Bakumatsu Gaikoku Kankei Monjo*, VIII, 391-2, Rōjū to America ōsetsu-kakari, kaibō-kakari, Shimoda and Hakodate bugyō, 5 Feb. 1855; XII, 288-9, Rōjū to various daimyō, 23 Sept. 1855.

[54] *Bakumatsu Gaikoku Kankei Monjo*, IX, 390-5, Shimoda bugyō to Rōjū, 1855, 2nd month (18 Mar.-16 Apr.); XI, 266-72, same to same, 15 June 1855.

[55] *Bakumatsu Gaikoku Kankei Monjo*, VII, appendix pp. 7-8, Shōgun to Hakodate bugyō, 7 Sept. 1854; pp. 8-11, Rōjū to Hakodate bugyō, 7 Sept. 1854; IX, 246-8, Hakodate bugyō to Rōjū, 4 Apr. 1855, and Rōjū minute thereon.

very much better than it had been earlier in the year.[56]

Nagasaki was the least satisfactory of the open ports. There, like Canton in China, the old habits of officials died hard, and they clung obstinately to the port regulations they had given Stirling. The summer of 1855 saw no improvement. British officers complained that the treaty had made no difference to the restrictions on their actions, that their protests were of no avail. The treaty, they said, was a dead letter.[57]

In September 1855 Commodore Elliot arrived at Nagasaki with his squadron, determined to obtain better treatment for his ships and men. Since he had an interpreter, Rikimatsu, a Japanese castaway from Hongkong, he demanded an interview with the two *bugyō*, Arao Iwami-no-kami and Kawamura Tsushima-no-kami.[58] Both were present in the port in anticipation of Stirling's arrival with the ratification of the previous year's convention. The meeting took place on 24 September and Elliot, confident in the support of seven warships, at once took an aggressive tone in complaining that the treatment of ships at Nagasaki was very much worse than that at Hakodate. The *bugyō* pointed out that each port made its own regulations and Stirling had agreed to abide by them. Elliot next objected to the ban on landing, since some crews had been in harbour for thirty days without being allowed exercise ashore. Once again he was referred to the terms of the convention. Thereupon, greatly incensed by the attitude taken by the two *bugyō*, the commodore launched into an acrimonious discussion of their interpretation of the treaty, especially of their insistence that all stores must be obtained through the officials, which resulted, he said, in the supply of goods poor in quality and insufficient in quantity. He threatened that unless this circumstance were changed, he would be forced to report to his government that the Japanese were breaking

---

[56] London *Times*, 13 Oct. 1855. Whittingham, *Expedition against the Russian settlements*, pp. 160-5.

[57] Tronson, *Voyage to Japan*, pp. 153-4, 159. Whittingham, *op. cit.*, pp. 216-7.

[58] Normally two bugyō were appointed, to carry out the duties of the office in rotation. One usually remained in Edo while the other was at Nagasaki.

the treaty. But his anger had no effect. The *bugyō*, too, regretted the strictness of the regulations. None the less, they had no power to alter either laws or treaty, and must in duty bound enforce them to the best of their ability. With this deadlock the discussion ended, on terms of rather distant friendship.[59]

Thus it was left to Stirling to make fresh arrangements. He had already decided to do so some months before, in May 1855, when he visited Nagasaki to inform the *bugyō* that he had been authorised to ratify the convention. He had said then that he would return himself or send a ship to exchange ratifications as soon as the Japanese were ready, but that first there were some questions of interpretation which he wanted settled. He demanded an interview with the *bugyō*, threatening to go to Edo if it were not granted, and moved his squadron into the inner harbour on the grounds that the outer anchorage was not safe in existing weather conditions.[60] The *bugyō* had little choice but to arrange a meeting.

The promised meeting took place ashore on 16 May, and dealt chiefly with the question of ratifications. Stirling allowed the Japanese to copy the Dutch translation of the British ratification, and agreed to return on 1 October, by which time they would have been able to check it and would be ready for the ceremony of exchange. This was all innocuous enough. Next day, however, he sent ashore a draft of the regulations he proposed to issue to British ships. They were, he emphasised, to clarify not to amend the convention, but to the Japanese they contained some ominous novelties. They affirmed that British ships must carry suitable papers of identification, but specifically relieved warships of any such obligation. They catalogued the port regulations to be observed at Nagasaki, but added that if weather conditions made such a course desirable, ships

[59] Whittingham, *op. cit.*, pp. 225-31. *Bakumatsu Gaikoku Kankei Monjo*, XII, 301-28, Japanese minutes of conference, 24 Sept. 1855 (2 versions); XII, 334-6, Nagasaki bugyō to Rōjū, 25 Sept. 1855.

[60] *Bakumatsu Gaikoku Kankei Monjo*, X, 191-2, translation, Stirling to Nagasaki bugyō, 13 May 1855; X, 219-22, translation, same to same, 15 May 1855.

might proceed direct to the inner harbour without stopping for examination. Finally, they enjoined observance of Japanese laws, but made it clear that the penalty for breach of those laws would be dismissal of the ship and punishments of the offenders, not the closing of the port.[61]

The *bugyō* could not let these statements pass unchallenged, and took up all three points in a written reply. Denying that the treatment of the *Winchester* constituted a precedent, he insisted that in future warships produce suitable papers and that all ships stop in the outer harbour until given permission to proceed. Moreover, he wrote, the port would certainly be closed if the laws were broken.[62] In fact, he took a firm stand on the letter of the treaty.

Stirling was evidently willing to let the matter drop until he returned in October, for no further discussions followed this exchange of notes. His report to the Admiralty gave no details of what had occurred,[63] and was, indeed, wilfully misleading. He claimed that he had been led to broach the subject of clarifying the convention by certain ' favorable indications ' in the attitude of the officials, a proposition which is inherently improbable and is supported neither by the Japanese records nor by the experience of other visitors to Nagasaki. He admitted that he found the officials ' extremely punctilious and evidently disposed to adhere strictly even to the minutiae of the Agreement ', but neither enclosed nor referred to the *bugyō*'s letter which categorically rejected his draft proclamation. Indeed, by stating that he could not ' report with any degree of certainty upon the prospects of success ', Stirling implied that while the discussions had revealed disagreement, they had not reached deadlock. This could be true only if Stirling himself planned to force the issue. One concludes that he was determined, with or without powers to negotiate, to effect some improvement in the treatment of British ships in

[61] *Bakumatsu Gaikoku Kankei Monjo*, X, 305-10, translation, Stirling to Nagasaki bugyō, 17 May 1855, and enclosed draft regulations.

[62] *Bakumatsu Gaikoku Kankei Monjo*, X, 349-51, Nagasaki bugyō to Stirling, 19 May 1855.

[63] F.O. *China Corres.*, vol. 240, Stirling to Adty., No. 51, 19 May 1855, in Adty. to For. Off., 18 Aug. 1855.

Japan, and did not wish to give the Admiralty too clear a picture of his intentions or of the methods such a course might entail, for fear they should tie his hands by issuing some over-cautious set of orders.

Before returning to Nagasaki, Stirling paid a visit to Hakodate to obtain copies of the port regulations and of the Russian treaty with Japan. His immediate interest in the latter was that section which defined the frontier between Russian and Japanese territories in the north, knowledge vital to him in planning attacks on the Russian settlements. For the moment, this was the only point on which he was prepared to insist, and he accordingly accepted instead of the treaty itself an abstract of the desired information, given him with a promise that he should have a copy of the whole treaty as soon as it became available.[64]

The Hakodate *bugyō*, although he denied it to Stirling, did in fact have a copy of the treaty. He was reluctant to reveal its terms because it opened Shimoda to the Russians in addition to Hakodate and Nagasaki, and allowed them to purchase supplies in the open market, privileges which the British would undoubtedly wish to claim under the most-favoured-nation clause of Stirling's convention. The *bugyō* declined to take such a responsibility without instructions from the Rōjū,[65] and in this he rightly judged the attitude of his superiors. They had already warned Shimoda that the British might insist on using that port, but that it was most undesirable that they should come so close to Edo and every effort must be made to discourage them. Similar instructions were sent to Hakodate. The *bugyō*'s previous decision was commended, and he was ordered to continue withholding the complete copy of the Russian treaty as long as that proved practicable.[66] The attitude did not augur well for the success of Stirling's negotiations at Nagasaki.

[64] *Bakumatsu Gaikoku Kankei Monjo*, XII, 14-5, Hakodate bugyō to Stirling, 21 July 1855; XII, 15-6, translation, Stirling to Hakodate bugyō, 21 July 1855.
[65] *Bakumatsu Gaikoku Kankei Monjo*, XII, 8-10, Hakodate bugyō to Rōjū, 19 July 1855.
[66] *Bakumatsu Gaikoku Kankei Monjo*, XI, 439-40, Rōjū to Shimoda bugyō, 11 July 1855; XII, 80-1, Rōjū to Hakodate bugyō, 3 Aug. 1855; XII, 94-5, Rōjū to Hakodate bugyō, 9 Aug. 1855.

By the time the admiral joined Commodore Elliot at Nagasaki at the end of September, the Japanese had been able to check the translation of his ratification which they had copied in May. The officials in Edo responsible for coast defence and foreign relations, comparing it with the Japanese text, found a few minor discrepancies in the wording of the article permitting ships in distress to enter Japanese ports for shelter, and proposed that when the ratifications were exchanged—an event they could see no means of preventing—Stirling should be asked to give a private undertaking that the Japanese version be accepted as the master-text. This proved unnecessary in the event, for Curtius was able to assure the *bugyō* that there was no essential difference in meaning between the two.[67] Nothing was said of the most-favoured-nation clause or the points raised by Stirling in May. Unlike Stirling, the Japanese had assumed that the matter ended with their rejection of his proposals. The only instructions known to have been sent to the Nagasaki *bugyō* by the Rōjū directed him to exchange ratifications in the same manner as had been used for the American treaty, and to grant the right to use Shimoda only if he could find no possible way of avoiding it.[68]

1 October was the date set by Stirling for the exchange of ratifications.[69] By 29 September eleven British and two French warships were gathered at Nagasaki, an exhibition of force which the admiral thought 'not without advantage '.[70] Some days passed before all questions arising out of the translation of the two documents had been settled,

[67] *Bakumatsu Gaikoku Kankei Monjo*, XII, 38-40, Kaibō-kakari kanjō-bugyō to Rōjū, 24 July 1855 ; XII, 346-7, Nagasaki interpreters to bugyō, 1855, 8th month (11 Sept.–10 Oct.).

[68] *Bakumatsu Gaikoku Kankei Monjo*, X, 240-1, Rōjū minute on Nagasaki bugyō to Rōjū, 1855, 3rd month (17 Apr.–15 May ; presumably 15 May, date of Stirling's request).

[69] F.O. *China Corres.*, vol. 255, Adty. to For. Off., 5 Jan. 1856, enclosed Stirling's full report on the negotiations, including Stirling to Adty., No. 78, 8 Nov. 1855 ; Diary of Events and Conferences kept by Capt. Currie (cited as Currie's Diary of Events) ; Journal of Conferences kept by Capt. Wilson of H.M.S. *Winchester* (cited as Wilson's Journal of Conferences). Parl. Papers 1856, vol. LXI (Cd. 2077), pp. 229-34 omits important passages from Stirling's dispatch and the whole of both diaries.

[70] Admiralty, *In-Letters*, vol. 5657, Stirling to Adty., No. 74, Nagasaki, 1 Oct. 1855.

but at last the negotiators exchanged notes affirming that the ratifications agreed with the texts of the convention as signed in the previous year, and on the morning of 9 October the formal ceremony of exchange took place.[71]

Not till this was done did Stirling turn to other matters. He knew that he had no power to treat and was ' thereby prevented from being a party to new conditions ',[72] and for this reason had resisted Japanese attempts to discuss points of interpretation during the first week's meetings. However he, too, was capable of observing the letter rather than the spirit of the law. Once the ratifications were exchaged, he shed the character of a diplomatic representative charged by his instructions with a single mission and unable to go beyond them, and reverted to that of naval Commander-in-Chief, whose duty it would be to see that British ships observed the provisions of the treaty just ratified. In this new capacity he drew up what he called ' a liberal Explanation ' of the convention's terms and began the task of obtaining from the Japanese ' their formal assent to as much of that exposition as they might be induced to concur in '.[73]

The admiral already knew something of the terms of the Russian and American treaties, copies of which he had demanded from the Japanese, and had announced that he considered Shimoda automatically opened to British ships under the most-favoured-nation clause of his own convention.[74] His exposition dealt rather with practical details of the treatment to be accorded British ships in the treaty ports. In effect, Stirling's ' liberal Explanation ' was equivalent to a demand for considerable changes both in the treaty and in the port regulations. It assumed the opening of the inner harbour at Nagasaki as a matter of right, provided for a hospital and burial-ground there and claimed

[71] F.O. *China Corres.*, vol. 255, Currie's Diary of Events and Wilson's Journal of Conferences for 1-9 Oct. 1855. *Bakumatsu Gaikoku Kankei Monjo*, XII, 367-84, Japanese minutes of conference, 9 Oct. 1855.

[72] Parl. Papers 1856, vol. LXI (Cd. 2077), pp. 229-30, Stirling to Adty., No. 78, 8 Nov. 1855.

[73] F.O. *China Corres.*, vol. 255, Stirling to Adty., No. 78, 8 Nov. 1855.

[74] F.O. *China Corres.*, vol. 255, Wilson's Journal of Conferences, 9 Oct. 1855. *Bakumatsu Gaikoku Kankei Monjo*, XII, 373-4, Japanese minutes of conference, 9 Oct. 1855.

the right of visitors to go ashore, all contrary to the existing arrangements ; it even included a statement to the effect that the Japanese would not ' impose unnecessary restrictions ' on British ships and subjects. The document further maintained that although breach of the laws might lead to the closing of the ports, no act of an individual, if it were neither authorised nor approved by his government, could set aside a treaty between sovereign rulers. It insisted that British warships could visit any Japanese port on showing good reason, whether it be officially open or not. Finally, it stated specifically that the Dutch and Chinese privileges excepted from the most-favoured-nation clause were only those ' existing previous to the 14th of October 1854 '.[75] It was on these points—apart from a few minor questions of phrasing—that the negotiations turned.

Stirling presented this draft to the two *bugyō* at a meeting ashore on 11 October. At that meeting and at later dis-discussions he employed two interpreters, the Japanese castaway Rikimatsu, borrowed from Commodore Elliot's squadron, and a surgeon from the flagship who had been learning Dutch specially for the purpose. Between them they prevented any such major misunderstandings as had occurred the year before. In handing over the draft, Stirling impressed on the Japanese that he did not regard it as a basis for discussion. It was his own interpretation of the treaty and must be wholly accepted or wholly rejected by them. If they did not accept it as accurate, then the matter was incapable of solution at Nagasaki and must be referred to Edo and London. He had not mentioned Shimoda, Stirling explained, because he considered it to have been opened automatically to British use by the operation of the most-favoured-nation clause. Other privileges might accrue from the Russian treaty, a copy of which he would expect to be ready for him when he sent a ship to fetch it in sixty days' time.[76]

[75] The text of this draft exposition is given as Appendix B, pp. 207-9, which also shows changes made in it as a result of the subsequent discussions.

[76] F.O. *China Corres.*, vol. 255, Wilson's Journal of Conferences and Currie's Diary of Events, 11 Oct. 1855. *Bakumatsu Gaikoku Kankei Monjo*, XII, 423-37, Japanese minutes of conference, 11 Oct. 1855.

Since the exposition would have to be translated before more could be done, the meeting of 11 October consisted of little more than Stirling's statement—which had many of the characteristics of an ultimatum. It was, in fact, four days before the two *bugyō* made any reply. On 15 October they sent to say that they could give no answer to the draft, since it touched on matters not contained in the treaty and was therefore outside their province, a reply very similar to that which had terminated the discussions in May.

This time Stirling was not prepared to accept such an answer as final. He warned the Japanese that their intransigent policy might force him to refer the whole question of the convention to his government, making it his own duty meanwhile ' to see that it is carried into full effect on both sides '.[77] Next day he stated that he would expect to receive, by the ship which was to fetch a copy of the Russian treaty, ' a full and distinct acceptance . . . or a specific refusal ' of his exposition, failing which he would go to Edo and demand one there.[78] The threat was enough to bring the offer of another conference ashore for the morning of 17 October.

This new meeting was no more successful than preceding ones. Stirling began by claiming that British ships had every right to enter the inner harbour at Nagasaki, since the convention expressly opened the port of Nagasaki and must necessarily be understood to mean the whole of that port. The *bugyō* denied this. He preferred to take his stand on the wording of the port regulations, which had been accepted in the previous year under Article II of the convention. Neither was willing to discuss a compromise. Stirling continued to insist on a specific answer, and when it became clear that none would be forthcoming he stormed out of the conference-room with the parting threat that he would immediately notify his government that the treaty had been broken by Japan, since the port of Nagasaki was not in fact open to British ships. He had little doubt, he

[77] F.O. *China Corres.*, vol. 255, Wilson's Journal of Conferences, 15 Oct. 1855.
[78] *ibid.*, 16 Oct. 1855.

said, that he would receive orders to enforce the treaty, ' to carry it out with a high hand '.[79]

With some difficulty the admiral was persuaded to wait for ten minutes while the two *bugyō* considered his terms in private consultation. The only result of their conference, however, was that they offered to send to Edo and get an answer within sixty days, provided that in the interval no British ship was to enter the inner harbour. At this Stirling again lost patience, and threatened to go out to the flagship and bring his entire force without further delay past the war-junks guarding the harbour entrance. The fear of open hostilities which this might cause brought the *bugyō* to terms. They agreed to admit the ships then present at Nagasaki, emphasising that this was all they had power to grant, and that the treatment of future squadrons must be left to the decision of the Bakufu.[80] With that temporary solution, consideration of the other points at issue was postponed to a meeting arranged for the following day.

When discussions were resumed on the morning of 18 October, the *bugyō* at once agreed to the clause opening ' the whole and every part ' of each of the treaty ports. This put Stirling in a tractable mood. He agreed to strike out the reference to a hospital and fix on a site for the burial ground, and when the *bugyō* objected to the right of landing which had been inserted in the exposition of Article I, contented himself with remarking that it seemed a necessary corollary of opening the ports, but might be omitted pending reference to the two governments. Article II was accepted with minor changes, and surprisingly enough, after a tedious discussion of detail, so was the right of warships to visit ports not opened by treaty. Article IV presented no difficulties.

The interpretation of Article V, the most-favoured-nation clause, brought fresh disputes, however. The *bugyō*

[79] F.O. *China Corres.*, vol. 255, Wilson's Journal of Conferences, 17 Oct. 1855.

[80] F.O. *China Corres.*, vol. 255, Wilson's Journal of Conferences, 17 Oct. 1855. *Bakumatsu Gaikoku Kankei Monjo*, XII, 479-86, Nagasaki bugyō and metsuke to Rōjū, 19 Oct. 1855; XII, 448-58, Japanese minutes of conference, 17 Oct. 1855.

objected to any mention of rights of residence, and assured Stirling that Japan had no intention of granting such privileges to any nation. Since the point was in any case covered by the wording of the clause in general, its omission was no great matter. But over Dutch and Chinese privileges there was complete deadlock. Stirling argued that it had always been his intention that only rights enjoyed by those nations *before* his own convention was signed should be excluded from the operation of the most-favoured-nation clause. Kawamura, on the other hand, maintained that in 1854 it had been agreed to exclude them altogether from the operation of the article, which thus entitled Britain to share neither existing nor future privileges granted to Dutch and Chinese in Japan. He even tried to persuade Stirling to alter the original convention to conform to this view. This, of course, the admiral refused to do, but as neither side would give way, the offending phrase was struck out of the exposition and left like others to the decision of the two governments.[81]

Next day officials came off to the *Winchester* to make a last attempt to get Article V of the convention amended to meet their ideas, but found Stirling obdurate. Indeed, he told them that the only change to which he might agree would be to cancel the existing agreement in its entirety and substitute the much more generous terms granted by Ieyasu to the English East India Company in 1613. He even gave them a copy of the document for future reference.[82]

Since further discussion was clearly useless, English and Japanese copies of the amended exposition were exchanged on 19 October, and next day Stirling sailed. Although he did not know it, the Japanese version differed from his own on one important point.[83] To meet objections, he had

[81] F.O. *China Corres.*, vol. 255, Wilson's Journal of Conferences and Currie's Diary of Events, 18 Oct. 1855. *Bakumatsu Gaikoku Kankei Monjo*, XII, 458-70, Japanese minutes of conference, 18 Oct. 1855.

[82] F.O. *China Corres.*, vol. 255, Wilson's Journal of Conferences, 19 Oct. 1855.

[83] For the English text see Appendix B, pp. 207-9. The Japanese text handed to Stirling is in F.O. *Protocols of Treaties, Japan*, I (F.O. 93/49-1). The Japanese version retained by the Bakufu, showing what are presumably later corrections, appears in *Bakumatsu Gaikoku Kankei Monjo*, XII, 437-42.

removed the expression 'existing previous to the 14th of October 1854' from that part of the English text which dealt with the exemption of Dutch and Chinese privileges from the most-favoured-nation provision. Elsewhere in the same article, however, they were referred to as those privileges ' hitherto conceded' to Dutch and Chinese, so that the change made the clause less specific but not essentially different in meaning. There were no corresponding alterations in the Japanese text handed to Stirling on 19 October. Under Article V it gave a direct translation of Stirling's original draft, including the disputed passages, followed by a note to the effect that agreement had not been reached in this article, which therefore remained in abeyance. This was an accurate statement of the position.

The Japanese text retained by the Bakufu provides yet a third variant. It applied to the translation of Stirling's original draft the same kind of corrections made in the English version—omission of some phrases, small changes in others—and since there can have been no time to draw it up on 19 October, must represent either the working copy used by the *bugyō* during the negotiations, or a fair copy made after Stirling's departure. With one exception, its terms correspond with those published in Britain. The exception is in Article V. The literary style (*sōrōbun*) used in the Japanese had no past tense, and this resulted in one important difference in meaning between the two versions. The removal of the date from the reference to Dutch and Chinese privileges in the Bakufu copy made it possible for the exemption to apply equally to future as to past concessions, which was undoubtedly the result the *bugyō* had intended to achieve by insisting on the date's omission. This was the interpretation on which the Japanese subsequently took their stand—another source of dispute which was a by-product of faulty translation.

Stirling's claim that the negotiations had been conducted ' with the utmost goodwill' and the exposition obtained ' without solicitation or menace '[84] is hardly borne out by

[84] F.O. *China Corres.*, vol. 255, Stirling to Adty., No. 78, 8 Nov. 1855.

the British, still less by the Japanese records. Even so, at least one of the British officers present at Nagasaki condemned him for getting so little with so strong a squadron, and thought his weakness might make it necessary later 'to strike a blow instead of pursuing the more magnanimous policy of only exhibiting strength '.[85]

Indeed, the negotiations had achieved very little. Stirling thought he had gained his points about the movement of warships and the right to enter Nagasaki's inner harbour, but both were subject to confirmation by Edo and were destined to arise again. He himself admitted that the very important questions of landing and the application of the most-favoured-nation clause to Dutch and Chinese privileges would have to be left until he received instructions from Her Majesty's Government. Yet he was satisfied that his two agreements together constituted ' as good a Treaty with Japan as any other nation has acquired or can by any possibility acquire hereafter '.[86] This was natural enough, for Stirling thought in terms of war and naval bases, not in terms of trade. To him, the justification for his actions lay in the statement that during 1855 Japan had been ' as useful to us as a British Colony in that locality ',[87] for he was well aware that naval superiority could turn an equal into an exclusive advantage.

Stirling's grandiose plans for the future throw additional light on the objectives he had set himself in Japan. He saw in Manchuria, ' the Turkey of the Eastern Seas ', the key to the Pacific trade as well as to the defence of China and India against Russia, and therefore the key to British power in the Far East. He wished Britain to extend her trade because of the revenue and influence it would bring, and to the same end she must suppress piracy and protect the coasting trade in the western Pacific, open all the ports of northeast Asia, obtain a new treaty with China and use to the full the resources of neighbouring countries. To accomplish this might require the use of force. Certainly

[85] Whittingham, *Expedition*, pp. 214-5.
[86] F.O. *China Corres.*, vol. 255, Stirling to Adty., No. 78, 8 Nov. 1855.
[87] *ibid.*

it must be accompanied by an unchallengeable naval supremacy in Pacific waters. ' In other words ', he wrote, ' we must establish a Maritime Empire with all its concomitant adjuncts of Naval Positions, Postal Communications, Hydrographical Surveys, and Steam Factories and Dockyards '.[88] In his own estimation, Stirling had made a beginning in Japan.

Stirling's personal views were representative of a section of British opinion which might justly be characterised as " imperialist ", but which was not dominant in Whitehall. Because he was in a position to put those ideas into practice in Japan at a time when detailed control of policy from London was an impossibility, they had, in the years 1854 and 1855, manifested themselves in action. Moreover, his conduct was officially commended[89] and his agreements ratified. His policy, however, did not thereby become official policy, for it was his results, not his objectives, that were acceptable. His plans for the future were never adopted by the Foreign Office and Board of Trade. Nor did they regard his convention as in the least satisfactory. They accepted it, in fact, not as the prelude to a new maritime empire, but because it might pave the way thereafter for some form of commercial agreement. Stirling's negotiations were in that sense a digression in the development of British policy towards Japan.

The admiral himself was to play no further part in the story. In 1856 he was recalled because he had failed in the primary naval duty of finding and destroying the Russian squadron[90]—partly, perhaps, because of his preoccupation with the self-imposed task of negotiating with Japan. For the future, British relations with Japan were to be conducted through more normal diplomatic channels.

---

[88] Admiralty, *In-Letters*, vol. 5660, Memoir on the Maritime Policy of England in the Eastern Seas, in Stirling to Sir C. Wood, private, Hongkong, 15 Nov. 1855.

[89] Parl. Papers 1856, vol. LXI (Cd. 2077), p. 235, For. Off. to Adty., 21 Jan. 1856.

[90] Admiralty, *In-Letters*, vol. 5672, Stirling to Adty., No. 101, 11 Dec. 1855 and No. 11, 8 Dec. 1856, and Admiralty minutes thereon.

CHAPTER VI

SIR JOHN BOWRING AND THE FOREIGN OFFICE : 1854–1857

STIRLING's diplomacy was not greeted with enthusiasm on the China coast. The *China Mail*, which represented chiefly the views of the Hongkong merchants, condemned it in no uncertain terms. It compared his convention unfavourably with that of Perry and ridiculed the Foreign Office for ratifying an agreement which entitled Britain only to pay dearly for stores originally provided free of charge.[1] Moreover, it said, in his preoccupation with this 'precious treaty' with Japan, Stirling had neglected the more important duty of protecting British ships and subjects in China. In the midst of dangers arising out of the T'aip'ing Rebellion and the Russian war, he had achieved 'nothing creditable to the arms of his country, and something rather discreditable to his own diplomacy'.[2] Even in the fleet similar sentiments were expressed.[3]

In England there was less criticism of this kind. On the other hand Stirling received little direct support. *The Times* gave no prominence to news of the convention and published the official correspondence without comment.[4] The subject was raised twice in the House of Commons during question time[5] but on each occasion it appeared as a request for information rather than a discussion of policy or results. In fact, public interest was centred on the Crimean War and events in Japan attracted very little attention.

[1] *China Mail*, 2 Nov. 1854, 9 Aug. 1855, 19 June 1856.
[2] *China Mail*, 25 Oct. 1855.
[3] Osborn, *A Cruise in Japanese Waters*, pp. 90-1.
[4] London *Times*, 16 Jan. and 7 May 1856.
[5] Hansard, *Parliamentary Debates*, 3rd Ser., vol. CXXXVIII, col. 834, Commons, 21 May 1855; vol. CXL, cols. 832-3, Commons, 15 Feb. 1856.

In 1854 the Foreign Office had decided to ratify the convention, but this meant no more than that there seemed to be some value in it. Clarendon did not necessarily think it satisfactory or approve of all its provisions. Stirling's own argument had been that the agreement was of immediate practical value and at the same time gave Britain equal advantages in Japan with all but the Dutch and Chinese. To him Japan was of greatest importance strategically, as a British foothold in northeast Asia where future dominance could be more surely attained if trade were postponed. The activities of British merchants, he said, judged by their record in China, seemed more likely to destroy confidence and cause Japan to deny Britain use of her invaluable harbours, coal and timber than to bring closer co-operation.[6]

Sir John Bowring, by contrast, was more interested in trading privileges. Comparing the terms of the convention with those he had been instructed to obtain, he came to the conclusion that Clarendon would not ratify. Whether ratified or not, however, he thought the existence of such an agreement would ' greatly add to the difficulties of after negotiations '.[7] He was most indignant at Stirling's action in assuming in this way functions properly belonging to the Superintendent,[8] and although he announced in March that he had accepted the Admiral's offer of a personal reconciliation,[9] he continued to comment bitterly on the terms of the convention and the policy that had produced it. He was obviously offended, too, that Clarendon decided to ratify despite these criticisms.[10]

Bowring's criticisms were reflected in London, where discussions between government departments continued

[6] Admiralty, *In-Letters*, vol. 5640, Stirling to Adty., No. 71, 26 Oct. 1854; Vol. 5657, Stirling to Graham, private, 27 Oct. 1854.
[7] F.O. *China Corres.*, vol. 217, Bowring to For. Off., No. 198, 29 Nov. 1854, recd. F.O. 27 Jan. 1855.
[8] *Clarendon Papers.* C vol. 19, ff. 527-8, Bowring to Clarendon, 26 Nov. 1854, ff. 549-50, same to same, 12 Dec. 1854 ; ff. 553-63, same to same, 18 Dec. 1854-5 Jan. 1855.
[9] *Clarendon Papers*, C vol. 37, ff. 173-4, Bowring to Clarendon, 7 Mar. 1855.
[10] *Clarendon Papers*, C vol. 37, ff. 198-9, Bowring to Clarendon, 7 May 1855.

despite the decision to ratify. The Board of Trade, rightly observing that the convention had ' very little to do with trade ', had not originally intended to take any action beyond arranging for the forms of identification to be carried by British ships.[11] When later requested to comment officially for Clarendon's information, it did so in distinctly unfavourable terms. The Board believed that the chief value of the convention lay in establishing relations with Japan through which trade might eventually be arranged, but confessed to some misgivings about the effect of the last article which denied the right of any ' High Officer ' to change the terms of the agreement in the future. It urged Clarendon to consider whether future negotiations ' might not be embarrassed if not precluded altogether by the retention in a Treaty of indefinite duration, of a provision which expressly pronounces the existing arrangements to be unalterable '.[12]

The Foreign Office came to Stirling's defence. Hammond, the permanent under-secretary, characterised the Board's letter as ' flippant ' and drafted a reply denying its interpretation of Article VII. The convention was not, he thought, ' of so immutable a nature as the Lords of the Committee apprehend ' ; first, because Article VII was intended only to prevent alteration by the commanders of ships, not by formally accredited diplomats ; second, because the most-favoured-nation clause would entitle Britain to share in the benefits obtained by other countries, and its inclusion implied that the Japanese expected to grant such benefits ; finally, because the prohibition of trade appeared not in the treaty itself, but in the Nagasaki port regulations, which could be changed without in any way altering the wording of the convention.[13] The arguments were not strictly accurate nor entirely compatible with each other. However, they indicated that the Foreign Office did not intend to be blocked at the outset of its relations with

[11] F.O. *China Corres.*, vol. 238, Cardwell (Bd. Trade) to Hammond, private, 24 Jan. 1855.
[12] F.O. *China Corres.*, vol. 238, Bd. Trade to For. Off., 30 Jan. 1855.
[13] F.O. *China Corres.*, vol. 238, Hammond minutes on Bd. Trade to For. Off., 30 Jan. 1855, and draft For. Off. to Bd. Trade, 8 Feb. 1855.

Japan by Stirling's inexperience in drawing up diplomatic documents.

Neither Bowring nor the Foreign Office showed any immediate inclination to give effect to these views or to take any positive steps to improve on Stirling's arrangement. The instructions given to Bowring in the previous year still held good. His plans to visit Japan had been postponed, not abandoned, when events in China and the outbreak of war had together made it impossible to spare the naval force which he thought indispensable to success. On the other hand, he regarded Stirling's convention not as a help but as a hindrance. He thought it would multiply the difficulties facing any attempt to negotiate a commercial treaty because of the precedent it had created, and, as he reported to Clarendon, this made him reluctant to undertake the mission. In his next dispatch on the subject, he recommended that these difficulties could best be overcome by sending a joint British and French squadron to Edo.[14] Since this was a course that could only be adopted after consultation between the two governments, it is clear that Bowring was not contemplating any immediate action.

Both these dispatches arrived in London on the same day. Apparently unwilling to force an issue in Japan while the Russian war still demanded so much of his attention, Clarendon decided that it would not be 'expedient' for Bowring to go there for the present and wrote to him accordingly.[15] However, in March 1855, before this dispatch reached Hongkong, Bowring changed his mind again and announced his intention of joining Stirling's fleet in the north as soon as the Siam mission, which had been planned for the spring of that year, had been completed.[16] The

---

[14] F.O. *China Corres.*, vol. 217, Bowring to For. Off., No. 192, 27 Nov. 1854 and No. 198, 29 Nov. 1854.

[15] F.O. *China Corres.*, vol. 217, Clarendon minute on Bowring to For. Off., No. 192, 27 Nov. 1854; vol. 224, For. Off. to Bowring, No. 51, 10 Feb. 1855. A later letter of Clarendon's throws some light on this decision. In June 1855 he told Bowring that Britain could only hope to check Russian progress in the Far East while the war lasted and that it was therefore 'very important to be on friendly terms with Japan'. (*Clarendon Papers*, C vol. 132, ff. 548-51).

[16] F.O. *China Corres.*, vol. 228, Bowring to For. Off., No. 131, 10 Mar., 1855.

exact purpose of this move was not specified, but Clarendon accepted it without comment. It was never carried out, however. Bowring had only suggested it with reluctance. Stirling, he said, had been 'jockied and jilted and laughed at by the Japanese' and the whole affair so 'botched and bungled' that he was quite unable to see his own way clearly. The only hope of success lay in providing him with naval support and complete authority to prevent any independent action by the admiral. Without such instructions he was unwilling to go to Japan at all.[17] When, therefore, he received Clarendon's dispatch of 10 February approving the earlier proposal to defer action for the time being, he gladly abandoned all thought of joining the fleet that spring.[18]

There the matter would presumably have rested had it been left entirely to Bowring's initiative. During the summer, however, Clarendon took up the question once more, and this time issued more positive directions. In April 1855 a Liverpool merchant had written to the Foreign Office for information about the terms of what he believed to be a commercial treaty negotiated by Stirling. When told that it actually made no provision for trade, he promptly pointed out that the Americans intended to trade under Perry's convention and urged the importance of obtaining a similar privilege for Britain, a statement which led Clarendon to call for a detailed comparison of the British and American agreements.[19]

The comparison of the two treaties was drawn up at the Foreign Office in July. It showed that the essential difference between them was that Perry had secured the right, under certain conditions, of exchanging coin and goods for Japanese products, which seemed tantamount to permitting

[17] *Clarendon Papers*, C vol. 37, ff. 200-3, Bowring to Clarendon, 29 May 1853. See also *ibid.*, ff. 198-9, same to same, 7 May 1855.
[18] F.O. *China Corres.*, vol. 230, Bowring to For. Off., No. 151, 14 May 1855 and No. 153, 15 May 1855; vol. 232, Bowring to For. Off., No. 249, 14 July 1855.
[19] F.O. *China Corres.*, vol. 239, Campbell to For. Off., 13 Apr. 1855; For. Off. to Campbell, 18 Apr. 1855; Campbell to For. Off., 23 Apr. 1855, and Clarendon minute thereon.

trade. This raised the question of how far the most-favoured-nation clause of Stirling's convention would enentitle Britain to do the same. Clarendon's first reaction was to order Bowring to sound the Japanese on this point. If they refused to admit such an interpretation, then he must take steps to amend the convention in such a way as to put British citizens visiting Japan on an equal footing with American. When it came to drafting a dispatch on the subject, however, the Foreign Secretary realised that it might be wiser to assume that there could be no doubt about British rights. He therefore amended the wording of his instructions. In their final form they ordered the plenipotentiary, without equivocation or condition, to claim from the Japanese ' whatever benefits, commercial or other, have been secured by the United States '.[20]

So explicit an order was not at all to Bowring's taste. During the summer he had been confirmed in his estimate of the difficulties in the way of obtaining a satisfactory treaty with Japan by reports that the Japanese consistently repudiated Perry's interpretation of the American treaty and had refused to admit Americans to residence or trade. Both in private letters and official dispatches he repeated his view that any British mission must be well supplied with warships and be completely under his own control. Indeed, he thought the situation so little encouraging that in August 1855 he wrote home to ask that even if it were decided to persist in the attempt to get a new agreement, he should himself be given discretion to decide the moment at which to make it.[21] He was, therefore, ' greatly embarrassed ' by the new instructions when they arrived in September. And he raised numerous objections. The Japanese recognised

[20] F.O. *China Corres.*, vol. 225, For. Off. to Bowring, No. 150, 27 July 1855. See also minutes on this dispatch and *ibid.*, vol. 240, For. Off. memo. of 20 July 1855 and Clarendon minute thereon ; *Clarendon Papers*, C Vol. 133, ff. 307-10, Clarendon to Bowring, 9 Aug. 1855, instructs the Superintendent that his three immediate tasks are to take Petropavlovsk, put an end to piracy, ' and come to a clear understanding with Japan about the Treaty with us being the same as with the U.S.'
[21] F.O. *China Corres.*, vol. 232, Bowring to For. Off., No. 249, 14 July 1855 ; vol. 233, same to same, No. 282, 24 Aug. 1855 ; *Clarendon Papers*, C vol. 37, Bowring to Clarendon, 5 Aug. 1855.

only the Dutch and Chinese as having any right to trade, and their rights were specifically excluded from the operation of Stirling's most-favoured-nation clause ; Article VII would cause difficulties in any attempt to revise the convention, and it would be impossible for him to submit to the port regulations which Stirling had accepted ; finally, the fleet was away (Stirling was then on his way to Nagasaki for the exchange of ratifications) which meant that the Superintendent had no immediate means of going to Japan.[22] It is clear, in fact, that Bowring was determined to avoid action if at all possible until he received an answer to his frequent requests for greater authority over the movements of the fleet. Fortunately the fleet did not return until the beginning of the northerly monsoon in October, and this enabled him to declare that a visit to Japan was now out of the question until the wind changed in the spring of 1856. Moreover, the same month brought news of Stirling's new diplomatic endeavour, negotiation of the Exposition of the 1854 convention, which gave fresh cause for seeking further instructions from the Foreign Office.[23]

Thus for the greater part of 1855 Bowring's reluctance to risk failure, and still more his hostility to Stirling, which led him to make extravagant demands for extending his own authority over the naval forces in China, had served to prevent any regular diplomatic mission to Japan. The Foreign Office, moreover, was content to await the Superintendent's action. Clarendon had never intended to dictate the timing of the expedition. His orders had referred to the terms he wished Bowring to obtain, and he had not meant to imply that the plenipotentiary must proceed posthaste to implement them. In December he readily approved Bowring's request that the date of the mission be left as a matter for decision at Hongkong.[24] On the same day he wrote a private letter to make it clear that despite the

---

[22] F.O. *China Corres.*, vol. 233, Bowring to For. Off., No. 309, 25 Sept. 1855.
[23] F.O. *China Corres.*, vol. 234, Bowring to For. Off., No. 326, 12 Oct. 1855, and No. 345, 29 Oct. 1855.
[24] F.O. *China Corres.*, vol. 225, For. Off. to Bowring, No. 233, 8 Dec. 1855.

difficulties, he expected Bowring to go to Japan 'as soon as practicable' and do the best he could there.[25]

Similarly, the Foreign Secretary refused to change his views about the interpretation of the Stirling convention, despite Bowring's opposition. The latter had announced the agreement in the *Hongkong Gazette* in July 1855, copying the official notice from the *London Gazette*, which, as he pointed out, made no mention of the port regulations restricting its application. In October Clarendon told him that he should also make public the terms on which trade could be carried on.[26] Bowring thereupon reiterated his opinion that no trade was permitted by the convention, which accounted for his 'hesitation in encouraging commercial adventures to Japan'.[27] When Clarendon replied that he saw no reason why traders should be discouraged from making the attempt so long as they were warned of the risks involved, the plenipotentiary countered maliciously that no discouragement was needed. Merchants, he said, showed no inclination to go to Japan under British registry.[28] It was a view for which he was able to muster considerable evidence.[29]

Meanwhile Stirling's exposition had been causing fresh discussions of interpretation and policy. On 5 January 1856, the Foreign Office received from the Admiralty a full account of the negotiations which followed the exchange of ratifications at Nagasaki. Stirling and the Nagasaki *bugyō* had left two disputed points for reference to their respective governments ; the first, whether the opening of the ports necessarily included the right of landing, as Stirling maintained ; the second, whether the Dutch and Chinese

[25] *Clarendon Papers*, C vol. 134, ff. 415-20, Clarendon to Bowring, 8 Dec. 1855. The letter also denied the rumour (somewhat petulantly reported by Bowring) that Stirling had been entrusted with the task of negotiating with Japan, and rebuked the Superintendent for constantly repeating his requests for ships for objects not directly related to the war.
[26] F.O. *China Corres.*, vol 232, Bowring to For. Off., No. 256, 28 July 1855 ; vol. 225, For. Off. to Bowring, No. 210, 8 Oct. 1855.
[27] F.O. *China Corres.*, vol. 235, Bowring to For. Off., No. 389, 4 Dec. 1855.
[28] F.O. *China Corres.*, vol. 242, For. Off. to Bowring, No. 60, 21 Feb. 1856; vol. 246, Bowring to For. Off., No. 142, 29 Apr. 1856.
[29] F.O. *China Corres.*, vol. 256, Bowring to Col. Off., Commercial No. 19, 1 Feb. 1856 in Col. Off. to For. Off., 18 Apr. 1856 ; vol. 246, Bowring to For. Off., No. 135, 21 Apr. 1856 ; vol. 250, same to same, No. 308, 29 Sept. 1856.

privileges excepted from the operation of the most-favoured-nation clause should be limited to those existing when the convention was signed. The Foreign Office upheld Stirling on both points. It asked the Admiralty to instruct him that he should ' courteously acquaint ' the Japanese of this fact were he to visit Japan again before Bowring. However, the *bugyō* had promised to obtain decisions from Edo on these matters, and there was some prospect that they would be favourable, or alternatively that as contacts increased, Japanese hostility would abate and cause such difficulties to disappear. Clarendon therefore concluded that for the time ' it would be well to avoid any practical misunderstanding with the Japanese authorities.'[30]

Two weeks later the Board of Trade forwarded its opinion on the exposition. Basically, the Board's ideas were the same as those it had expressed in the previous year, but it saw some new difficulties over Dutch and Chinese privileges. The exposition seemed to cloud rather than clarify this issue. While its intention was clear enough, the actual wording was self-contradictory and might be taken to mean that the ports of Hakodate and Nagasaki were themselves excluded from the operation of the most-favoured-nation clause. The Board suggested that the best course would be to undertake fresh negotiations to remove the obscurity.[31]

On 4 February the Board of Trade's letter was sent to the Admiralty for Stirling's information. Since it appeared to contradict the Foreign Office instructions of the previous month, and was not accompanied by any Foreign Office comment, the Admiralty asked whether it was intended that Stirling be ordered to open the fresh negotiations which the Board of Trade proposed.[32] This was far from being Clarendon's intention. He had earlier described Stirling's handling of the most-favoured-nation clause as ' a bungle ' and was determined that Bowring should make the next visit to Japan. For this reason he had been careful to amend his

---

[30] Foreign Office, General Correspondence, *Japan* (F.O. 46 ; hereafter cited as F.O. *Japan Corres.*), vol. 1, For. Off. to Adty., 21 Jan. 1856.
[31] F.O. *Japan Corres.*, vol. 1, Bd. Trade to For. Off., 4 Feb. 1856.
[32] F.O. *Japan Corres.*, vol. 1, For. Off. to Adty., 6 Feb. 1856 ; Adty. to For. Off., 7 Feb. 1856.

earlier letter to the Admiralty so as to avoid giving the impression that any special action was required from Stirling.[33] He now put a definite end to Stirling's unauthorised career as a diplomat. On receipt of the Admiralty letter the Treaty Department at the Foreign Office observed that the admiral could do little good and might do some harm by going specially to discuss the points at issue. Since the convention was in any case only 'the thin end of the wedge', it recommended that negotiations be left until Bowring could revise the agreement more thoroughly. At Clarendon's direction, a reply was sent to the Admiralty in these terms.[34]

Copies of this correspondence were sent to Bowring,[35] but although it seemed clear that he was expected to act on the opinions expressed, he was not directly ordered to do so. Bowring himself was convinced that the exposition, like the original convention, had made his task all the harder. In this view he was confirmed by the Board of Trade's arguments. His experience was, he said, that oriental nations excelled in ' verbal controversies ' such as would arise over the exact meaning of the convention and its exposition. The Foreign Office had claimed that the sense of the convention precluded the Japanese from imposing such port regulations as they had introduced at Nagasaki, but Bowring failed to see the force of this reasoning. No ' vague generality ' could supersede ' a specific condition '. Even Stirling had never claimed that this treaty permitted trade. And the Superintendent rejected with scorn any idea that other nations be left ' to open the doors through which we may hereafter enter '. Britain's dignity would not permit her to wait for such privileges as were likely to be arranged by ' inferior maritime powers '.[36]

The fact was that Bowring had already evolved a different plan of his own. It was one which would enable him to

[33] F.O. *Japan Corres.*, vol. 1, Clarendon notes and alterations on draft, For. Off. to Adty., 21 Jan. 1856.
[34] F.O. *Japan Corres.*, vol. 1, F.O. minutes on Adty. to For. Off., 7 Feb. 1856; For. Off. to Adty., 9 Feb., 1856.
[35] F.O. *China Corres.*, vol. 242, For. Off. to Bowring, No. 37, 23 Jan. 1856; No. 41, 31 Jan. 1856; No. 46, 6 Feb. 1856; No. 50, 9 Feb. 1856.
[36] F.O. *China Corres.*, vol. 246, Bowring to For. Off., No. 110, 5 Apr. 1856.

play a distinguished role. There had been suggestions for some time past that treaty revision in China should be undertaken jointly by the Treaty Powers, and late in 1855 he began to link this idea with that of negotiations in Japan, hoping that success in China would make the Japanese more amenable to changes.[37] By February 1856 his ideas were taking definite shape. He reported that there seemed no prospect of Stirling providing naval support for a visit to Japan without direct orders from the Admiralty, and suggested that until such orders should arrive he might usefully spend some time in sounding the French and American representatives on their views and intentions towards Japan. He felt that a combined fleet sent there could effect far more than either Perry or Stirling had done. The French were not embarrassed by any earlier agreement, and it would be possible to concentrate on getting suitable terms for them, which both Britain and the United States could share under their respective most-favoured-nation clauses.[38] In March he put forward the proposal that a joint Anglo-French squadron be sent to Edo. If the fleet received orders that ' naval arrangements should be made subservient and subordinate to diplomatic action ', he said, then it should be possible by ' a proper union of firmness and amenity ' to overcome Japanese objections to a commercial treaty.[39]

The initial arrangements for such an expedition would obviously have to be made in Paris and London, not in China. Bowring therefore decided that he would take no further steps about the Japan negotiations until he received a reply from the Foreign Office about his latest suggestion. This fact was not made clear in his letters to Clarendon. In April 1856 he again urged the need for naval support and his desire to co-operate with the French, in a dispatch which implied, but did not actually state, that he was still

[37] F.O. *China Corres.*, vol. 235, Bowring to For. Off., No. 382, 4 Dec. 1855.
[38] F.O. *China Corres.*, vol. 245, Bowring to For. Off., No. 46, 2 Feb. 1856 ; same to same, Confidential, 6 Feb. 1856.
[39] F.O. *China Corres.*, vol. 245, Bowring to For. Off., No. 81, 12 Mar. 1856. See also *Clarendon Papers*, C vol. 57, ff. 400-3, Bowring to Clarendon, 10 Feb. 1856, describing Stirling's offer to let him have 2 ships for the purpose for 2 months during the winter monsoon as ' a mauvaise plaisanterie '.

awaiting instructions despite the arrival of the correspondence about the London discussions of the exposition.[40] Another letter of 26 July conveyed the same impression.[41]

To Rear Admiral Sir Michael Seymour, Stirling's successor as Commander-in-Chief, Bowring was more explicit. He said that while he still hoped and expected to go to Japan, he would make no move without a considerable force and orders from home authorising him to use it in the way he proposed.[42] In August, Seymour left with his squadron to visit Japan and other lands in the north, expecting to return late in September. Since the northerly monsoon would begin again in October and there were still no instructions for his proposed Anglo-French expedition to the Peiho and Japan, Bowring saw in this the end of his hopes of putting the plan into execution during 1856. He began to look to the spring of 1857 as the next suitable opportunity.[43]

In September there was encouraging news from Townshend Harris, American consul in Japan. Harris reported that the Japanese confessed ' great anxiety ' about future British movements, now that the end of the Crimean War left both Britain and Russia free to pursue their ambitions in northeast Asia. In forwarding this information to Clarendon, Bowring expressed the hope that he would be authorised to go to Japan ' when the season is favourable ' with a proper fleet and in co-operation with representatives of other nations.[44] It was the first time since February that he had asked openly for instructions.

It seems that during these months the Foreign Office

---

[40] F.O. *China Corres.*, vol. 246, Bowring to For. Off., No. 110, 5 Apr. 1856, and No. 135, 21 Apr. 1856. On 5 May he wrote to Clarendon privately that ' Japan still floats before me in very misty shape' (*Clarendon Papers*, C. vol. 57, ff. 410-2).

[41] F.O. *China Corres.*, vol. 249, Bowring to For. Off., No. 230, 26 July 1856.

[42] F.O. *China Emb. Arch.*, vol. 210, Bowring to Seymour, No. 118, 3 June, and No. 150, 7 July 1856.

[43] F.O. *China Corres.*, vol. 249, Bowring to For. Off., No. 236, 6 Aug. 1856. F.O. *China Emb. Arch.*, vol. 210, Bowring to U.S. Commissioner, 11 Aug. 1856.

[44] F.O. *China Corres.*, vol. 250, Bowring to For. Off., No. 297, 25 Sept. 1856. See also *Clarendon Papers*, C. vol. 57, ff. 440-3, Bowring to Clarendon, 9 Sept. 1856.

was, with some justice, expecting Bowring to take action on the instructions he had already received. Certainly it showed no inclination to send new ones. The only point in his dispatches which was thought in London to need further action was that of naval strength. During 1855 he had often warned Clarendon that the Russians were steadily building up a position in northeast Asia which might soon enable them to dominate Japan, Korea and North China. In February 1856, with this in mind, the Foreign Office asked the Admiralty for information on the existing naval strength in Chinese waters and the extent to which it would be possible to reinforce it.[45] The reply was unhelpful. The Admiralty observed that reinforcement must depend in the last resort on whether the war with Russia was to continue,[46] and the matter was therefore allowed to drop until April.

By the time the Crimean War ended, a crisis had arisen in British relations with the United States, chiefly because of accusations that Crampton, British minister in Washington, had abused diplomatic privilege in his war-time recruiting activities there. The American government demanded his recall and American public opinion became so vehemently anti-British that war seemed possible, even probable, in the spring of 1856. The situation greatly complicated the problem of negotiations with China and Japan. Clarendon had long been working to secure Anglo-American co-operation on the China coast, and was still doing so in March 1856, at the height of the disputes leading to Crampton's departure from Washington.[47] He had hoped that the two countries might also work together in Japan.[48] There was for the moment, however, no opportunity of raising the subject officially. Indeed, it became necessary early in April to give serious thought to the

[45] F.O. *China Corres.*, vol. 255, For. Off. to Aaty., 22 Feb. 1856.
[46] F.O. *China Corres.*, vol. 255, Adty. to For. Off., 23 Feb. 1856.
[47] F.O. *United States Corres.*, vol. 638, For. Off. to Crampton, No. 63, 14 Mar. 1856.
[48] *Clarendon Papers*, C vol. 134, ff. 415-20, Clarendon to Bowring, 8 Dec. 1855, in which he states his belief that ' joint action with the U.S. Commissioner and Naval force would be the best means of bringing the Japanese to view us with favor '.

danger of war with the United States, and the Admiralty was therefore instructed that the China squadron must be strengthened on that account under the guise of taking steps to suppress piracy on the China coast. The force so collected, according to Clarendon, would be none the less useful if war should not occur, for it could be used to support the negotiations with China and Japan.[49]

As a result of this correspondence more ships were sent out to China. In view of their real purpose, however, no immediate instructions were sent to put them at Bowring's disposal. Ships in themselves were no satisfaction to the plenipotentiary. He wanted authority to determine their use, and without it he continued to complain. In September, in reply to one of his complaints, the Admiralty somewhat acidly pointed out that Seymour already had twelve ships, that ten more were being sent ; and as the American squadron contained only two and the French had none at all in China, it failed to see in what respect the force was inadequate to the duties required of it.[50]

Bowring's difficulty had, in fact, been disposed of in July, when instructions were sent to Seymour to support the negotiations in the north.[51] However, he did not receive them until the beginning of October. By that time it was too late to organise the expedition before the monsoon changed, and Bowring decided to postpone the attempt until May 1857. He thought the delay might enable him to arrange effective French and American co-operation, and would give Seymour time to collect the necessary force ' for giving to the expedition such a character as would most likely secure us against disappointment or defeat '.[52]

While Bowring spent the summer and early autumn of 1856 waiting for instructions and collecting such information as he could about the activities of Dutch and Americans in Japan, the Royal Navy again intervened actively in

[49] F.O. *China Corres.*, vol. 256, For. Off. to Adty., Secret, 9 Apr. 1856.
[50] F.O. *China Corres.*, vol. 258, Adty. to For. Off., 10 Sept. 1856.
[51] F.O. *China Corres.*, vol. 257, For. Off. to Adty., 22 July 1856 ; Adty. to For. Off., 24 July 1856.
[52] F.O. *China Corres.*, vol. 251, Bowring to For. Off., No. 317, 3 Oct. 1856, encl. correspondence with Seymour.

Anglo-Japanese relations. In 1855 Stirling had agreed to send a ship to Nagasaki sixty days after the signing of the exposition to fetch the replies of the Japanese government on the points left unsolved by himself and the *bugyō*. The Foreign Office, although anxious to prevent any further naval diplomacy, had agreed that these letters must be obtained. It had also ordered Stirling that he was at the same time to secure copies of any new port regulations which might have been introduced as a result of his actions.[53] Stirling did nothing to follow out these instructions before he was recalled. It was not until 3 September 1856 that his successor, Seymour, arrived at Nagasaki to do so. He was accompanied by no more than three ships, but quickly found an opportunity to show himself something more than a mere carrier of messages.

Seymour's first move was to insist on the right to enter the inner harbour, a right which Stirling had already claimed the year before. Immediately on arrival he announced his intention of entering with the squadron and gave the Japanese one hour in which to remove the line of war-junks blocking the entrance. There is some doubt whether they did so,[54] but the ships certainly entered at the end of that period without provoking armed opposition.

At a meeting with the *bugyō* two days later, Seymour obtained a copy of the Russian treaty with Japan and officially announced the end of Britain's war with Russia. But the discussion chiefly concerned the question of port facilities. A depot had been built at Nagasaki for British seamen to use as a recreation space, and also as a place at which supplies might be purchased and stored. This was an improvement, of course, on the arrangements for previous visits, but Seymour complained vigorously because the depot was surrounded by a stockade, refusing to believe that such protection against the Japanese people could be

---

[53] F.O. *Japan Corres.*, vol. 1, For. Off. to Adty., 21 Jan. 1856.
[54] Tronson (*Voyage to Japan*, pp. 397-9) describes the forcing of an entry, but Seymour's report (F.O. *Japan Corres.*, vol. 1, Seymour to Adty., 22 Sept. 1856, in Adty. to For. Off., 1 Dec. 1856) makes no reference to such an incident —perhaps deliberately so. The Japanese records are of no assistance on this point.

necessary. He went on to request the same facilities for landing at Nagasaki as were already enjoyed at Hakodate. To this he received the usual reply, that what happened at Hakodate was no concern of the Nagasaki *bugyō*. Seymour's request became a demand. The *bugyō*, fearing he would resort to force, offered to permit him the necessary privilege on this occasion and refer to Edo for authority to do so in future, at which the admiral declared that he considered permission had now been given and that it was irrevocable.[55] There the matter was left, though the point was scarcely settled.

The chief difficulties, however, arose over the Japanese government's policy respecting the questions left unsettled by Stirling and the *bugyō* in the previous year, notably the right of landing at Nagasaki and the extent to which Article V of the convention barred Britain from sharing any privileges granted to Dutch and Chinese in Japan subsequent to October 1854. These and several minor points were referred to Edo in November 1855. There was little difficulty in agreeing to hand over a copy of the Russian treaty, since that could not be indefinitely delayed, but neither Rōjū nor subordinate officials showed any inclination to give way in other matters. The *kaibō-kakari bugyō*, it is true, said they could see no alternative but to allow British visitors to land at Nagasaki—and then gave their attention to the problem of how that could be arranged so as to prevent contact with the local inhabitants. The depot to which Seymour objected was the result of their deliberations.[56] The Rōjū themselves debated the question of the most-favoured-nation clause. They decided that only two courses were acceptable. Either all reference to the date must be omitted, thus making Dutch and Chinese privileges an exception for the future as well as for the past, or mention of the Dutch and Chinese must be deleted entirely, as had been done in the Russian

---

[55] F.O. *Japan Corres.*, vol. 1, Seymour to Adty., No. 66, 22 Sept. 1856 in Adty. to For. Off., 1 Dec. 1856. *Bakumatsu Gaikoku Kankei Monjo*, XIV, 663-76, Japanese minutes of conference, 5 Sept. 1856 ; XIV, 692-5, Nagasaki bugyō and metsuke to Rōjū, 7 Sept. 1856.
[56] *Bakumatsu Gaikoku Kankei Monjo*, XIII, 18-20, Kaibō-kakari kanjō-bugyō to Rōjū, 4 Nov. 1855 ; XIII, 30-1, same to same, 7 Nov. 1855.

and American treaties. Any other decision, they said, would involve Japan in constant disputes.[57]

On 5 September 1856, in accordance with the instructions he had received, the Nagasaki *bugyō* handed Seymour two notes addressed to Stirling, denying the validity of the British interpretation of the treaty on two major questions, the rights of warships and the Dutch and Chinese privileges.[58] Next day, Seymour replied, in wording which followed closely the Foreign Office instructions of January, that the British government upheld Stirling's views on both points.[59]

At the *bugyō*'s request, a conference was arranged to discuss the disagreement. This took place on 10 September and achieved nothing. The *bugyō*, despite the answer he had received from Seymour, insisted that his notes of 5 September must be sent to England, and spent most of the meeting trying to persuade the admiral not to exercise his new-found right of landing until there had been time to refer to Edo. This request Seymour consistently refused, though he did agree to instruct British ships not to enter the inner harbour without first identifying themselves to the appropriate officials.[60]

Since the discussions showed Seymour to be adamant, the *bugyō* bowed to the inevitable and drafted a set of regulations which he hoped would keep the privilege of landing within reasonable bounds. He restricted it to the territory directly administered by the Bakufu—that is, not forming part of the neighbouring fiefs—and to parties of officers. They were to be accompanied at all times by guides and

[57] *Bakumatsu Gaikoku Kankei Monjo*, XII, 474-4, Rōjū notes on Japanese copy of Exposition of Oct. 1855; XIII, 71-2, Rōjū to Nagasaki bugyō, 20 Nov. 1855.

[58] *Bakumatsu Gaikoku Kankei Monjo*, XIV, 676-8, Nagasaki bugyō to Stirling, undated (2 letters). F.O. *Japan Corres.*, vol. 1, Adty. to For. Off., 1 Dec. 1856, encl. English translation of these notes.

[59] F.O. *Japan Corres.*, vol. 1, Adty. to For. Off., 1 Dec. 1856, encl. Seymour to Nagasaki bugyō, 6 Sept. 1856 (2 notes). *Bakumatsu Gaikoku Kankei Monjo*, XIV, 680-5, translations of Seymour's notes of 6 Sept. 1856.

[60] F.O. *Japan Corres.*, vol. 1, Seymour's report in Adty. to For. Off., 1 Dec. 1856. *Bakumatsu Gaikoku Kankei Monjo*, XIV, 704-14, Japanese minutes of conference, 10 Sept. 1856; XIV, 722-4, Seymour to Nagasaki bugyō, 12 Sept. 1856.

were not to separate, enter private houses or purchase goods. All this Seymour was prepared to accept for the time being. He indicated, however, that he would expect these restrictions, in their turn, to be lifted by the following year.[61]

Seymour had also requested a copy of any new port regulations. When they arrived, he found that they incorporated a reference to the new depot to be used ashore but were otherwise little changed in spirit from those of 1854. He only accepted them, he told the *bugyō*, because the prohibition of landing was followed by a note to the effect that its revision was being undertaken.[62]

Seymour, with fewer ships but an equally threatening manner, had succeeded in improving slightly on Stirling's work at Nagasaki. His own feeling was that although the officials were obviously afraid of making any concessions which would arouse ' the jealous suspicion of their Government', the atmosphere was gradually becoming more friendly and the prejudices against Europeans might in time be expected to disappear.[63] The Foreign Office approved his ' great ability and tact '.[64] Bowring was convinced that his methods not only secured ' becoming respect and attention ', but would also make smoother future relations with Japan.[65]

In this view Bowring was confirmed by the news of H.M.S. *Nankin*'s experiences at Nagasaki in October 1856. Her captain reported to Seymour that when forced to put in there by contrary winds, his men had been allowed to land and his boats to pull about the harbour without supervision, an improvement which he attributed entirely to the

[61] F.O. *Japan Corres.*, vol. 1, Adty. to For. Off., 1 Dec. 1856, encl. Seymour to bugyō, 13 Sept. 1856 and translation of landing regulations. *Bakumatsu Gaikoku Kankei Monjo*, XIV, 724-5, Nagasaki bugyō to Seymour, 12 Sept. 1856 ; XIV, 739-42, translation, Seymour to bugyō, 13 Sept. 1856.

[62] F.O. *Japan Corres.*, vol. 1, Adty. to For. Off., 1 Dec. 1856, encl. Nagasaki port regulations and Seymour to bugyō [13 Sept.. 1856] referring to them. *Bakumatsu Gaikoku Kankei Monjo*, XIV, 726-7, revised Nagasaki port regulations ; XIV, 743-5, translation Seymour to Nagasaki bugyō, 13 Sept. 1856.

[63] F.O. *Japan Corres.*, vol. 1, Seymour to Adty., No. 66, in Adty. to For. Off., 1 Dec. 1856.

[64] F.O. *China Corres.*, vol. 259, For. Off. to Adty., 4 Dec. 1856.

[65] F.O. *China Corres.*, vol. 269, Bowring to For. Off., No. 265, 26 May 1857.

admiral's ' decisive measures ' of the previous month. It was obvious, he said, that the *bugyō* entertained 'a very wholesome respect ' for Seymour. He did not seem at all anxious to renew his acquaintance, however, saying the Japanese ' were afraid the English ships would knock the town down '.[66] The reply to this statement was not calculated to ease the *bugyō*'s mind. Captain Stewart assured him that there was no danger of such an untoward event so long as the British were well treated !

A question on which Seymour obtained no satisfaction, and on which his instructions did not permit him to negotiate, was that of the Dutch and Chinese privileges. After September 1856, however, this ceased to be of major importance to the Foreign Office. Whether or not Stirling's most-favoured-nation clause was admitted to apply to the Dutch, there could be no doubt that it applied fully to any treaties made with Japan by other western nations. This even the Japanese recognised. The American convention of 1854 had contained no commercial provisions, or at least none which it was worthwhile claiming. But the Russian treaty of February 1855, a copy of which Seymour had just obtained, provided a much more satisfactory basis for trade. It entitled the Russians to pay for the supplies they required either in cash or by exchanging goods of their own, and the accompanying explanatory articles not only gave them much personal freedom in the ports of Shimoda and Hakodate, but also laid it down that arrangements for supplies and exchange could be made directly with the Japanese merchants, payment alone being effected through the officials.[67] The treaty gave no specific permission to trade, but its advantages over previous agreements were obvious. Bowring reported on them at length, and the Foreign Office was quick to see that at Shimoda and Hakodate, at least, Britain could claim equal privileges.[68]

[66] F.O. *China Corres.*, vol. 251, Capt. Stewart to Seymour, 25 Oct. 1856, in Bowring to For. Off., No. 351, 30 Oct. 1856 ; vol. 279, For. Off. to Adty., 3 Jan. 1857 conveyed F.O. satisfaction at this evidence of Seymour's success.
[67] For the text of the Russian treaty and explanatory articles, see Gubbins, *Progress of Japan*, pp. 235-9.
[68] F.O. *China Corres.*, vol. 250, Bowring to For. Off., No. 305, 27 Sept. 1856 and F.O. minutes thereon.

One result of the Russian treaty was that Bowring received fresh instructions, something for which he had long been waiting. In November 1856 Clarendon wrote privately to him that he had warned the Dutch not to make difficulties for Britain in Japan, and Bowring's reply expressed a confidence which had been lacking in his letters hitherto.[69] The decision to make the attempt was confirmed almost at once by an exchange of official dispatches.[70] The object was to be to get terms at least as good as those granted Russia. Seymour had orders to provide the necessary ships, and there seemed every chance that the mission to Japan would take place as soon as the monsoon changed in March. Once again, however, external factors interfered with the plans. Bowring had missed his best opportunity in 1856, when he failed to take advantage of the period of comparative quiet which followed the end of the Crimean War. In June 1857, before he was able to carry out his new instructions, he learned that it had been decided to entrust the Japan mission to other hands.

The change was brought about by the outbreak of a fresh war with China. Ever since the Treaty of Nanking, Anglo-Chinese relations had been strained. The British believed that the treaty settlement must be enforced to the full and improved if possible ; the Chinese that the treaties already made too many concessions and that complete exploitation of their terms must therefore be prevented. In October 1856 the crew of the *Arrow*, a Chinese-owned lorcha under Hongkong registry, were arrested on a charge of piracy by the Chinese at Canton, and the circumstances surrounding the arrest led to a local dispute over treaty rights. Bowring had already been cautioned by Clarendon not to use force in such disputes. Apparently he decided that this was a temporary rule, occasioned by the need to concentrate on the war with Russia, and no longer held good now that the war had ended. He and Parkes, the consul at Canton,

[69] *Clarendon Papers*, C vol. 137, ff. 172-5, Clarendon to Bowring, 10 Nov. 1856 ; C vol. 57, ff. 470-1, Bowring to Clarendon, 30 Dec. 1856.
[70] F.O. *China Corres.*, vol. 243, For. Off. to Bowring, No. 235, 9 Dec. 1856 ; vol. 264, Bowring to For. Off., No. 61, 4 Feb. 1857.

consequently refused to accept the Chinese offer to return the arrested men. They insisted that Britain receive a full public apology, and when this was not forthcoming, brought the fleet up the river to capture the forts and bombard official residences in the city as a means of exerting pressure. To their surprise the Chinese chose to resist, and the result was open war.

The news caused a political crisis in England. The Foreign Office had no advance warning of Bowring's intentions, but Palmerston and Clarendon agreed that they had no option but to support his actions and seize the opportunity of negotiating a new settlement with China. Russell, Gladstone, Disraeli and Cobden, a formidable if unusual alliance, thought differently. They violently attacked the honesty, legality and political wisdom of Bowring's actions, and early in 1857 succeeded in defeating the government in the House of Commons on the question of approving them. Palmerston promptly dissolved Parliament and won a general election on the issue of peace or war in China.[71]

This success meant that the war was to continue. But in view of the attacks on his conduct and the undoubted rashness of his action in precipitating hostilities, Bowring was clearly not the man to direct either the operations themselves or the negotiations to which it was hoped they would lead. He had originally been instructed to open negotiations for treaty revision with China in addition to going to Japan. In March 1857 he was informed that the Cabinet had decided to send out a special envoy, and that his plenipotentiary powers for China would therefore lapse for the period of the war.[72] Towards the end of the month Clarendon announced the appointment of Lord Elgin, a Palmerston supporter of some political independence who had an excellent record in Jamaica and Canada.[73]

In these first exchanges there had been no suggestion that Elgin was also to be responsible for negotiations with

[71] For a detailed account of the charges and debates see Costin, *Great Britain and China*, pp. 219-30.
[72] F.O. *China Corres.*, vol. 261, For. Off. to Bowring, No. 72, 10 Mar. 1857.
[73] F.O. *China Corres.*, vol. 261, For. Off. to Bowring, No. 88, 25 Mar. 1857. Morison, *The Eighth Earl of Elgin*, pp. 192-4.

Japan. Bowring, who in February had reported that he continued to receive news favourable to British prospects there and that he would go 'when Chinese questions are arranged', remained optimistic despite Elgin's appointment. He still hoped to be allowed to conduct the mission.[74] However, there seemed no good reason why the two series of negotiations should be conducted by different men, and Bowring was not popular at home. In April he was informed that the Foreign Office had decided to send Elgin to Japan as well as to China. It was a decision to which he bowed with reluctance.[75]

Some months later the Superintendent wrote a postscript on his own accomplishments in the matter of the Japan expedition. Confessing himself 'grieved and disappointed' at being deprived of the opportunity of completing an important task, he reported that Townshend Harris, U.S. consul at Shimoda, had been authorised to conclude a commercial treaty with Japan. Since the time when he had himself been given such powers, he wrote, he had continued, through Harris and other correspondents, 'to gather such intelligence and to convey such information to the Japanese as was likely to prepare the way for success'.[76] This statement was true enough, and Bowring's communications to the Japanese through Townshend Harris certainly played a part in smoothing the way for Elgin's negotiations. But this seems a small achievement for over three years' work. Since 1854 Bowring had possessed both instructions and authority to negotiate with Japan. He would undoubtedly have objected that events in China and war with Russia had made it impossible for him to make use of them. This is partly true, of course. But there had been several opportunities of going to Japan had he been content with an escort of one or two ships. Fundamentally the Japan mission was prevented not so much by the international

[74] F.O. *China Corres.*, vol. 264, Bowring to For. Off., No. 57, 3 Feb. 1857 ; vol. 268, same to same, No. 216, 4 May 1857.

[75] F.O. *China Corres.*, vol. 261, For. Off. to Bowring, No. 105, 21 Apr. 1857 ; vol. 295, Bowring to For. Off., No. 295, 11 June 1857.

[76] F.O. *China Corres.*, vol. 272, Bowring to For. Off., No. 383, 21 Sept. 1857.

situation as by Bowring's insistence on the need for a large naval force and orders putting it under the control of the plenipotentiary. Elgin had different ideas. In 1858 he demonstrated that to the Japanese the appearance of two British warships in Edo Bay was sufficient reminder that many more were within a few days' sail.

CHAPTER VII

THE ELGIN MISSION : 1857–1858

WHEN Lord Elgin was entrusted with the task of conducting negotiations in China and Japan, his instructions were based on drafts originally intended for Bowring. They had been circulated to the Cabinet early in January 1857 and met with serious opposition from Sir G. C. Lewis, who objected that in China, at least, they could lead only to a difficult and costly war. As the problem had existed for centuries, he said, there could be no urgency about sending new orders. As for Japan, action was in any case to be deferred until matters had been settled in China, and this could not be for some years. It would on every count be 'more prudent', therefore, to wait on the progress of events.[1]

Lewis's arguments were reinforced by news of the outbreak of hostilities at Canton. Within a few days Clarendon wrote to Bowring that this had led the Foreign Office to hold back his new instructions,[2] and in the following month he advised him that to make fresh plans for Japan 'would be looking too far ahead just now'.[3] Thereafter the rising tide of criticism about Bowring's actions in China made it inevitable that some other envoy supersede him there, and Elgin was appointed in March. In April he was authorised to visit Japan, too, once the China treaty had been concluded.

It had long been British policy to seek French and American co-operation in negotiations for treaty revision in China. In September 1856 Bowring had renewed his

[1] *Clarendon Papers*, C vol. 70, ff. 123-33, Sir G. C. Lewis memo. on China and Japan, 4 Jan. 1857.
[2] *Clarendon Papers*, C vol. 138, ff. 18-23, Clarendon to Bowring, 10 Jan. 1857.
[3] *Clarendon Papers*, C vol. 138, ff. 187-90, Clarendon to Bowring, 10 Feb. 1857.

proposal that joint action be attempted in Japan as well.[4] Clarendon undoubtedly agreed with him in principle, and in the case of France there was no reason to expect a refusal.[5] The Americans had shown themselves less willing to engage in active collaboration, however, and the Foreign Secretary therefore confined his discussions with them to the problems of China, where British help might seem more valuable.[6] This was reflected in the wording of Elgin's instructions for Japan.

These instructions were neither pugnacious nor very detailed. The Foreign Office ignored the more extravagant suggestions made by private correspondents—one of whom urged that the time was ripe for the abolition of polygamy in China and Japan[7]—and showed no signs of 'trying its hand with Japan' (as its recent policy was characterised by one of the government's opponents in the House of Lords).[8] Elgin was provided with copies of the American, Dutch and Russian treaties and of the papers relating to Stirling's negotiations, and was instructed to co-operate closely with the French plenipotentiary, but was given wide discretion in matters of detail. The only specific points brought to his attention were the need to make the English version the master text of his treaty, as he was also to do in China, and to ensure that any provision for extraterritoriality was clear, easily enforceable and did not give the same privileges to Japanese subjects in Britain as it was desired to obtain for British subjects in Japan.

His object was to be to establish commercial relations with Japan upon terms 'at least as favourable' as those he had been instructed to obtain in China. To that end he was to regard the proposed treaty with China, which

---

[4] *Clarendon Papers*, C vol. 57, ff. 440-3, Bowring to Clarendon, 9 Sept. 1856 ; F.O. *China Corres.*, vol. 250, Bowring to For. Off., No. 297, 25 Sept. 1856.

[5] F.O. *China Corres.*, vol. 250, Clarendon minute of 5 December on Bowring to For. Off., No. 297, 25 Sept. 1856.

[6] This appears clearly in Clarendon's letters to Napier (at Washington) in March, April and May 1857. See *Clarendon Papers*, C vol. 138, ff. 331-2, 571-2, 621.

[7] F.O. *China Corres.*, vol. 259, James Stewart to Clarendon, 6 Dec. 1856.

[8] Hansard 3rd. Ser., vol CXLIV, cols. 2429-30, Lords, 19 Mar. 1857.

had already been fully discussed, as the model on which to base his subsequent negotiations in Japan. In one respect however, the two negotiations would differ markedly. The treaty with Japan was not to be obtained by the use of force, as the final paragraph of his instructions strongly emphasised :—

> 'I have only to add that Your Excellency will understand that it is not the intention of Her Majesty's Government to impose a new Treaty on Japan by forcible means. We wish to conciliate the goodwill of the Government and people of Japan ; but we have no cause of quarrel with them to justify our having recourse to coercive measures on any account, and least of all in order to compel them to conclude a Treaty the provisions of which might be repugnant to their wishes or interests.'[9]

This prohibition of the use of force was repeated in the dispatch which ordered Seymour to provide Elgin with a suitable escort.[10]   Although H.M.S. *Furious* was sent out with fourteen gunboats to reinforce the China squadron, this was for the prosecution of the war with China, not to overawe the Japanese negotiators.

After April 1857 the Foreign Office continued to send Elgin frequent reports from Europe and America about the activities of other western diplomats in Japan, but by February 1858, the end of his period in office, Clarendon had made no major addition or alteration to the instructions for the proposed treaty.   In October 1857 both Dutch and Russians succeeded in obtaining supplementary treaties which gave them new privileges at Nagasaki and Hakodate, and in particular increased rights of trade under somewhat less rigid control by the officials.[11]   Elgin had already been directed to include in his own treaty all the provisions of the earlier Russian agreement[12] and no new instructions seemed necessary.   When he reported the new terms

[9] Parl. Papers 1859, vol. XXXIII (Cd. 2571), pp. 18-9, For. Off. to Elgin, No. 16, 20 Apr. 1857.

[10] F.O. *China Corres.*, vol. 280, For. Off. to Adty., 21 Apr. 1857. Admiralty, *Out-Letters*, vol. 1613, Adty. to Seymour, No. 166, 24 Apr. 1857.

[11] Gubbins, *Progress of Japan*, pp. 255 65, Additional articles to Dutch treaty, 16 Oct. 1857 ; pp. 239-45. Russian supplementary treaty, 24 Oct. 1857.

[12] F.O. *China Corres.*, vol. 274, For. Off. to Elgin, No. 46, 19 June 1857.

obtained by Russia both Foreign Office and Board of Trade agreed that they were a great improvement on all previous concessions, but held to their original idea that a new British treaty incorporating these terms would be more satisfactory than any attempt to claim them under the most-favoured-nation clause of Stirling's convention.[13]

At about the same time Bowring's dispatch reporting his correspondence with Townshend Harris arrived in London. It led Clarendon to raise the question of sending a British consul to Japan. The permanent under-secretary opposed such a move on the grounds that there were no British interests immediately in need of protection. Moreover the presence of a consul might hamper Elgin and Elgin's arrival with plenipotentiary powers would certainly lower the consul's prestige. Nothing was done, therefore, except to refer to Elgin for his opinion.[14]

Elgin arrived in Hongkong in 1857 in time to conduct the summer campaign, but the outbreak of the Sepoy Mutiny in India robbed him of many troops and some ships. After visiting India to investigate the situation at first hand, he decided to postpone full-scale operations in China until the 1858 season. Since negotiations with Japan were to follow those in China, his visit to Japan, too, was necessarily postponed.

In Britain the Palmerston government fell early in 1858 and Malmesbury succeeded Clarendon as Foreign Secretary. He took the unusual step of preparing a circular to announce to British diplomats and the governments to which they were accredited the principles on which his foreign policy was to be conducted. This document emphasised the peaceful intentions of Great Britain and denied that she had any wish for territorial expansion or exclusive privileges in any part of the world. It implied strong criticism of the policies of aggression and of interference in the domestic politics of foreign countries which had so often been

[13] F.O. *China Corres.*, vol. 276, F.O. minutes on Elgin to For. Off., No. 63, confidential, 19 Nov. 1857 ; vol. 303, Bd. Trade to For. Off., 3 Feb. 1858.
[14] F.O. *China Corres.*, vol. 272, Clarendon and Hammond minutes of Nov. 1857 on Bowring to For. Off., No. 383, 21 Sept. 1857 ; vol. 274, For. Off. to Elgin, No. 110, 7 Dec. 1857

attributed to Palmerston by his opponents. It might have been taken as heralding a reversal of British policy towards China and Japan. In fact no change resulted, presumably because, as the circular also stated, the government was 'convinced that no surer guarantee for peace is to be found than in the maintenance and extension of commercial and social intercourse between nations'.[15] That Malmesbury was anxious to end the war in China was beyond doubt,[16] but it seemed that in China, at least, peace and the extension of commerce were temporarily incompatible objectives.

The change in government brought no change in Elgin's instructions for China and Japan. Indeed, it was difficult to see what changes Malmesbury could make. The war with China was a fact he could not alter, and the instructions about Japan were already as peaceable as he could wish. Moreover, he had fallen heir to a very complex problem, and it was some time before he could see his way clearly in it. In April 1858 he confessed to Elgin that he was faced with such 'a mass of correspondence' that it was quite impossible to appreciate the situation properly. He asked him to send home a summary of events and a statement of his own opinions and intentions in order that the Foreign Office could draw up fresh instructions if they seemed necessary.[17] As if in answer to this, a dispatch arrived from Elgin three days later announcing that he was about to go to Shanghai to open negotiations, and thence to Peking or Japan.[18] In fact the negotiations were transferred to the Peiho, and it was not until he had signed the Treaty of Tientsin in July 1858 that Elgin found it possible to visit Japan.

Since 1854, while British policy towards Japan had been slowly taking shape, the attitude of the Japanese towards

[15] F.O. *China Emb. Arch.*, vol. 250, F.O. circular of 8 Mar. 1858

[16] See, for example, his premature attempt to recall part of the China squadron. (Admiralty, *Out-Letters*, vol. 1615, Adty. to Seymour, No. 256, 19 May 1858 ; No. 257, 20 May 1858 ; No. 265, 24 May 1858.)

[17] F.O. *China Corres.*, vol. 284, For. Off. to Elgin, No. 3, 9 Apr. 1858.

[18] Parl. Papers 1859, vol. XXXIII (Cd. 2571), pp. 231-2, Elgin to For. Off., No. 51, 27 Feb. 1858. Recd. F.O. 12 Apr. 1858.

foreign relations had undergone a gradual change. This change was due in no small measure to British activities in China. It played a vital part in determining the character and results of Elgin's negotiations in 1858, and before proceeding with an account of the Elgin mission, therefore, it is necessary to give some consideration to the development of Japanese policy in this period. In particular, we must consider Japanese reactions to news of British plans.

In and after 1854 the principal influences on Bakufu policy were the Rōjū ; the Go-sanke and other close family connections of the Shōgun ; the great outside feudatories or *tozama daimyō* ; and the lords of the *tamari-no-mazume*, leaders of the *fudai daimyō*. The Go-sanke, led by Nariaki of Mito, together with such related lords as Matsudaira Echizen-no-kami, Matsudaira Awa-no-kami (son of a previous *shōgun*) and Matsudaira Sagami-no-kami (son of Nariaki), were the leaders of the seclusion party and fierce opponents of every attempt to relax the laws governing treatment of foreigners. The *tozama* lords were traditional rivals of the Tokugawa. Some of them, like Shimazu and Nabeshima, were moderates in foreign affairs ; others like Mōri, Hosogawa and Yamanouchi seemed ready to resort even to force to prevent the opening of the ports. The *tamari-no-mazume*, on the other hand, was dominated by Ii Naosuke and Hotta Bitchū-no-kami, both advocates of a so-called ' liberal ' foreign policy, which meant in practice that they advocated an extension of foreign intercourse not as being desirable in itself, but as being the only safe and sensible course in face of Western military superiority. This group was represented in the Rōjū by Matsudaira Iga-no-kami and Matsudaira Izumi-no-kami. As *kaibō-kakari* these two were the officials most closely concerned with the conduct of foreign affairs, and Iga, at least, was a man of strong will and forceful character. Abe Ise-no-kami and Makino Bizen-no-kami were the senior members of the Rōjū. Both saw the urgent necessity of finding some formula that would prevent foreign war, but they were equally convinced that no policy could long succeed if it did not have the support of Nariaki, with whom, therefore, they did their utmost to co-operate. The other two members of the Council were nonentities.

The split within the ranks of its supporters over foreign relations, the differences between the Go-sanke and the *fudai* of the *tamari-no-mazume*, certainly constituted a notable danger to the Bakufu's political position in Japan. The full support of both would be required if the Tokugawa were successfully to resist the new challenge to their power represented by a growing movement to restore to the Emperor his ancient rights as active head of the State. Abe recognised the danger, though not, perhaps, its precise form. It was in an attempt to close the ranks that after Perry's visit in 1853 he brought Nariaki back into active politics as an adviser to the Rōjū, especially on problems of defence. But Iga and Izumi consistently opposed Nariaki's recommendations, and the breach if anything widened.

Nariaki's power and influence grew steadily, and by the autumn of 1855 he was able to force the dismissal of both Iga and Izumi from the Rōjū. His success was shortlived, however. If it was impossible for Abe to run directly counter to Nariaki's views, it was equally dangerous to alienate the leaders of the *fudai*. The latter began at once to press for the appointment of Hotta to replace Iga and Izumi, a move which would make their representation stronger even than before. Within a few weeks they had gained their end. Within a year, Hotta had replaced Abe as acknowledged head of the Rōjū.[19]

Up to the time of Hotta's appointment and for some months thereafter, Bakufu foreign policy remained essentially unchanged. Although Imperial approval of the early treaties was given in 1855, they continued to be the object of widespread criticism. This criticism forced the Bakufu into expensive defence measures in preparation for the expected trial of strength with the Western Powers, the financing of which presented ever-increasing difficulties. Further concessions, it seemed, might well lead to a domestic

[19] Akimoto, *Ii Naosuke*, pp. 135-9. Kobayashi, *Bakumatsu-shi*, pp. 262-5. Ōmori, *Dai Nihon Zenshi*, III, 738-40.

crisis. Thus Stirling at Nagasaki in 1855 and Seymour in 1856 met with stubborn opposition when they tried to obtain them. The methods they chose to employ to overcome that opposition not only gained them small advantage, but also tended to confirm Japanese suspicions of British policy. But while Seymour was still at Nagasaki in September 1856, the Rōjū was giving much thought to new reports of British intentions respecting Japan and the possible ways of countering them. These were deliberations which led in time to a new phase in Japanese policy.

In August 1856 a Dutch ship arrived at Nagasaki with the news that Bowring planned to visit Japan within a few weeks, accompanied by a large fleet, for the purpose of demanding a commercial treaty. Donker Curtius took the opportunity of urging that only a treaty with the Dutch, laying down terms on which trade could be conducted by all foreigners, could possibly avert the obvious danger of attack and minimise the concessions Japan would be forced to make. The Nagasaki *bugyō*, confessing that he could see no feasible alternative to this plan, promptly appealed to Edo for support and instructions.[20]

The first action of the Rōjū, on the advice of the *bugyō* responsible for defence, was to ensure that the Nagasaki officials would do nothing on their own initiative. They were accordingly instructed to refer any such British request to Edo, though without permitting the mission itself to go there.[21] At the same time, the Rōjū called for the advice of the officials most closely concerned with foreign affairs, in a letter which indicated a growing feeling that trade, however unwelcome, had become inevitable, and might be put to good use in strengthening the finances—and through them the defences—of the country.[22] This was the policy

[20] Japan, Foreign Office, *Nichi-ei gaikō-shi*, I, 42-4. *Bakumatsu Gaikoku Kankei Monjo*, XIV, 421-4, Bugyō in Nagasaki to Kanjō-bugyō and Nagasaki bugyō in Edo, 10 Aug. 1856; XIV, 445-9, same to same, 21 Aug. 1856.

[21] *Bakumatsu Gaikoku Kankei Monjo*, XIV, 544-8, Kaibō-kakari kanjō-bugyō to Rōjū, 28 Aug. 1856; XIV, 687-8, Rōjū to Nagasaki bugyō and metsuke, c. 6 Sept. 1856. These orders could not have arrived in Nagasaki in time to affect Seymour's discussions.

[22] *Bakumatsu Gaikoku Kankei Monjo*, XIV, 652-3, Rōjū to various officials, 2 Sept. 1856.

of Hotta. However, the replies to this and a later request revealed considerable differences of opinion among the officials. Most of them, since they were much more aware of Japan's weakness than the generality of the *daimyō*, recognised the need for concessions and recommended trade in such goods as camphor and lacquerware. The *metsuke* and *ōmetsuke* were unwilling to countenance even this. The Nagasaki *metsuke*, in contrast, wanted a public announcement that trade would be permitted, followed by discussions to decide the conditions under which it should be carried on. Some were even optimistic enough to hope that if the foreigners were supplied with beef, women, and such other luxuries as they might require during their visits to Japanese ports, they might agree not to press their demands for trade.[23]

Probably because opinions were conflicting, no definite decision on policy was taken at once. Mizuno Chikugo-no-kami, who had negotiated with Stirling in 1854, was sent to Nagasaki to discuss general policy and the Dutch request with the *bugyō*, with orders that any settlement must be based on the Russian and American treaties. A group of envoys was appointed to negotiate with Bowring when he came.[24] In the event, however, Bowring did not come and the Rōjū was not therefore forced to commit itself to a specific policy at all.

Shortly after these discussions, Hotta assumed the direction of foreign relations in person, and instituted a formal investigation of the trade problem by appointing special *bugyō* to study it. Progress was slow, and by the spring of 1857 the investigators had still produced no solution. Hotta therefore called on them for an interim report. The wording of his request makes it clear that he had already decided that trade in •some form was inevitable,

[23] e.g. *Bakumatsu Gaikoku Kankei Monjo*, XV, 118-9, ōmetsuke and metsuke to Rōjū, 1856, 9th month (29 Sept.–28 Oct.); XIV, 825-8, Nagasaki metsuke to [Wakadoshiyori], 1856, 8th month (30 Aug.–28 Sept.); XIV, 799-802, Kaibō-kakari kanjō-bugyō to Rōjū, 24 Sept. 1856.
[24] *Bakumatsu Gaikoku Kankei Monjo*, XIV, 781-2, Rōjū to Kanjō-bugyō Mizuno Chikugo-no-kami, 20 Sept. 1856; XV, 70-1, Rōjū to ōmetsuke Tosa Tamba-no-kami, Kanjō-bugyō Kawaji Saemon and Mizuno Chikugo-no-kami and others, 14 Oct. 1856.

and that to him the real issues were whether Japan should take the initiative or wait for the British envoy, and what laws would enable her best to use the profits from trade to strengthen her own position.[25]   To that, of course, must be added the problem of what support he could expect for his policy in Japan.

Once again Hotta's advisors were not unanimous.   The *kanjō-bugyō* were anxious to limit trade to the minimum that would satisfy the West, and proposed that a restriction be put on the number of ships to be sent by each nation. Moreover, they wanted to permit trade only at Nagasaki in the first instance, as this would enable Japan to offer Shimoda and Hakodate if the foreigners later demanded trade at the Inland Sea ports of Hyōgo and Osaka, which were uncomfortably close to the Imperial capital at Kyōto.[26] The *kaibō-kakari metsuke* and *ōmetuke* dissented from this opinion.   They pointed out that such half-measures would never satisfy Britain and the other maritime powers, and that it would be better, therefore, to permit extensive private trade without government interference and use the revenue derived from it to build up Japanese military strength.[27] News of the British attack on Canton, reaching Japan at about this time, provided the occasion for other statements of policy.   Most officials thought that this event underlined the need for concessions to Britain,[28] and Hotta undoubtedly agreed.   But such was not the temper of the capital at large. Moriyama, the senior interpreter, reported to Townshend Harris on 28 March 1857 that of every ten men in authority, three would favour opening the ports at once and two opening them after some delay ; three would be prepared

---

[25] *Bakumatsu Gaikoku Kankei Monjo*, XV, 669-71, Rōjū to Kaibō-kakari, 20 Apr. 1857 ; XV, 682-7, Hotta draft memo. to Bōeki Torishirabe-kakari, 1857, 3rd month (26 Mar.-23 Apr.).

[26] *Bakumatsu Gaikoku Kankei Monjo*, XV, 687-97, Kaibō-kakari kanjō-bugyō to Rōjū, 1857, 3rd month (26 Mar.-23 Apr.) ; XVI, 183-7, same to to same, 1857, 5th month (23 May-21 June).

[27] *Bakumatsu Gaikoku Kankei Monjo*, XV, 819-24, Kaibō-kakari ōmetuke and metsuke to Rōjū, 1857, 4th month (24 Apr.-22 May).

[28] e.g. *Bakumatsu Gaikoku Kankei Monjo*, XV, 700-5, Kaibō-kakari ōmetuke and metsuke to Rōjū, 1857, 3rd month (26 Mar.-23 Apr.) ; XV, 831-4, Shimoda bugyō to Rōjū, 1857, 4th month (24 Apr.-22 May) ; XV, 781-3, Hakodate bugyō to Rōjū, 6 May 1857.

to yield without resistance to a threat of force, but two would fight to the last.[29]

The death of Abe in the summer of 1857 greatly strengthened Hotta's position in the Rōjū and reduced the influence of the Mito group. Thereafter Nariaki was no longer consulted by the Bakufu on important questions of policy. In October treaties were concluded with the Dutch and Russians which incorporated the results of the previous twelve months' discussions among Edo officials, and which Hotta intended to be models for all future agreements. The terms were not generous, for trade was still to be restricted and supervised, but they were acceptable to the Dutch, who planned to effect improvement in their position by stages rather than by a single coup,[30] while the commercial interests of the Russians were relatively small.

During the same period the Rōjū were considering a more ambitious plan. It was clear that the Japanese lacked experience of international trade and relied heavily on Dutch and Chinese traders for estimates of Britain's future intentions, especially on the vital question of whether or not she was prepared to use force against Japan. The Rōjū was aware of this difficulty, and in October 1857 asked the advice of the officials about a plan to send a mission to Hongkong to gather first-hand information on trade and international affairs.[31] The *kaibō-kakari bugyō* and *metsuke* differed over this as they had on the topic of trade in general, and along the same lines. The *hyōjōsho* (the highest feudal court of Japan)[32] envisaged all kinds of legal and practical difficulties. Hayashi Daigaku-no-kami, head of the Confucian school which trained most of the Bakufu officials, feared the effect it might have on British officials at Hongkong and the danger of involving the mission in the Anglo-Chinese war. He would have preferred sending it

[29] Harris, *Complete Journal*, pp. 336-7.
[30] For an account and justification of Dutch policy at this period see van Doren, *De Openstelling van Japan voor de Vreemde Natien in 1856*, especially pp. 111-2, 204-8.
[31] *Bakumatsu Gaikoku Kankei Monjo*, XVII, 338-40, Rōjū to various Officials, 5 Oct. 1857.
[32] In this instance, *hyōjōsho* is a collective term for the *jisha-bugyō, machi-bugyō, kanjō-bugyō* and *ōmetsuke*, who together composed the court.

direct to Batavia.[33]   Hotta, summarising the conflict of opinions in a report to the Shōgun, was not prepared to say that the advantages of such a mission would be greater than the risks it involved.   He proposed that the matter be considered again at some future date.[34]

The problem of British intentions, already a recurrent theme in Japanese discussions of foreign policy, was also being urged on the Bakufu from another quarter. Townshend Harris had been appointed American consul at Shimoda in 1856 under the terms of the Perry convention He had met Bowring before this appointment, and called again at Hongkong on his way to Japan and discussed his plans with the Superintendent.   The two men probably talked over the terms of the commercial treaty Harris hoped to obtain, and Harris was certainly told of Bowring's plan to visit Japan and given permission to disclose the fact to the Japanese.[35]

After Harris reached Shimoda he continued to correspond with Bowring and was able to put his knowledge of Bowring's plans to some use in his own negotiations with the Japanese.   After spending several weeks impressing them with his friendliness, he revealed that he was empowered to treat and asked permission to visit Edo to present his credentials.   He promised, if this request were granted, to put the Japanese in full possession of his information about British intentions, but insisted that he was only willing to do so in the capital itself.[36]   The Japanese, of course, had already received Dutch reports of Bowring's proposed visit and were probably less anxious to hear more than Harris thought.   However, his proposal in some respects fitted in with Hotta's decision that treaties must

[33] *Bakumatsu Gaikoku Kankei Monjo*, XVII, 340-2, Hyōjōsho to Rōjū, 1857, 8th month (18 Sept.–17 Oct.) ; XVII, 342-6, ōmetsuke and metsuke to Rōjū, 1857, 8th month ; XVII, 658-61, Kaibō-kakari kanjō-bugyō to Rōjū, 24 Oct. 1857 ; XVII, 755-7, Hayashi Daigaku-no-kami to Rōjū, c. 29 Oct. 1857.
[34] *Bakumatsu Gaikoku Kankei Monjo*, XVII, 812-5, Rōjū to Sbōgun, 1857, 9th month (18 Oct.–16 Nov).
[35] Crow, *Harris of Japan*, pp. 105-7, 257. Harris, *Complete Journal*, pp. 165-7.
[36] Crow, *Harris of Japan*, pp. 163-4. Harris, *Complete Journal*, pp. 247 note, 300 note.

soon be made, and in September 1857, after consulting the Go-sanke and the *daimyō*, the Rōjū agreed to his visit to Edo despite fierce opposition from Nariaki.

In December Harris travelled in state to the capital, and after a formal audience with the Shōgun, had a long private interview with Hotta at the latter's *yashiki*. According to the accounts left by Harris and his secretary Heusken,[37] the consul's argument was that in changing world conditions Japan could not indefinitely maintain her seclusion, and it would be easier for her to negotiate with him, free from the threat of action by foreign warships, than to wait until other nations lost all patience and forced greater concessions at the point of a gun. From the Japanese records[38] it appears that Harris was, in fact, much more specific as to the source of danger. He warned Hotta that Britain would take the lead in any move against Japan, that she was willing to fight to open Japanese ports, and even that she had territorial as well as commercial ambitions. Whether or not that was an accurate summary of Harris's statement, it was the one made by the Japanese and presumably, therefore, the gist of what they believed him to have said.

Harris was dealing with men already convinced of the reality of these dangers, and he accordingly had little difficulty in opening negotiations or in overcoming most Japanese objections to specific points in his proposals. Always his argument was that what he did was for the ultimate good of Japan in that it would prevent worse from happening. On one occasion, when the negotiators proved obstinate, he much impressed them by quoting from one of Bowring's letters written nearly a year before. ' Japan, of course, occupies much of my thoughts ', wrote Bowring, ' and if I had reason to know that I should have a becoming reception and a disposition to give me such a treaty as I could accept with propriety . . . I have no desire to be

[37] Harris, *Complete Journal*, pp. 484-7 (12 Dec. 1857). Wagener, ' Aus dem Tagebuche Hendrik Heuskens ', *Mittheilungen der Deutschen Gesellschaft fur Natur- und Volkerkunde Ostasiens*, III, 29 (June 1883), pp. 382-3.
[38] Japanese accounts have been translated and summarised in Murdoch, *History of Japan*, III, 636-8, and Treat, *Early Diplomatic Relations between the United States and Japan* 1853-1865, pp. 75-9.

accompanied by so great a fleet as to ·cause alarms and apprehensions '.[39] A quotation more apt to Harris's purpose it would be difficult to find.

It would be unjust to Harris's ability to say that he obtained his treaty entirely by using the British fleet as a threat to support his diplomacy. He was but emphasising and documenting a danger which many Japanese had recognised before his arrival. It is clear from the record of their policy discussions since 1855 that Japanese officials needed little persuasion to believe the course he proposed the safest one for their country. The difficulty was to persuade the *daimyō* in general of this fact. At the end of 1857 and again in 1858 Hotta called for advice about the American treaty, as had been done in 1853. This time the replies showed some important changes, but not enough to solve Hotta's problem.

Nariaki and his son, with a few supporters, still argued that the danger of admitting foreigners was greater than that of excluding them altogether. At all costs, they said, foreigners must be kept out of the provinces near Kyōto. Many agreed with this last point, though prepared to open trade elsewhere in Japan. There had been some defections from the seclusion party in recent years, notably Matsudaira Echizen-no-kami, but nearly all the replies urged that Imperial approval be obtained before the treaty were signed, an attitude adopted only by Ii Naosuke in 1853. Most *daimyō* felt, like Shimazu of Satsuma, that Japan had no choice but to open trade, but there were few among them who did not wish to put restrictions on it, either of time or place.[40] There is no doubt that the treaty sought by Harris went much farther than most were willing to accept. In February 1858, after the draft had been agreed by the negotiators, one of them told Heusken he estimated that only about a third of the *daimyō* would be in favour of signing it.[41]

[39] Harris, *Complete Journal*, p. 554 note, quoting Bowring to Harris, 18 March 1857.
[40] Gubbins, *Progress of Japan*, pp. 102-11, 289-91. Kobayashi, *Bakumatsu-shi*, pp. 308-9. Ōmori, *Dai Nihon Zenshi*, III, 748-9.
[41] Wagener, ' Tagebuche Hendrik Heuskens ', p. 387.

In face of such opinions, Hotta decided that it would be wise to obtain Imperial sanction before signing the treaty he had arranged with Harris. Consequently Hayashi Daigaku-no-kami was sent to Kyōto to plead the Rōjū case. This had at first seemed a mere formality, but the intrigues of Nariaki and the anti-foreign feeling of the court nobles persuaded the Emperor to refuse the request, and Hotta was unable to reverse this decision though he went himself to Kyōto and spent the months of March, April and May there. His failure was not due entirely to the question of foreign policy. The Shōgun was without an heir, and one was to be chosen from among the Tokugawa branch houses, with the result that intrigues on behalf of rival candidates from Owari and Mito complicated the political situation. In Edo, the coincidence of these two crises and Hotta's failure to solve them soon led to a widespread demand for the appointment of a Tairō, or Regent, to bolster the waning Tokugawa prestige. Early in June 1858, while Hotta was still on his way back from Kyōto, Ii Naosuke was appointed to the office.[42]

As Tairō Naosuke assumed general supervision of policy and sometimes of administrative detail. He was, of course, as anxious as Hotta to sign the American treaty, and for the same reasons. Having arranged another postponement with Harris, promising that whatever happened the American treaty would be the first to be signed, Naosuke set himself to the task of securing the agreement of *daimyō* and court nobles. He was given little time to succeed. In July occurred the very crisis which the treaty had been designed to prevent. In that month news reached Japan that the Treaty of Tientsin had been concluded and that the British and French envoys were on their way to Japan with a large fleet. Harris, first to get the news, went at once to Kanagawa to meet the officials with whom he had negotiated his treaty. He urged that unless it were signed at once, Elgin would be able to start negotiations on his own terms untramelled by any precedent, and would

[42] Kobayashi, *Bakumatsu-shi*, pp. 309-12, 345-59, 371-2. Ōmori, *Dai Nihon Zenshi*, III, 754-61.

probably insist on an agreement very similar to the Treaty of Tientsin. On the other hand, Harris promised, if the American treaty were signed before Elgin arrived, he would do his best to persuade the British ambassador to accept a similar one.[43]

Harris's treaty was already formally drawn up and required only the addition of the signatures, and on 28 July the Bakufu ministers met to discuss his request. Naosuke still preferred to delay until Imperial approval was received, but he was supported only by the Wakadoshiyori Honda Etchū-no-kami. Hotta made no contribution to the discussion. Matsudaira Iga-no-kami, now restored to his old position in the Rōjū, urged strongly that the Bakufu had made treaties without Imperial approval in the past and should certainly do so in a crisis such as now faced Japan. The others agreed that it was hopeless to think of resisting British and French power. Still reluctant, Naosuke finally decided that the negotiators must delay as far as possible but sign if they saw no alternative, and on 29 July, at Harris's insistence, the Treaty of Kanagawa was signed.[44]

Now that the die was cast, Naosuke took decisive steps to strengthen his own position before Elgin's arrival. He announced the signing of the treaty to the *daimyō*, but before doing so dispatched another mission to Kyōto to obtain Imperial approval. Partly because of their unpopularity with the Court and the seclusion party, partly because of their differences with himself, he dismissed both Hotta and Iga-no-kami, replacing them in the Rōjū with men who were competent administrators unlikely to have a decisive effect on policy. He thereby greatly increased his personal control over that body. He had already taken steps to decide the succession question against the Mito candidate, and as soon as Imperial sanction for the choice was received, found an excuse to order the confinement of Nariaki and

---

[43] Griffis, *Townshend Harris*, pp. 315-21. Ōmori, *Dai Nihon Zenshi*, III, 767-9.

[44] Akimoto, *Ii Naosuke*, pp. 156-9. Kobayashi, *Bakumatsu-shi*, pp. 385-7. Ōmori, *Dai Nihon Zenshi*, III, 770-5.

his immediate supporters.[45] ˙This took place the day after Elgin reached Kanagawa. The domestic crisis continued throughout the discussions with Britain, but Naosuke had ensured that for a time, at least, Bakufu foreign policy would conform to his own ideas.

Harris claimed that Elgin and Gros would ' find their work all done to their hands ' when they arrived, and that they would have no need of a large fleet to help them secure the terms they sought.[46] There was much truth in his statement. During his protracted negotiations, Harris had educated the Japanese in the ideas of Western diplomacy, the language of which their interpreters had begun to learn. Moreover, if Elgin chose to accept the American treaty as a model, there was little doubt that he would be spared the tedious discussions of detail that had gone to the making of it. It is probable that Harris was also thinking that his own frequent warnings about British power and intentions had predisposed the Japanese to submit to Elgin's demands. But he had been by no means alone in this, and it is doubtful whether his influence was decisive. More important were the political repercussions of the American treaty in Japan. Harris, by his persistence and persuasions, had brought to a head the conflict between those who were and those who were not willing to open the ports to trade, and while he cannot claim credit for the victory of the former —that must go to Hotta and Ii Naosuke—his treaty had established a precedent, and no other diplomat was likely to suffer the same delays. In the event, Elgin's negotiations were almost a formality.

On 6 July 1858, as soon as he heard that the Chinese Emperor had approved the Treaty of Tientsin, Elgin decided that his next task was to negotiate with Japan. He therefore arranged with Seymour for a suitable naval escort, emphasising, however, that his intentions were entirely peaceful.[47] He went first to Shanghai, intending

---

[45] Satoh, *Agitated Japan*, pp. 72-94. Kobayashi, *Bakumatsu-shi*, pp. 392-9.
[46] Griffis, *Townshend Harris*, p. 321, quoting Harris to Bowring, 2 Aug. 1858.
[47] F.O. *China Corres.*, vol. 289, Elgin to For. Off., No. 145, 6 July 1858 and encl. Admiralty, *In-Letters*, vol. 5693, Seymour to Admiralty, No 228, 6 July 1858.

to make arrangements for the negotiation of a tariff agreement supplementary to the Tientsin treaty, but at the end of the month, finding that the Chinese envoys for these negotiations would not arrive for another two weeks, he decided that the resultant delay would be sufficient for a visit to Japan. Seymour had originally planned to accompany him, but the situation at Canton was unsatisfactory, and both agreed that after a brief visit to Nagasaki the admiral had better go south.[48]

The visit was in any case expected to be no more than an exploratory one, for Elgin did not know what he could accomplish in the time at his disposal.[49] Baron Gros, the French envoy, had been ordered to stay in China, and the *China Mail*, at least, thought that Elgin should have done the same. His first duty, it maintained, was to ensure the protection of Hongkong in the new hostilities that had broken out at Canton, instead of which he was taking Seymour off on what seemed to be no more than a pleasure excursion.[50] From the light-hearted spirit in which the adventure was undertaken one might almost think the *China Mail*'s strictures to be justified. Most members of the mission seemed more interested in shopping than diplomacy, while the tone of the account given by Oliphant, Elgin's secretary, even suggests that the discomfort of Shanghai's summer heat had something to do with the decision to escape for a few weeks from China.

Elgin reached Nagasaki on 3 August aboard H.M.S. *Furious*, escorted by two other ships. Seymour arrived on the following day. Despite the attempts of an ' officious signalman ' on the flagship to draw attention to them, the captain of *Furious* had studiously ignored all Japanese boats and officials on his way into harbour, for fear that they should impose unacceptable restrictions on his ship's movements under the terms of Stirling's convention. Once in, however, he submitted to the usual detailed interrogation,

[48] Elgin, *The Letters and Journals of James, eighth Earl of Elgin*, pp. 260-1.
[49] Parl. Papers 1859, vol. XXXIII (Cd. 2571), pp. 374-5, Elgin to For. Off., No. 163, 30 July 1858. Admiralty, *In-Letters*, vol. 5693, Seymour to Adty., No. 263, 30 July 1858.
[50] *China Mail*, 5 and 19 Aug. 1858.

allowing the officials ' to see, touch, smell and hear every-thing, except the British Ambassador '.[51]   This somewhat cavalier assumption of the right to choose which Japanese laws were to be observed and which ignored was to characterise the actions of all Elgin's subordinates, and sometimes of the ambassador himself.

Conditions at Nagasaki had much improved since Seymour's previous visit, but Elgin had no intention of negotiating there.   After a brief stay he continued to Shimoda.   There he had a long talk with Harris about the terms of the American treaty and then left for Edo Bay, despite the almost tearful protests of the Shimoda *bugyō* that such a course would endanger both Elgin and himself. Once again the guard-boats were ignored, and on the morning of 12 August *Furious* passed Kanagawa, where Poutiatine was opening negotiations, and at Elgin's orders and in defiance of all precedent, moved on up the channel towards Edo itself, followed at lengthy intervals by boats bringing the officials from Uraga, Kanagawa and elsewhere whose duty it would have been to meet her had the speed of her passage not defeated their purpose.[52]

Once anchored in sight of the capital, Elgin refused all requests that he return to Kanagawa, an attitude accepted without great demur by Japanese officials who had orders to be tactful.[53]   He now officially informed the Rōjū that he had come to negotiate and wished to do so in Edo, and after necessary arrangements had been made (on practically identical lines with those made for Harris and Poutiatine), he landed and entered Edo on 17 August.

Despite the evidence of his actions so far, Elgin's approach to the question of negotiations with Japan was very different from that of Bowring.   He had been instructed to avoid the use of force and hoped to avoid the threat of it, although it seemed that the situation created before his arrival, especially by the activities of Stirling and Seymour, might

[51] Osborn, *Cruise in Japanese Waters*, pp. 18-20, 25-9.
[52] Osborn, *Cruise in Japanese Waters*, pp. 120-9.   Oliphant, *Elgin Mission*, II, 92.
[53] Oliphant, *Elgin Mission*, II, 95-9.   *Bakumatsu Gaikoku Kankei Monjo*, XX, 678-9, Rōjū to Machi-bugyō and kanjō-bugyō, 12 Aug. 1858.

make inevitable some sort of recourse to 'gunboat diplomacy'. Osborn, captain of the *Furious*, thought that 'the hour had arrived for Japan to yield to reason, or to be prepared to suffer, as the Court of Pekin had done, for its obstinacy'.[54] But Elgin had no desire to transfer to Japan the methods he had found necessary in China. He had little sympathy with Britain's record in what he called 'this abominable East—abominable not so much in itself as because it is strewed all over with the records of our violence and fraud, and disregard of right'.[55] He wanted to like the Japanese. He knew that they had been encouraged to fear Britain and that it would be difficult to overcome their suspicions, but he was resolved not to be any more 'peremptory' in his relations with them than was absolutely necessary.[56] On the other hand, he had a duty to perform and must perform it, even though, like Harris,[57] he sometimes wondered whether Japan might not be better without treaty relations, whether, indeed, treaties might not bring her only 'misery and ruin'.

His task did not seem at first an easy one. The problem, as Elgin saw it, was that he had to make a treaty against time, for he must soon return to China ; without an interpreter, which put him at the mercy of any the Japanese might provide ; and without proper credentials, for although he had full powers, he had no right to demand an audience with the Shōgun as Harris had done, and this might lower his prestige in the eyes of the Japanese.[58]

The last difficulty was easily solved, for the Japanese were inexperienced in the niceties of diplomatic credentials. When Stirling had completed his convention at Nagasaki in 1854, he had promised, on behalf of the British government, to send a yacht as a present to the Shōgun—whom he, like most of his contemporaries, thought to be 'the Emperor'. This promise was confirmed by the Foreign

[54] Osborn, *Cruise in Japanese Waters*, p. 127.
[55] Elgin, *Letters*, p. 274. See also Morison, *Elgin*, pp. 212-5.
[56] Elgin, *Letters*, pp. 263, 267-8. Oliphant, *Elgin Mission*, II, 15.
[57] Compare, for example, Elgin, *Letters*, pp. 264-5, 271 and Harris, *Complete Journal*, p. 225.
[58] Elgin, *Letters*, p. 263 (12 Aug. 1858).

Office, and a steam yacht built for the purpose was finally
made ready in the spring of 1857. It was sent out to be
handed over by Seymour with a complimentary letter to
the ' Prime Minister ' from Clarendon.[59] Even before
leaving China, Elgin had seen in this yacht, which had
by then reached Shanghai, a useful means of introduction
to the Japanese capital. He suggested that it might be
left to him to deliver it, but Seymour at first insisted on
carrring out the Admiralty's instructions that he was to
do so himself.[60] At Nagasaki the admiral changed his
mind. Before leaving for Canton, he arranged that the
present should be handed over by a naval officer, but in
a manner and at a time convenient to the ambassador,
which gave Elgin the excuse he needed to go to Edo rather
than Nagasaki, and to insist on the ceremonial due to a
friendly envoy.[61]

The interpreter problem was solved by Harris. He lent
Elgin his secretary, Heusken, who spoke some Japanese
as well as Dutch, and whose experience during the American
negotiations made him invaluable not only as an interpreter
but as an adviser, almost First Secretary, to the mission.[62]
The time factor was much more likely to prove a real
difficulty, especially, Elgin thought, as the Japanese were
' not much disposed to do things in a hurry '.[63] He had
been told to base his treaty on that which he negotiated
with China, but such a course would have involved him
in lengthy discussions of the form and content of every
article. These he could only avoid by accepting Harris's
treaty as the basis of his own. It was neither so detailed
nor so generous as the Treaty of Tientsin, but it provided

[59] F.O. *China Corres.*, vol. 280, Adty. to For. Off., 3 Apr. 1857, ana For.
Off. to Adty., 16 Apr. 1857; vol. 278, draft, Clarendon to Prime Minister
of Japan, 15 Apr. 1857. Admiralty, *Out-Letters*, vol. 1613, Adty. to Seymour,
No. 153, 20 Apr. 1857.
[60] F.O. *China Corres.*, vol. 289, Elgin to For. Off., No. 145, 6 July 1858.
Parl. Papers 1859, vol. XXXIII (Cd. 2571), pp. 374-7, Elgin to For. Off., No.
163, 30 July 1858.
[61] Oliphant, *Elgin Mission*, Il, 56. Admiralty, *In-Letters*, vol. 5693,
Seymour to Adty., No. 272, 20 Aug. 1858. Parl. Papers 1859, vol. XXXIII
(Cd. 2571), p. 378, Elgin to For. Off., No. 165, 28 Aug. 1858.
[62] Elgin, *Letters*, p. 263; Oliphant, *Elgin Mission*, II, 90; Crow, *Harris
of Japan*, p. 296.
[63] Elgin, *Letters*, p. 265 (14 Aug. 1858).

an adequate foundation for commercial relations, and so anxious was Elgin to return to China that he decided to accept it despite its minor imperfections. This would enable him, he said, to avoid delay and ' to obviate, as far as possible, the risk of confusion and complication at the outset of a regular trade '.[64]

His first formal meetings were with two of the new members of the Rōjū, whom both he and Oliphant thought stupid.[65] The same was not true of the five bugyō appointed to conduct the negotiations, however. The most important of them were Mizuno Chikugo-no-kami and Nagai Gemba-no-kami, who had negotiated with Stirling at Nagasaki in 1854, and Iwase Higo-no-kami, one of the commissioners for Harris's treaty. Iwase, according to Oliphant, was the wit of the party and Nagai the most intelligent, and when Nagai and Mizuno agreed, the rest seldom failed to follow.[66] Elgin found them ' business-like ' and ' very shrewd '.[67] Moriyama, the senior Japanese linguist, who spoke both Dutch and English, was not only an efficient interpreter but ' a diplomat of the Talleyrand school '.[68] All insisted on the fullest discussion of any proposal which departed from the text of the American treaty, and it was only with difficulty that Elgin succeeded in making a few alterations—which was not surprising, since the avowed policy of the Rōjū was to whittle down the British requests to the greatest possible extent.[69]

After some discussion of the full powers given to the Japanese plenipotentiaries, the first meeting to discuss the terms of the treaty took place on 21 August. On that and the two following days the draft was gone through article by article. By the evening of 23 August all outstanding points were settled, and it was agreed that the treaty should

[64] Parl. Papers 1859, vol. XXXIII (Cd. 2571), pp. 382-5, Elgin to For. Off., No. 172, 30 Aug. 1858.
[65] Oliphant, Elgin Mission, II, 152. Elgin, Letters, p. 268.
[66] Oliphant, Elgin Mission, II, 160-1.
[67] Parl. Papers 1859, vol. XXXIII (Cd. 2571), pp. 382-5, Elgin to For. Off., No. 172, 30 Aug. 1858.
[68] Oliphant, Elgin Mission, II, 104-5.
[69] Bakumatsu Gaikoku Kankei Monjo, XX, 776-7, Rōjū to ōmetsuke and metsuke, 21 Aug. 1858.

be signed and the yacht handed over on the twenty-sixth. Elgin promised, though with little hope of good result, that he would pass on to his government a Japanese request that Britain should not exercise the right to send a permanent diplomatic representative to Edo until 1861. By that time it was hoped, Japanese opinion would be reconciled to such an unparalleled event. He also refused an audience with the Shōgun's heir, because although the Shōgun himself was ill, Elgin feared to establish a precedent by waiting on anyone of lesser rank.[70]

Three days later the treaty was signed and the yacht handed over with all due ceremony. Elgin departed well satisfied that his ' daring exploit ' had ended ' in an illumination of the forts in our honour '.[71]

Elgin's treaty, as he pointed out to the Foreign Office, differed in some respects from that concluded by Harris.[72] It omitted the promise of mediation and friendly aid which had been included in Article II of the American treaty, and where the latter prohibited the import of opium into Japan, Elgin, mindful of events in China, was careful to place the responsibility for checking smuggling squarely on the Japanese authorities. He also inserted a most-favoured-nation clause, a thing which Harris had unaccountably omitted.

The regulations for trade which formed an appendix to both documents were almost identical. Exports were to pay a uniform duty of 5 per cent. ; imports of gold and silver (both coin and bullion) and the personal effects of foreign residents were to be admitted free of duty, and all intoxicating liquors were to carry an import duty of 35 per cent. Harris had arranged that supplies for rigging and repairing ships, coal, timber, steam machinery, zinc, lead, tin and various foodstuffs could be imported at a 5 per cent. duty, and to this list Elgin succeeded in adding

[70] Parl. Papers 1859, vol. XXXIII (Cd. 2571), pp. 382-5, Elgin to For. Off., No. 172, 30 Aug. 1858.
[71] Elgin, *Letters*, p. 273.
[72] Parl. Papers 1859, vol. XXXIII (Cd. 2571), pp. 386-7, Elgin to For. Off., No. 174, 31 Aug. 1858 ; pp. 387-94, Treaty of Edo and Regulations for Trade, 26 Aug. 1858. The text of the American treaty will be found in Gubbins, *Progress of Japan*, pp. 269-77.

cotton and woollen manufactured goods. On all other imports a duty of 20 per cent. was to be paid. The American agreement provided that these categories could be revised after five years at the request of the Japanese government, but Elgin again went a little farther by making revision depend on the wishes of either signatory.

On major issues, however, the two treaties were alike. Both opened the ports of Hakodate, Nagasaki and Kanagawa at once, Niigata or some other port on the Japan Sea coast from 1 January 1860 and Hyōgo (later known as Kōbe) from 1 January 1863. They gave foreigners the right of residence in Edo from 1 January 1862 and in Osaka from 1 January 1863. Both conceded diplomatic or consular representation in Edo and the open ports, arranged for consular jurisdiction and extraterritoriality, and provided that trade should be carried on freely between private subjects without government intervention. The two treaties, in fact, incorporated many of the ideas which had been originated or developed in the course of Western relations with China.

The Japanese text of Elgin's treaty,[73] although a little looser in its phraseology and sometimes vague in its dates —for example, the date of revision, ' on or after 1 July 1872 ', became ' after about fourteen years from now '— differed from the English text in only one notable respect. That difference lay in the most-favoured-nation clause. The English version entitled British subjects to share ' all privileges, immunities, and advantages, that may have been or may be hereafter, granted ' in Japan to other countries. The Japanese text left out the reference to existing privileges and mentioned only ' special rights which may hereafter be granted '. It was the same sort of change that had appeared in the Japanese text of Stirling's convention. This time, however, it had little practical importance, for there were no existing rights of any value that were not incorporated in the treaty itself. British interest would be in future not in past concessions.

[73] *Bakumatsu Gaikoku Kankei Monjo*, XX, 791-810, Japanese text of Treaty of Edo and trade regulations .

The treaty met with general approbation if not enthusiasm. Of those most immediately concerned, the Japanese were satisfied that they had conceded as little as possible,[74] while Elgin thought the settlement would be of advantage to both countries if British merchants ' did not, by injudicious and aggressive acts, rouse against themselves the fears and hostility of the natives '.[75] The Foreign Office, having indicated its ' interest ' and ' satisfaction ',[76] began to make arrangements to establish consular representation in Japan. It did not choose at first to send anyone of full diplomatic status because it expected that Japanese ports would ' principally be resorted to by vessels engaged in the Whale Fishery ',[77] but in this it was rapidly disillusioned by news that a number of merchants were fitting out ships for the trade even before the exchange of ratifications had made it legal to do so. Steps were accordingly taken to restrain their impatience.[78]

Outside official circles, the merchants of Belfast and Dundee complained that linen had not been included in the list of goods bearing import duty of only 5 per cent.,[79] but there was little other criticism. The *China Mail* approved the treaty and contrasted it favourably with that of Stirling.[80] *The Times* thought it of less commercial importance than the Treaty of Tientsin, but ' with even a higher character of historical and political significance '.[81] And if the *Edinburgh Review* doubted the permanence of Elgin's accomplishment,[82] the treaty was sufficiently popular

---

[74] *Bakumatsu Gaikoku Kankei Monjo*, XX, Rōjū to ōmetsuke and metsuke, 28 Aug. 1858 ; XX, 825-6, Rōjū to negotiators of treaty, 30 Aug. 1858.

[75] Elgin, *Letters*, p. 274.

[76] Parl. Papers 1859, vol. XXXIII (Cd. 2571), pp. 394-5, For. Off. to Elgin, No. 65, 8 Nov. 1858.

[77] F.O. *China Corres.*, vol. 307, For. Off. to Treasury, 4 Dec. 1858.

[78] F.O. *China Corres.*, vol. 307, For. Off. to Adty., 24 Nov. 1858. London *Times*, 3 Feb. 1859.

[79] F.O. *China Corres.*, vol. 307, Memorial of Belfast Chamber of Commerce, 4 Dec. 1858 ; Bd. Trade to For. Off., 13 Nov. 1858, encl. memorial of Dundee Chamber of Commerce.

[80] *China Mail*, 9 and 16 Sept. 1858.

[81] London *Times*, 2 Nov. 1858.

[82] *Edinburgh Review*, CXI, 225 (Jan. 1860), p. 118.

to cause the political parties in England to vie publicly for the credit of having initiated and directed it.[83]

It was, however, left to a Frenchman, a member of the Gros embassy which followed Elgin to Japan to pay tribute to Japanese policy, to commend ' cette rare intuition que possède le gouvernement japonais et qui le porte à accorder de bonne grâce et spontanément ce qu'il sent pouvoir lui être enlevé par la force '.[84] The praise was perhaps a little high, certainly a little premature. Recent Anglo-Japanese relations had been confined to treaty negotiations and the use of Japanese ports for naval operations. With the opening of trade, as British merchants, missionaries and officials claimed the right of residence in Japan, fresh occasions of dispute would undoubtedly arise. In the existing state of opinion in the two countries, it seemed unlikely that they would be ignored. The real test of British intentions and Japanese policy had still to come.

[83] London *Times*, 4 Feb. 1859, reports of Parliamentary debates.
[84] Marquis de Moges, *Souvenirs d'une Ambassade en Chine et au Japon en* 1857 *et* 1858, p. 333.

The East India Company's Japan factory, founded early in the seventeenth century in the first flush of English expansion, proved a disappointment. Japan produced few of the exotic oriental goods that the traders sought. Indeed, she sought them herself as imports. There was no great market for European products other than arms, no basis for a flourishing trade, and no gateway was to be opened through Japan to the mysterious and fabulously wealthy China. In face of Dutch competition, of increasing Japanese restrictions and the ineffective trading methods of Richard Cocks, the factory inevitably proved a commercial failure. It was withdrawn only ten years after its foundation.

Thereafter the directors of the Company were not easily persuaded of the value of markets in Japan. A few men remained convinced that great wealth could be found there and, despite evidence to the contrary, that British woollens could be sold in quantity. Their efforts led the Company to make an attempt to renew the trade in the reign of Charles II, but the attempt failed, as did those to open an indirect trade through other countries of East Asia. After 1700, still not convinced that the trade would repay the cost of opening it, the East India Company sought its profits elsewhere.

This pattern of opinion was repeated after 1775. Once more the efforts of a few individuals, some of them officials of the Company, some private merchants, brought about a revival of interest in Japan. The directors, who had access to seventeenth century records, were reluctant to make any new attempt on the trade. The government proved easier to persuade and in the Macartney mission of 1791–3 made half-hearted plans to establish contact with Japan. Nothing came of these plans. Thereafter, however, unofficial visits to Japan increased in number through enthusiasts like Raffles and adventurers like Peter Gordon ; still more through the expansion and northward movement of the Pacific whale fishery, which brought British seamen in increasing numbers to the Japanese coast.

There came, too, greater knowledge of Japanese opposition to trade. It was realised that Japan's policy of seclusion, directed not specifically against Great Britain, but against all foreigners outside the group of Dutch and Chinese merchants allowed to trade at Nagasaki, put an obstacle in the way that could not be overcome by the undirected efforts of a few individuals. The task would have to be undertaken by the Company or by the government, and probably on a large scale. For that there was still not enough incentive.

In 1834, with the end of the East India Company's monopoly of the China trade, the Foreign Office became directly responsible for British policy in East Asia. This made no immediate difference. Like the Company, whose policy it inherited, the Foreign Office paid lip-service to the desirability of opening Japan but was not sufficiently convinced of the trade's value to take direct action. It was, of course, susceptible to the pressure of merchant opinion. But Japan had not captured the imagination of the merchants as China had done, nor was there any general belief that Japan had unlimited sources of wealth waiting to be tapped by British enterprise. There was, after all, some solid basis for the ' myth ' of the China trade. A valuable trade already existed there ; the greater part of the country was still untouched by it ; and it was logical to believe that a vast expansion was possible in remoter Chinese markets. As seen by British merchants and officials, the war of 1839 to 1842 was fought to gain access to those markets. There was no such basis on which they could erect a similar structure of belief about Japan. Japan was obviously smaller, reputedly less wealthy than China. There was no British trade by which prospects might be judged ; the trade of the Dutch was reported to be small and declining ;

and even those who did advocate establishing relations with Japan did not presume to claim that its possibilities were as great as those of China. Moreover, a beginning had been made in China. Its exploitation was not only more attractive but more practical. Success in China, therefore, brought no immediate attempt to open Japan.

Even so, the China war did bring the opening of Japan one step nearer. By opening to British ships ports to the north of Canton, it increased the possibility of unofficial —or unpremeditated—visits to Japan out of which conflict might grow. More important, it led to the creation of a consular service and a new naval squadron permanently stationed on the China coast. Where in the past the organisation of an expedition to Japan would have required a special effort on the part of the Foreign Office and Admiralty, and did not seem likely to repay the expenditure of time and money involved, it could now be carried out by the use of purely local resources and might therefore be worth the attempting. This fact explains the plans of 1845. Davis saw that the evacuation of Chusan provided a convenient and inexpensive opportunity of going to Japan, a view in which Aberdeen concurred.

Yet it was another thirteen years before Britain concluded a treaty of the kind Davis planned. Why was this? Practically, it was because the officials directly responsible for implementing the plans were convinced that negotiations, to be successful, must be accompanied by a display of ' naval pomp ' ; and the warships they required for this purpose seemed never to be available when the plenipotentiary was ready to sail. Fundamentally, it was because there was no deep interest in the project, either in London or in China, among officials or among merchants, to lend drive and persistence to the policy which had been formulated. It is a measure of Japan's unimportance that in 1846 the suppression of piracy in Borneo was numbered among the more important duties which prevented the China squadron from visiting Japan.

The unimportance of Japan in British policy was confirmed after 1847 by the failure of attempts to force revival of the plans abandoned by Davis. In Bonham there was a new Superintendent who naturally did not have an author's interest in the project ; in Palmerston a new Foreign Secretary much occupied with events in Europe. Moreover, the pressure brought to bear on them was neither great nor effective. Men like Gutzlaff and Bettelheim had little political influence. Montgomery Martin worked up a public campaign of a kind much more likely to succeed, but it was obviously the work of one man and aroused only a superficial interest. None of the commercial organisations approached by Martin ever saw fit to press the matter once their initial memorials had been answered by the Foreign Office.

British policy towards the Perry expedition provides further evidence. Despite the arguments of a number of private correspondents, neither Malmesbury nor Clarendon showed any inclination to emulate, still less to forestall the Americans. They preferred to await the expedition's results and benefit by them if they could. It was not until after Perry's success—or rather, a premature report of his success—that Clarendon took action. Even then he did so only because the American treaty seemed to create a new opportunity of opening relations with Japan without special risk or expense. Early in 1854, presumably in a belief that where America led Britain could follow with little difficulty, he instructed Bowring to go to Japan on the first suitable occasion for the purpose of concluding a satisfactory commercial treaty. This time the plan remained in being. It was the subject of frequent discussion in the course of the next four years, but it was still not put into effect.

The twin problems of providing naval support and of overcoming Japanese opposition to trade continued to render British policy ineffective. The Foreign Office, aware that its instructions might be four months out of date by the time they reached Hongkong, was unwilling to give specific directions about the date of the mission. Bowring, though eager enough to accomplish a task that might bring him fame, tended to over-estimate its difficulties. He was sure that the Japanese would not willingly grant the kind of treaty he meant to demand, and from that premise argued that nothing effective could be done without the help of a large naval squadron. First the Crimean War, then the new war with China made it impossible to provide such a squadron as he desired. In the interval between these wars it would have been possible, but Bowring missed this opportunity by waiting for Foreign Office permission to organise a joint Anglo-French expedition. Had he been content with an escort of one or two ships, there would have been other opportunities. He might have gone in the winter, for example, during the northerly monsoon. The advent of the steamer had made such a course possible, but he continued to think of the Japan mission as something for the summer months, perhaps because he had not fully realised the possibilities of the steamer, more probably because there were still not enough steamers on the China coast to form an impressive squadron.

On the other hand, the events that prevented Bowring from taking action actually operated to create an opportunity for the Royal Navy to do so. The two wars brought considerable reinforcements to the China squadron. Bowring could not use them because his Japan expedition required a predictable interval in naval operations, a thing it was almost impossible to find in time of war. The commander-in-chief was not so handicapped, for he could make decisions about the use of his ships at very much shorter notice. Moreover, his duties took him to Japan and gave him a valid reason to negotiate.

Stirling's desire to use Japanese ports against the Russians took him to Nagasaki, where the errors of the interpreters and the preconceived ideas of the Japanese negotiators provided him with a convention very similar to that secured by Perry—and very different from that desired in London and Hongkong. That it was criticised because it omitted all mention of trade gave Stirling but little concern. However, when he found that it was also proving unsatisfactory as a means of providing bases for the fleet, he attempted to expand its provisions by negotiating an Exposition in 1855.

Stirling received no support in his attempt to introduce a stragetic factor into Anglo-Japanese relations. Bowring, the Board of Trade, the Foreign Office all continued to think in terms of trade. To some, a treaty containing no commercial privileges was worse than no treaty at all. In January 1856 Clarendon took steps to put an end to naval diplomacy in Japan, and the responsibility for future negotiations fell once again to Bowring, now more than ever convinced of the difficulty of the task and the impossibility of accomplishing it by mere persuasion.

The war with China and the consequent criticism of Bowring's conduct made it desirable to send a special envoy to assume control of British interests there. In April 1857 the Foreign Office took the opportunity of putting the Japan mission, too, in different hands. Elgin, like Bowring, was forced to postpone negotiations, but not for the same reasons. He was not dominated by the China coast traditions of diplomacy and had, moreover, been instructed not to use force against Japan. He was therefore willing to dispense with much of the 'naval pomp', but on the other hand his visit to Japan was contingent on success in China and that in its turn was delayed by events in India.

This delay proved to have certain advantages, however. By 1858, when Elgin was ready to leave China for a time, events had taken place in Japan which made his work much easier. Perry's negotiations in 1854 had made it easier for Stirling to obtain similar terms if he cared to accept them. Harris performed much the same office for Elgin, and Elgin, because he was anxious to return to China with the least possible delay, was ready to follow the lead he had been given. The British treaty of 1858 confirmed the fact of American leadership in the opening of Japan.

From this narrative of British policy towards Japan it is possible to draw certain general conclusions. In the first place, it is clear that the initiative rested usually with British officials in the East. They were frequently the first to put forward such plans as were adopted, and were always given wide discretion in carrying them out. The function of the Foreign Office—like that of the East India Company's

Court of Directors before 1834—was to approve or reject the suggestions of its representatives in China, to ensure that they conformed in methods and objectives to the general lines of government policy. It was seldom that a policy was formulated in London that did not originate in an in-coming dispatch. Sometimes an over-enthusiastic or over-ambitious official had to be restrained, for in so remote a field of action he might easily involve Britain in embarrassment or even war, but rarely was any attempt made to urge a reluctant one to take action.

Foreign Office failure to take the initiative is a measure of Japan's importance to British Foreign Secretaries. Palmerston and Aberdeen, Clarendon and Malmesbury, despite their political differences, were remarkably consistent in their attitude to Japan. They showed by their actions, sometimes by their words, that the opening of Japanese ports, however desirable in theory, was not an object of sufficient value to warrant the expenditure of much effort or the acceptance of much risk. And there was never enough public interest at home to make a change in that attitude politically profitable.

The Royal Navy's influence lay in the execution rather than the formulation of policy. Stirling's negotiations are an obvious exception, but they were an accident of personality, a temporary diversion from the main stream of policy, made possible by the freedom of action enjoyed by the commander of a distant station in the days before the telegraph. In the plans of Davis and Bowring the China squadron was to play a supporting, not a leading role. It was to provide the prestige, the ceremonial and the thinly-veiled threat of force which alone, they thought, would make a plenipotentiary's arguments convincing to the Japanese.

This technique is the one that became known as ' gunboat diplomacy ', and it is interesting that it was always the Superintendent who insisted on its necessity, the Foreign Office who bowed to his judgment, often reluctantly. Even Palmerston, with whose name such methods are normally associated, was more willing to approve than to advocate their application to Japan. And their effect was very different from their purpose. Since the plenipotentiary would not go without ships, the timing of the Japan expedition was controlled by the duties of the China squadron, and there seemed always to be more important duties to perform. The methods that were to have ensured success served only to delay the attempt itself.

British policy towards Japan in the period 1834 to 1858 is marked off from what is usually termed British foreign policy by the fact that it was concerned not with the day-to-day relations between two countries but with the plans and negotiations aimed at establishing such relations. This gives it an appearance of independence, even of isolation. It was, however, closely related to British policy in China. China was always recognised as being the more important of the two countries, and it was usually the protection or extension of British interests there, requiring the full attention of the China squadron, that prevented the plenipotentiary from assembling a suitable force to support his Japan negotiations.

More directly, Anglo-Chinese relations did much to determine the type of treaty Britain sought to conclude with Japan. Japan was a near neighbour of China, akin to her in language and culture and equally averse to foreign intercourse. It was natural enough that British officials should assume that both presented the same problems. By 1845, when the first plans were made for negotiating with Japan, they already had much experience of dealing with such problems. The instructions sent to Davis were based on that experience, anticipating the same difficulties and providing for their solution in terms identical with those then being applied in China. The same was true of the instructions to Bowring in 1854. They differed from earlier ones precisely to the extent that the immediate issues engaging Foreign Office attention in China had changed. Elgin in his turn was told to base his treaty on that to be concluded with China. That he did not do so was due to circumstances which neither he nor the Foreign Office had foreseen, and it made little difference in the result, for Harris, too, had been impressed with the desirability of incorporating into his agreement many of the provisions which governed western relations with China.

The same tendency is apparent in British policy immediately after 1858. The consular service established in Japan as a result of Elgin's agreement was openly modelled on, and almost entirely staffed from, that existing in China. In fact, Britain entered upon treaty relations with Japan with certain fixed ideas—belief in the " treaty port " system, extraterritoriality and tariff control being chief among them —which owed nothing of their development to the situation in which they were to be applied.

If China played an important part in British policy towards Japan, it played a still more important one in Japanese policy towards Britain. As a demonstration of British power, events in China undoubtedly inclined the Japanese to submit to the demands of an enemy whose military might they knew themselves unable to withstand. As a demonstration of British expansion, they bred fear of the results of foreign intercourse. British military operations in China, the reports brought by Dutch, Chinese and Americans, the actions of Stirling and Seymour at Nagasaki, even the treaty negotiated by Elgin, all helped to convince the Japanese that their national sovereignty was threatened by British imperialism. The extension of British political control for the protection of trade to them seemed naked aggression. A re-examination of that imperialism is outside the scope of this study, as is any new analysis of the associated problem of British policy in China. However, an attempt must be made to answer the question of how far British policy towards Japan in the years 1834 to 1858 represented a real threat to Japan's political and economic independence. The discussion may throw light on these wider problems.

On one point it is possible to be definite. There is no evidence of any policy of *deliberate* British political and territorial expansion in Japan before 1858. Stirling's emphasis on strategic interests and his plans for a new ' maritime empire ' were never accepted by the British Cabinet, to whom the government of colonial territories was a burden to be undertaken—if at all—only in return for very real advantages.

On the other hand, the story of British interest in Japan before treaty relations began is inevitably one of plans and intentions, and it is argued that in the mid-nineteenth century British imperialism was less a matter of intentions than of unpremeditated results, of a gradual and often unwilling assumption of political authority as the only way of providing the law and order in which trade might flourish. To contemporaries, it seemed unlikely that the Bakufu would be able to provide the administrative efficiency which alone could prevent such a development. Its policy was one of grudging concessions unlikely to breed goodwill. Moreover, most of the *samurai* were unshaken in their hatred of foreigners, and Tokugawa control of them was precarious —as appeared after 1858 in the frequent attacks on foreign ships and citizens. Yet it does not follow from these facts alone that disputes would have led to war, and war to British economic and political domination of Japan.

The danger to China lay not so much in Manchu weakness as in the belief of British merchants, diplomats and officials that the China trade was but a fraction of what it might be and that only political obstacles—the policy of the Chinese government—prevented access to vast new markets. On this estimate the China trade was worth fighting for, and two wars were indeed fought for it. It was, too, a consideration that might make China worth governing if all else failed. The reasoning does not apply equally to Japan. The threat to Chinese independence existed only so long as the Foreign Office and Board of Trade retained their faith in the roseate promises of the ' old China hands ', and there was no equivalent body of belief behind the attempt to secure trade with Japan. Admittedly elements of economic and political control which had already been introduced in China were incorporated in the first treaties with Japan —not only by Britain but by all the Treaty Powers—but this was because the China treaty-pattern had become almost a habit of mind with Western diplomats. Moral considerations apart, Britain was not prepared to fight to impose such terms unless convinced both that they were necessary and that the returns would repay her effort. With few exceptions, neither Foreign Office nor merchants were convinced of either. If they had been, they would never have delayed so long in face of Japanese opposition to the opening of the ports.

That is only to say that in 1858 Japan was not facing the same dangers as China. It was still possible that danger would arise thereafter, for the treaty of 1858 was potentially not the end but the beginning of difficulties. Stirling in 1855 and Seymour in 1856 had shown that friction was more likely to arise out of the expansion or interpretation of existing treaties than out of the negotiations to obtain them in the first place—a fact already amply demonstrated in China. British merchants could certainly be expected to show greater interest in the extension of an existing trade than they had in the attempt to establish a new one in a country relatively unknown to them. They might even create a new ' myth ' of the Japan trade if the policy of the Japanese government denied them the opportunity of assessing its true worth.

In the event these dangers proved illusory, for both British and Japanese policies were eventually to undergo a change. That change, however, was not immediately apparent. In the interval there occurred events which were decisive for the future course of Japanese history, since the years 1858 to 1868 saw the struggle for power within Japan come to a head, and its result brought new rulers and a new form of government. Throughout that vital formative period, the Japanese held to the estimate of British policy which they had formed before the signing of the treaties. British actions, reflecting as they did most of the characteristics of British policy in China, gave them no good cause to revise their estimate. In fact, by convincing many Japanese statesmen that only modern economic, political and military organisation on Western lines could preserve their country's independence in face of Western aggression, British policy, both before and after 1858, played an important part in determining the nature and objectives of the new Japan.

APPENDIX A

The Anglo-Japanese Convention of 14 October 1854

The text of the convention given below, omitting preamble and signatures, is taken from Parliamentary Papers 1856, vol. LXI (Cd. 2014), pp. 209–12. The phrases in italics and enclosed between square brackets were omitted from the Japanese text of the agreement (*Bakumatsu Gaikoku Kankei Monjo*, VII, 439–41). Other variations in the Japanese text are indicated by italics and footnotes. Since the phrasing of the English and Japanese documents does not exactly correspond, it is emphasised that the differences between them indicated here are differences of *meaning*, not exact differences of *wording*.

* * * *

Article I. The ports of Nagasaki (Fisen)[1] and Hakodadi (Matsmai)[2] shall be open to British ships for the purpose of effecting repairs, and obtaining fresh water, provisions, *and other supplies of any sort they may absolutely want*[3] for the use of the ships.

Article II. Nagasaki shall be open for the purposes aforesaid from and after the present date; and Hakodate from and after the end of fifty days from the Admiral's departure from this port. The rules and regulations of each of these ports are to be complied with.

Article III. Only ships in distress from weather or unmanageable, will be permitted to enter other ports than those specified in the foregoing Articles, without permission from the Imperial government.

[1] Nagasaki (Hizen).
[2] Hakodate (Matsumai).
[3] In Japanese, " and indispensable necessities."

ARTICLE IV. British ships in Japanese ports shall conform to the laws of Japan. If high officers or commanders of ships shall break any such laws, it will lead to the ports being closed. Should inferior persons break them, they are to be delivered over to the Commanders of their ships for punishment.

ARTICLE V. In the ports of Japan, [*either now open, or*] which may hereafter be opened, to the ships or subjects of any foreign nations, British ships and subjects shall be entitled to admission, and to the enjoyment of an equality of advantages with those of *the most favoured nation,*[4] [*always excepting the advantages accruing to the Dutch and Chinese from their existing relations with Japan.*]

ARTICLE VI. This Convention shall be ratified, and the ratifications shall be exchanged at Nagasaki on behalf of Her Majesty the Queen of Great Britain, and on behalf of His Highness the Emperor of Japan, within twelve months from the present date.

ARTICLE VII. When this Convention shall be ratified, no *high officer*[5] coming to Japan shall alter it.

[4] In Japanese, " other countries ".
[5] In Japanese, " ship's commander ".

APPENDIX B

DRAFT EXPOSITION HANDED BY REAR ADMIRAL SIR JAMES
STIRLING TO THE NAGASAKI BUGYŌ, 11 OCTOBER 1855

The text is taken from F.O. *China Corres.*, Vol. 255,
enclosure in Admiralty to Foreign Office, 5 January
1856. Passages omitted from the final form of the
exposition as a result of the negotiations of October
1855 are shown in italics and enclosed in square
brackets. Other changes made during the negotiations are indicated by italics and footnotes.

* * * *

The First Article of the Convention opens the Ports of
Nagasaki and Hakodadi[1] to British Ships for Repairs and
Supplies. It opens the whole and every part of those Ports,
but Ships must be guided in anchoring by the Directions of
the Local Government. Safe and convenient Places will be
assigned where Ships may be repaired. Workmen, Materials,
and Supplies will be provided by the Local Government
according to a Tariff to be agreed upon, by which also the
modes of Payment will be regulated. All Official Communications *will be made in the English Language.*[2] [*An Hospital
in case of need will be provided,*] a British Burial Ground *set apart,
fenced in, and*[3] properly protected [*and permission given to land
under Regulations to be hereafter agreed upon*].
The Second Article provides that at each of the Ports of
Nagasaki and Hakodadi,[4] the Port Regulations shall be obeyed;
but the Japanese Government will take care that they shall
not be of a nature [*to impose unnecessary Restrictions nor*] to

---

[1] Hakodate.
[2] The final text reads, " will hereafter, when Japanese shall have time to
learn English, be made in that language ".
[3] The final text reads, " shall be set apart on Medsume Sima, fenced in
by a stone wall, and ".
[4] Hakodate.

create embarrassment [s *and quarrels,*] nor to contradict in any other way the general tenor and Intent of the Treaty, the main object of which is to promote a friendly Intercourse between Great Britain and Japan.

The Third Article declares that only ships in distress from weather or unmanageable shall enter other Ports than Nagasaki and Hakodadi[4] without permission from the Imperial Government ; but [*this Article is not intended to apply to Her Majesty's*] Ships of War, *whose general Right*[5] to enter the Ports of Friendly Powers in the unavoidable performance of *Public Duties can*[5] neither be waived nor restricted, but *they*[6] will not enter any other than Open Ports without necessity or without offering proper explanations to the Imperial Authorities.

The Fourth Article provides that British Ships and Subjects in Japanese Ports shall conform to the Laws of Japan, and that if any Subordinate British Subjects commit offences against the Laws, they shall be handed over to their own officers for Punishment, and that if High Officers or Commanders of Ships shall break the Laws, it will lead to the closing of the Ports specified. All this is as it should be, but it is not intended by this Article that any Acts of Individuals, whether High or Low, previously unauthorised or subsequently disapproved of by Her Majesty the Queen of Great Britain, can set aside the Convention entered into with Her Majesty alone by His Imperial Highness the Emperor of Japan.

The Fifth Article secures in the fullest sense to British Ships and Subjects in every Port of Japan, either now open or hereafter to be opened, an Equality in point of advantage and accommodation with the Ships and Subjects or Citizens of any other Foreign Nation, excepting any peculiar Privilege hitherto conceded to the Dutch and Chinese in the Port of Nagasaki. If therefore any other Nation or People be now or hereafter permitted to enter other Ports than Nagasaki and Hakodadi,[7] [*or to reside in any part of the Empire,*] or to appoint Consuls, or to open Trade, or to enjoy any Advantage or

---

[5] The final text reads, "have a general right . . . public duties, which right can ".

[6] The final text reads, " Her Majesty's Ships ".

[7] Hakodate.

Privilege whatever, [(*the Dutch and Chinese Privileges existing previous to the 14th of October 1854 alone excepted*)] British Ships and Subjects shall, as of Right, enter upon the enjoyment of the same.

BIBLIOGRAPHY

GENERAL NOTE.

This bibliography lists all the important works used in preparing chapters I to VII. Those used for the introduction are not included here, but are given more fully in footnote references.

The chief manuscript sources were the two Foreign Office series of correspondence relating to China in the Public Record Office. No separate series was started for Japan until 1859, except for a single volume for the year 1856. F.O. 17, the general China correspondence originally housed in the Foreign Office itself, contains originals of dispatches from China, with their enclosures, and drafts of dispatches to China, together with some Foreign Office minutes on them. In addition, it includes the valuable collection of letters, listed as " Domestic Various ", which were exchanged between the Foreign Office, other government departments, and private citizens and organisations in Britain. F.O. 228, the archive collected at and returned from Hongkong, contains originals of dispatches from London and drafts of dispatches to London, including some dispatches and many enclosures which are missing from F.O. 17. The letter-books containing copies of the Superintendents' letters to local correspondents (the Commander-in-Chief, merchants, etc.) were occasionally useful, but the series does not include the letters received from those correspondents.

These were supplemented by the few but important Foreign Office minutes and memoranda relating to Japan in F.O. 96, and by occasional use of Foreign Office correspondence with other Western countries (e.g. the United States), though the latter proved to be fairly represented by the extracts found in the China series. Except for the Clarendon Papers, which contain the private letters exchanged by Bowring and Clarendon in the period 1853–8, the private correspondence of Secretaries of State served rather as background information, since direct references to China and Japan are rare. Such Board of Trade records as are available add little to the information contained in the Board of Trade letters to the Foreign Office, which appear in the " Domestic Various " volumes of F.O. 17. The Admiralty papers throw relatively little light on the formation of policy, but are, of course, essential for the study of Stirling's negotiations, of which they contain very detailed accounts. Many dispatches are missing from the correspondence with the Commander-in-Chief East Indies, especially for the years 1848–51.

The Japanese records published in the *Dai Nihon Komonjo* series are a very full collection of documents for the years 1853 to 1858. They include contemporary translations of foreign letters ; reports to and instructions from the Rōjū ; detailed minutes of negotiations ; memoranda and private correspondence of officials and others ; extracts from diaries ; and texts of treaties and conventions. They are invaluable both in supplementing British records of the actual negotiations —though they contain no good account of the Elgin discussions —and also in providing a means of assessing Japanese policy generally, especially necessary because little of the recent work of Japanese historians is available in this country.

The published letters of British statesmen (with the notable exception of those of the Earl of Elgin) make little reference to Japan. Like contemporary journals and travels, they sometimes contain useful comment of a general kind, e.g. on British activities or representatives in East Asia, but are interesting rather than important to the study of policy. Reliable and detailed modern works of direct relevance are few, as the list itself will show.

I. BIBLIOGRAPHIES

Wenckstern, Fr. von, *A Bibliography of the Japanese Empire* vol. I, 1477–1893, Leiden, 1895 ; vol. II, 1894–1906, Tokyo, 1907.
Lists works in Western languages only.

Nachod, O., *Bibliography of the Japanese Empire*, 1906–26, 2 vols., London and Leipzig, 1928.

—— *Bibliographie von Japan*, 1927–1929 ; 1930–1932 ; 1933–1935 ; 1936–1937, 4 vols., Leipzig, 1931–40.
A continuation of Wenckstern's work.

Kerner, R. J., *Northeastern Asia : A Selected Bibliography*, 2 vols., Berkeley, 1939. Lists some works in Japanese.

II. CONTEMPORARY MATERIAL

(*a*) MANUSCRIPT MATERIAL.

Government archives at the Public Record Office.

Foreign Office, General Correspondence, *China* (F.O. 17 : cited as F.O. *China Corres.*).
Volumes 1 to 307, covering the years 1834 to 1858.

Foreign Office, Embassy and Consular Archives, *China, Correspondence* (F.O. 228 : cited as F.O. *China Emb. Arch.*).
Volumes 1 to 260, excluding consular correspondence.

Foreign Office, General Correspondence, *Japan* (F.O. 46 : cited as F.O. *Japan Corres.*).
Volume 1, Domestic Various, 1856, is the only volume for the years before 1859.

Foreign Office, General Correspondence, *America, United States, Series II* (F.O. 5 : cited as F.O. *United States Corres.*).
A few dispatches of importance, chiefly on treaty revision in China, in the years 1854–7.

Foreign Office, *Protocols of Treaties, Japan* (F.O. 93/49).
Number 1 (F.O. 93/49–I) contains both English and Japanese originals of Stirling's convention and exposition of 1854–5.

Foreign Office, *Miscellanea, Series II* (F.O. 96).
Volumes 17 to 25, Foreign Office minutes and memoranda, 1830–58.

Admiralty, Secretary's Department, *Indexes and Compilations, Series III* (cited as *Admiralty Digests*).
Contains digests of Admiralty correspondence, valuable when the originals have been weeded and destroyed.

Admiralty, Secretary's Department, *In-letters, New General Series* (Adm. 1 : cited as Admiralty, *In-letters*).

Dispatches from East Indies station in volumes 5496, 5514, 5530, 5539, 5629, 5640, 5657, 5660, 5672, 5693, covering the years 1840 to 1858.

Admiralty, Secretary's Department, *Out-letters, Modern series* (Adm. 2 : cited as Admiralty, *Out-letters*).
Dispatches to East Indies station in volumes 1597, 1599, 1600, 1603–5, 1608–9, 1611, 1613, 1615, covering the years 1840 to 1858.

Admiralty, *Supplementary* (Adm. 13).
Volume 4, Port and Standing Instructions for the East Indies station.

Board of Trade, *Minutes* (B.T. 5).
Volumes 41, 43, 50, 55, 58.

Board of Trade, *Out-letters* (B.T. 3).
Volume 26, correspondence about the Bonin Islands, 1835.

Treasury, *Minutes* (T. 29).
Volume 348, correspondence concerning abolition of China trade monopoly, 1833–4.

Treasury, *Out-letters, Various* (T. 28).
Volume 57, correspondence with Secretaries of State, 1834, concerning China trade monopoly.

Colonial Office, *East Indies* (C.O. 77).
Volume 45, correspondence concerning Bonin Islands, 1836.

At the India Office.

East India Company, *Letters from the Board of Control.*
Volume 9, correspondence concerning abolition of China trade monopoly.

East India Company, *Letters to the Board of Control.*
Volume 12, correspondence concerning abolition of China trade monopoly.

India Board, Secret Department, *China.*
Volume 7, correspondence concerning abolition of China trade monopoly.

Hudson's Bay Company Archives.
Correspondence concerning Japanese castaways, 1834–5 :—
Vancouver Fort, Correspondence Books, Out (B. 223), b. 10.
London Correspondence, Outward, Official (A. 6), vol. 23.
London Correspondence, Outward, General (A. 5), vol. 11.

Private Papers.

British Museum, Additional Manuscripts, *Aberdeen Papers.*
Volumes XXVI (Add. MSS. 43064), XXVII (Add. MSS. 43065), and CXXIV (Add. MSS. 43162).

Public Record Office, Gifts and Deposits, *Granville Papers* (G.D. 29). Volumes 18 to 20.

Public Record Office, Gifts and Deposits, *Russell Papers* (G.D. 22). Volumes 4–8, 11.

Bodleian Library, *Clarendon Papers.*
The semi-official correspondence (listed as *MS. Clarendon* Dep. C), especially the correspondence between Clarendon and Bowring in volumes 19, 29, 37, 57, 70 and 129–38.

(*b*) PRINTED PAPERS.

Parliamentary Papers 1830, vol. V (Sess. No. 644), *First Report from the Select Committee on the Affairs of the East India Company (China Trade).*

Parliamentary Papers 1830, vol. VI (Sess. No. 646), *Report from the Select Committee of the House of Lords appointed to inquire into the present state of the Affairs of the East India Company.*

Parliamentary Papers 1856, vol. LXI (Cd. 2014), *Convention between Her Majesty and the Emperor of Japan, signed at Nagasaki in the English and Japanese Languages, October 14, 1854.*
This also includes the text of the Exposition of 1855.

Parliamentary Papers 1856, vol. LXI (Cd. 2077), *Correspondence respecting the late Negotiation with Japan.*
Omits some important passages and several enclosures from Stirling's reports.

Parliamentary Papers 1859, vol. XXXIII (Cd. 2571), *Correspondence relative to the Earl of Elgin's Special Mission to China and Japan, 1857–1859.*
The Japan papers are printed with only minor omissions.

East India Company, *The Third Report of the Select Committee Appointed to take into Consideration the Export Trade from Great Britain to the East Indies*, London, 1793.

East India Company, *Papers respecting the negotiations with His Majesty's Ministers on the subject of the East-India Company's Charter*, London, 1833.

Sir T. S. Raffles Report on Japan to the Secret Committee of the East India Company, ed. M. B. Paske-Smith, Kobe, 1929.
A print *in extenso* of East India Company, *Factory Records, China and Japan*, vol. 195.

Hansard, *Parliamentary Debates*, Third Series.

Dai Nihon Komonjo—Bakumatsu Gaikoku Kankei Monjo [Old Japanese Documents—Documents on late-Tokugawa Foreign Relations], 21 volumes and 4-volume appendix, Tokyo, 1911–35.
Covers the years 1853 to 1858.

(c) NEWSPAPERS AND PERIODICALS.

The Times, London (for the years 1833–59).

The Edinburgh Review, Edinburgh (for the years 1802–59).

The Quarterly Review, London (for the years 1809–59).

Bentley's Miscellany, London (vol. xxxi, 1852).

Lawson's Merchants' Magazine, London (vol. i, 1852).

The Chinese Repository, Canton (for the years 1832–51 ; ceased publication in 1851).

The China Mail, Hongkong (for the years 1845–59).

(*d*) LETTERS, JOURNALS, VOYAGES, ETC.

Alcock, Sir R., *The Capital of the Tycoon : a Narrative of a Three Years Residence in Japan*, 2 vols., London, 1863.

Ashley, E., *The Life of Henry John Temple, Viscount Palmerston : 1846–1865. With selections from His Speeches and Correspondence*, 2 vols. (3rd ed.), London, 1877.

Belcher, Capt. Sir E., *Narrative of the Voyage of H.M.S. Samarang during the years 1843–46*, 2 vols., London, 1848.

Bulwer, Sir H. Lytton, *The Life of Henry John Temple, Viscount Palmerston : with Selections from his Diaries and Correspondence*, 3 vols., London, 1870–4.

Colnett, J., *The Journal of Captain James Colnett aboard the Argonaut*, Champlain Society, Toronto, 1940.

Doeff, H., *Herinneringen uit Japan*, Haarlem, 1833.

Elgin (James Bruce, Earl of Elgin), *The Letters and Journals of James, eighth Earl of Elgin*, ed. T. Walrond, London, 1872.

Halloran, A. L., *Wae Yang Jin. Eight Months' Journal kept on board one of Her Majesty's Sloops of War during visits to Loochoo, Japan, and Pootoo*, London, 1856.
Halloran was Master of H.M.S. *Mariner* when she visited Japan in 1849.

Harris, Townshend, *The Complete Journal of Townshend Harris, First American Consul General and Minister to Japan*, ed. M. E. Cosenza, New York, 1930.
The journal ends with the entry for 27 February 1858, except for a few scattered entries in May and June of that year. This edition contains valuable notes based on Harris's unpublished letters.

King, C. W. and Lay, G. T., *The Claims of Japan and Malaysia upon Christendom, exhibited in notes of voyages made in 1837 from Canton, in the Ship Morrison and the Brig Himmaleh under the direction of the owners*, 2 vols., New York, 1839.

Maxwell, Sir H., *The Life and Letters of George William Frederick, fourth Earl of Clarendon, K.G., G.C.B.*, 2 vols., London, 1913.

Moges, Marquis de, *Souvenirs d'une Ambassade en Chine et au Japon en 1857 et 1858*, Paris, 1860.

Oliphant, L., *Narrative of the Earl of Elgin's Mission to China and Japan in the years 1857, '58, '59*, 2 vols., Edinburgh and London, 1859.

Osborn, S., *A Cruise in Japanese Waters*, Edinburgh and London, 1859.
An interesting account of the Elgin mission by the captain of H.M.S. *Furious*, the ship which took Elgin to Japan. Osborn took no part in the negotiations, however.

Rich, E. E., ed., *The Letters of John McLoughlin from Fort Vancouver to the Governor and Committee, First series, 1825–38* (Champlain Society and Hudson's Bay Record Society), Toronto and London, 1941.

Russell, Lord John, *The Later Correspondence of Lord John Russell, 1840–1878*, ed. G. P. Gooch, 2 vols., London, 1925.

Staunton, Sir G., *An Authentic Account of an Embassy from the King of Great Britain to the Emperor of China*, 3 vols., London, 1797.

Tronson, J. M., *Personal Narrative of a Voyage to Japan, Kamtschatka, Siberia, Tartary, and Various Parts of the Coast of China; in H.M.S. Barracouta*, London, 1859.
Tronson was with the fleet at Nagasaki during Stirling's and Seymour's negotiations of 1854–6, but his account is more useful for " local colour " than for the negotiations themselves.

Wagener, G., 'Aus dem Tagebuche Hendrik Heuskens', *Mittheilungen der Deutschen Gesellschaft fur Natur- und Volkerkunde Ostasiens*, III, 29 (June 1883), pp. 372–90.
German summary, with some extracts from the French original, of the diary of Townshend Harris's secretary; covers the period August 1856 to June 1858, and also January 1861.

Whittingham, B., *Notes on the late Expedition against the Russian Settlements in Eastern Siberia*, London, 1856.
Whittingham was an army officer who accompanied

Commodore Elliot's squadron in 1855–6. He was present during the negotiation of the Exposition in 1855, but like Tronson has little of value to say about it.

Williams, S. Wells, ' Narrative of a voyage of the ship Morrison, captain D. Ingersoll, to Lewchew and Japan, in the months of July and August, 1837 ', *Chinese Repository*, vol. VI (December, 1837).

III. LATER PUBLISHED WORKS

Akao, T., ' Perry torai zengo ni okeru taigai kokumin shisō no kōsatsu (A Study of Popular Thought in Regard to Foreigners at the Time of Perry's Arrival) ', *Shirin*, vol. XXII (1937), pp. 529–54, 753–82.

Akimoto, S., *Lord Ii Naosuke and New Japan*, trans. and adapted from *Ii Tairo to Kaiko* by K. Nakamura, [Yokohama], 1909.

Ballard, S., ' A Sketch of the Life of Noboru Watanabe (Kwazan) ', *Trans. Asiatic Soc. Japan*, XXXII (1905), pp. 1–23.

Beasley, W. G., ' The language problem in the Anglo-Japanese negotiations of 1854 ', *Bulletin Sch. Oriental and African Studies*, XIII, 3 (1950).

Bell, H. C. F., *Lord Palmerston*, 2 vols., London & New York, 1936.

Boxer, C. R., *Jan Compagnie in Japan*, 1600–1817, The Hague, 1936.

van der Chijs, J. A., *Neerlands Streven tot Openstelling van Japan voor den Wereldhandel*, Amsterdam, 1867.

Coleman, H. E., ' The Life of Shoin Yoshida, being a translation from the Japanese Life of Shoin Yoshida by Mr. Iichiro Tokutomi ', *Trans. Asiatic Soc. Japan*, XLV (1917), pp. 119–88.

Costin, W. C., *Great Britain and China* 1833–1860, Oxford, 1937.

Crow, C., *Harris of Japan. The Story of Townshend Harris and his Amazing Adventures in Establishing Relations with the Far East*, London, 1939.

van Doren, J. B. J., *De Openstelling van Japan voor de Vreemde Natien in* 1856, Amsterdam, 1861.
Quotes extensively from Dutch official documents.

Drury, C. M., ' Early American Contacts with the Japanese ', *Pacific Northwest Quarterly*, XXXVI (1945), pp. 319–30.

Eckel, P. E., ' A Russian Expedition to Japan in 1852 ', *Pacific Northwest Quarterly*, XXXIV (1943), pp. 159–67.

Eckel, P. E., ' The Crimean War and Japan ', *Far Eastern Quarterly*, III (1944), pp. 109–18.

Fox, Grace, ' The Anglo-Japanese Convention of 1854 ', *Pacific Historical Review*, X (1941), pp. 411–34.
A detailed account of Stirling's negotiations of 1854–5 based chiefly on the Admiralty records.

Greene, D. C., ' Correspondence between William II of Holland and the Shogun of Japan, A.D. 1844 ', *Trans. Asiatic Soc. Japan*, XXXIV (1907), pp. 99–132.

Greene, D. C., ' Osada's Life of Takano Nagahide ', *Trans. Asiatic Soc. Japan*, XLI (1913), pp. 379–492.

Griffis, W. E., *Townshend Harris. First American Envoy in Japan*, Boston and New York, 1895.
Includes Harris's journal for 1856–8, with some minor omissions.

Gubbins, J. H., *The Progress of Japan* 1853–1871, Oxford, 1911.
Includes texts of several treaties and some useful translations.

van Gulik, R. H., ' Kakkaron, a Japanese echo of the Opium War ', *Monumenta Serica*, IV (1939–40), pp. 478–545.
Contains very valuable information on the attitude of the Japanese Confucian scholars to foreign affairs in the late-Tokugawa period.

Heibonsha, *Dai Hyakka Jiten* [Encyclopaedic Dictionary], 28 vols., Tokyo, 1932–5.

Inobe, S., ' Perry torai no sai ni okeru kokuron no kisū (The National Opinion provoked by the Arrival of American Expedition of Commodore M. C. Perry to Japan) ', *Shirin*, XIII (1928), pp. 343–70.
Chiefly useful for its detailed analysis of the replies to the Bakufu request for advice on handling the Perry mission in the winter of 1853–4.

Japan, Gaimushō Chōsa-bu [Foreign Office Research Section], *Nichi-ei Gaikō-shi* [History of Anglo-Japanese Relations], 2 vols., Tokyo, 1937–8.
An official history. It contains a few printed documents for the period 1854–8.

Kobayashi, S., *Bakumatsu-shi* [History of the late-Tokugawa period], (*Nihon Jidai-shi* series, vol. XI), Tokyo, 1927.
A detailed but pedestrian political history.

Michie, A., *The Englishman in China during the Victorian Era as illustrated in the career of Sir Rutherford Alcock*, 2 vols., Edinburgh and London, 1900.

Morison, J. L., *The Eighth Earl of Elgin. A Chapter in Nineteenth Century Imperial History*, London, 1928.

Morse, H. B., *The International Relations of the Chinese Empire*, (3 vols.), vol. I, *The Period of Conflict*, 1834–1860, London, 1910.

Murdoch, J. and Yamagata, I., *History of Japan*, 3 vols., London, 1925–6.

Mutō, C., *Nichi-ei kōtsū-shi no kenkyū* (*A Study of the History of Anglo-Japanese Relations*), rev. ed., Kyoto, 1941.
Chiefly used for its extensive bibliography, which takes up the greater part of the book and often quotes long extracts from the works cited.

Ōmori, K., *Dai Nihon Zenshi* [Complete History of Japan], 3 vols., Tokyo, 8th/9th impr., 1934–6 (1921–2).

Pelcovits, N. A., *Old China Hands and the Foreign Office*, American I. P. R., New York, 1948.

Q

BIBLIOGRAPHY

Philips, C. H., *The East India Company*, 1784–1834, Manchester, 1940.

Sakamaki, S., ' Japan and the United States, 1790–1853 ', *Trans. Asiatic Soc. Japan*, 2nd series, XVIII, Tokyo, 1939.

Sansom, G. B., *Japan : A Short Cultural History*, rev. ed., London, 1946 (1931).

Satoh, H., *Agitated Japan : the Life of Baron Ii Kamon-no-kami Naosuke (based on the Kaikoku Shimatsu of Shimada Saburo)*, revised by W. E. Griffis, Tokyo, 1896.

Satoh, H., *Lord Hotta, the Pioneer Diplomat of Japan*, Tokyo, 1908.
Contains both English and Japanese texts.

Satow, E. M., ed., *Japan 1853–1864, or Genji Yume Monogatari*, Tokyo, 1905.

Treat, P. J., *The Early Diplomatic Relations between the United States and Japan 1853–1865*, Baltimore, 1917.

Tokutomi, I., *Yoshida Shōin*, rev. ed., Tokyo, 1934 (1908).

Tsuchiya, T., ' Bakumatsu Shishi no mita Shina Mondai ' [The China problem as seen by loyalists of the late Tokugawa period], *Kaizō*, XX (July, 1938), pp. 154–67.
An article outlining Japanese reactions to European activities in China before 1860.

INDEX